OUR MR. WRENN

LECTOR HOUSE PUBLIC DOMAIN WORKS

OUR MR. WRENN

SINCLAIR LEWIS

ISBN: 978-93-90058-76-1

Published: 1914

LECTOR HOUSE LLP
E-MAIL: lectorpublishing@gmail.com

OUR MR. WRENN
THE ROMANTIC ADVENTURES
OF A GENTLE MAN

BY

SINCLAIR LEWIS

MCMXIV

TO
GRACE LIVINGSTONE HEGGER

CONTENTS

CHAPTER I

MR. WRENN IS LONELY

The ticket-taker of the Nickelorion Moving-Picture Show is a public personage, who stands out on Fourteenth Street, New York, wearing a gorgeous light-blue coat of numerous brass buttons. He nods to all the patrons, and his nod is the most cordial in town. Mr. Wrenn used to trot down to Fourteenth Street, passing ever so many other shows, just to get that cordial nod, because he had a lonely furnished room for evenings, and for daytime a tedious job that always made his head stuffy.

He stands out in the correspondence of the Souvenir and Art Novelty Company as "Our Mr. Wrenn," who would be writing you directly and explaining everything most satisfactorily. At thirty-four Mr. Wrenn was the sales-entry clerk of the Souvenir Company. He was always bending over bills and columns of figures at a desk behind the stock-room. He was a meek little bachlor—a person of inconspicuous blue ready-made suits, and a small unsuccessful mustache.

To-day—historians have established the date as April 9, 1910—there had been some confusing mixed orders from the Wisconsin retailers, and Mr. Wrenn had been "called down" by the office manager, Mr. Mortimer R. Guilfogle. He needed the friendly nod of the Nickelorion ticket-taker. He found Fourteenth Street, after office hours, swept by a dusty wind that whisked the skirts of countless plump Jewish girls, whose V-necked blouses showed soft throats of a warm brown. Under the elevated station he secretly made believe that he was in Paris, for here beautiful Italian boys swayed with trays of violets; a tramp displayed crimson mechanical rabbits, which squeaked, on silvery leading-strings; and a newsstand was heaped with the orange and green and gold of magazine covers.

"Gee!" inarticulated Mr. Wrenn. "Lots of colors. Hope I see foreign stuff like that in the moving pictures."

He came primly up to the Nickelorion, feeling in his vest pockets for a nickel and peering around the booth at the friendly ticket-taker. But the latter was thinking about buying Johnny's pants. Should he get them at the Fourteenth Street Store, or Siegel-Cooper's, or over at Aronson's, near home? So ruminating, he twiddled his wheel mechanically, and Mr. Wrenn's pasteboard slip was indifferently received in the plate-glass gullet of the grinder without the taker's even seeing the clerk's bow and smile.

Mr. Wrenn trembled into the door of the Nickelorion. He wanted to turn back and rebuke this fellow, but was restrained by shyness. He *had* liked the man's

"Fine evenin', sir "—rain or shine—but he wouldn't stand for being cut. Wasn't he making nineteen dollars a week, as against the ticket-taker's ten or twelve? He shook his head with the defiance of a cornered mouse, fussed with his mustache, and regarded the moving pictures gloomily.

They helped him. After a Selig domestic drama came a stirring Vitagraph Western scene, "The Goat of the Rancho," which depicted with much humor and tumult the revolt of a ranch cook, a Chinaman. Mr. Wrenn was really seeing, not cow-punchers and sage-brush, but himself, defying the office manager's surliness and revolting against the ticket-man's rudeness. Now he was ready for the nearly overpowering delight of travel-pictures. He bounced slightly as a Gaumont film presented Java.

He was a connoisseur of travel-pictures, for all his life he had been planning a great journey. Though he had done Staten Island and patronized an excursion to Bound Brook, neither of these was his grand tour. It was yet to be taken. In Mr. Wrenn, apparently fastened to New York like a domestic-minded barnacle, lay the possibilities of heroic roaming. He knew it. He, too, like the man who had taken the Gaumont pictures, would saunter among dusky Javan natives in "markets with tiles on the roofs and temples and—and—uh, well—places!" The scent of Oriental spices was in his broadened nostrils as he scampered out of the Nick-elorion, without a look at the ticket-taker, and headed for "home"—for his third-floor-front on West Sixteenth Street. He wanted to prowl through his collection of steamship brochures for a description of Java. But, of course, when one's landlady has both the sciatica and a case of Patient Suffering one stops in the basement din-ing-room to inquire how she is.

Mrs. Zapp was a fat landlady. When she sat down there was a straight line from her chin to her knees. She was usually sitting down. When she moved she groaned, and her apparel creaked. She groaned and creaked from bed to breakfast, and ate five griddle-cakes, two helpin's of scrapple, an egg, some rump steak, and three cups of coffee, slowly and resentfully. She creaked and groaned from break-fast to her rocking-chair, and sat about wondering why Providence had inflicted upon her a weak digestion. Mr. Wrenn also wondered why, sympathetically, but Mrs. Zapp was too conscientiously dolorous to be much cheered by the sympathy of a nigger-lovin' Yankee, who couldn't appreciate the subtle sorrows of a Zapp of Zapp's Bog, allied to all the First Families of Virginia.

Mr. Wrenn did nothing more presumptuous than sit still, in the stuffy furni-ture-crowded basement room, which smelled of dead food and deader pride in a race that had never existed. He sat still because the chair was broken. It had been broken now for four years.

For the hundred and twenty-ninth time in those years Mrs. Zapp said, in her rich corruption of Southern negro dialect, which can only be indicated here, "Ah been meaning to get that chair mended, Mist' Wrenn." He looked gratified and gazed upon the crayon enlargements of Lee Theresa, the older Zapp daughter (who was forewoman in a factory), and of Godiva. Godiva Zapp was usually called "Goaty," and many times a day was she called by Mrs. Zapp. A tamed child drudge was Goaty, with adenoids, which Mrs. Zapp had been meanin' to have removed, and which she would continue to have benevolent meanin's about till it should be too late, and she should discover that Providence never would let Goaty go to school.

"Yes, Mist' Wrenn, Ah told Goaty she was to see the man about getting that chair fixed, but she nev' does nothing Ah tell her."

In the kitchen was the noise of Goaty, ungovernable Goaty, aged eight, still snivelingly washing, though not cleaning, the incredible pile of dinner dishes. With a trail of hesitating remarks on the sadness of sciatica and windy evenings Mr. Wrenn sneaked forth from the august presence of Mrs. Zapp and mounted to paradise—his third-floor-front.

It was an abjectly respectable room—the bedspread patched; no two pieces of furniture from the same family; half-tones from the magazines pinned on the wall. But on the old marble mantelpiece lived his friends, books from wanderland. Other friends the room had rarely known. It was hard enough for Mr. Wrenn to get acquainted with people, anyway, and Mrs. Zapp did not expect her gennulman lodgers to entertain. So Mr. Wrenn had given up asking even Charley Carpenter, the assistant bookkeeper at the Souvenir Company, to call. That left him the books, which he now caressed with small eager finger-tips. He picked out a P. & O. circular, and hastily left for fairyland.

The April skies glowed with benevolence this Saturday morning. The Metropolitan Tower was singing, bright ivory tipped with gold, uplifted and intensely glad of the morning. The buildings walling in Madison Square were jubilant; the honest red-brick fronts, radiant; the new marble, witty. The sparrows in the middle of Fifth Avenue were all talking at once, scandalously but cleverly. The polished brass of limousines threw off teethy smiles. At least so Mr. Wrenn fancied as he whisked up Fifth Avenue, the skirts of his small blue double-breasted coat wagging. He was going blocks out of his way to the office; ready to defy time and eternity, yes, and even the office manager. He had awakened with Defiance as his bedfellow, and throughout breakfast at the hustler Dairy Lunch sunshine had flickered over the dirty tessellated floor.

He pranced up to the Souvenir Company's brick building, on Twenty-eighth Street near Sixth Avenue. In the office he chuckled at his ink-well and the untorn blotters on his orderly desk. Though he sat under the weary unnatural brilliance of a mercury-vapor light, he dashed into his work, and was too keen about this business of living merrily to be much flustered by the bustle of the lady buyer's superior "*Good* morning." Even up to ten-thirty he was still slamming down papers on his desk. Just let any one try to stop his course, his readiness for snapping fingers at The Job; just let them *try* it, that was all he wanted!

Then he was shot out of his chair and four feet along the corridor, in reflex response to the surly "Bur-r-r-r" of the buzzer. Mr. Mortimer R. Guilfogle, the manager, desired to see him. He scampered along the corridor and slid decorously through the manager's doorway into the long sun-bright room, ornate with rugs and souvenirs. Seven Novelties glittered on the desk alone, including a large rococo Shakespeare-style glass ink-well containing cloves and a small iron Pitts-burg-style one containing ink. Mr. Wrenn blinked like a noon-roused owlet in the brilliance. The manager dropped his fist on the desk, glared, smoothed his flow-ered prairie of waistcoat, and growled, his red jowls quivering:

"Look here, Wrenn, what's the matter with you? The Bronx Emporium order for May Day novelties was filled twice, they write me."

"They ordered twice, sir. By 'phone," smiled Mr. Wrenn, in an agony of po-liteness.

"They ordered hell, sir! Twice—the same order?"

"Yes, sir; their buyer was prob—"

"They say they've looked it up. Anyway, they won't pay twice. I know, em. We'll have to crawl down graceful, and all because you—I want to know why you ain't more careful!"

The announcement that Mr. Wrenn twice wriggled his head, and once tossed it, would not half denote his wrath. At last! It was here—the time for revolt, when he was going to be defiant. He had been careful; old Goglefogle was only barking; but why should *he* be barked at? With his voice palpitating and his heart thudding so that he felt sick he declared:

"I'm *sure*, sir, about that order. I looked it up. Their buyer was drunk!"

It was done. And now would he be discharged? The manager was speaking:

"Probably. You looked it up, eh? Um! Send me in the two order-records. Well. But, anyway, I want you to be more careful after this, Wrenn. You're pretty sloppy. Now get out. Expect me to make firms pay twice for the same order, cause of your carelessness?"

Mr. Wrenn found himself outside in the dark corridor. The manager hadn't seemed much impressed by his revolt.

The manager wasn't. He called a stenographer and dictated:

"Bronx Emporium:

"GENTLEMEN:—Our Mr. Wrenn has again (underline that `again,' Miss Blaustein), again looked up your order for May Day novelties. As we wrote before, order certainly was duplicated by 'phone. Our Mr. Wrenn is thoroughly reliable, and we have his records of these two orders. We shall therefore have to push col-lection on both—"

After all, Mr. Wrenn was thinking, the crafty manager might be merely con-cealing his hand. Perhaps he had understood the defiance. That gladdened him till after lunch. But at three, when his head was again foggy with work and he had forgotten whether there was still April anywhere, he began to dread what the manager might do to him. Suppose he lost his job; The Job! He worked unneces-sarily late, hoping that the manager would learn of it. As he wavered home, drunk with weariness, his fear of losing The Job was almost equal to his desire to resign from The Job.

He had worked so late that when he awoke on Sunday morning he was still in a whirl of figures. As he went out to his breakfast of coffee and whisked wheat at the Hustler Lunch the lines between the blocks of the cement walk, radiant in a white flare of sunshine, irritatingly recalled the cross-lines of order-lists, with the narrow cement blocks at the curb standing for unfilled column-headings. Even the ridges of the Hustler Lunch's imitation steel ceiling, running in parallel lines, jeered down at him that he was a prosaic man whose path was a ruler.

He went clear up to the branch post-office after breakfast to get the Sunday mail, but the mail was a disappointment. He was awaiting a wonderful fully illustrated guide to the Land of the Midnight Sun, a suggestion of possible and coyly improbable trips, whereas he got only a letter from his oldest acquaintance— Cousin John, of Parthenon, New York, the boy-who-comes-to-play of Mr. Wrenn's back-yard days in Parthenon. Without opening the letter Mr. Wrenn tucked it into his inside coat pocket, threw away his toothpick, and turned to Sunday wayfaring.

He jogged down Twenty-third Street to the North River ferries afoot. Trolleys took money, and of course one saves up for future great traveling. Over him the April clouds were fetterless vagabonds whose gaiety made him shrug with excitement and take a curb with a frisk as gambolsome as a Central Park lamb. There was no hint of sales-lists in the clouds, at least. And with them Mr. Wrenn's soul swept along, while his half-soled Cum-Fee-Best $3.80 shoes were ambling past warehouses. Only once did he condescend to being really on Twenty-third Street. At the Ninth Avenue corner, under the grimy Elevated, he sighted two blocks down to the General Theological Seminary's brick Gothic and found in a pointed doorway suggestions of alien beauty.

But his real object was to loll on a West and South Railroad in luxury, and go sailing out into the foam and perilous seas of North River. He passed through the smoking-cabin. He didn't smoke—the habit used up travel-money. Once seated on the upper deck, he knew that at last he was outward-bound on a liner. True, there was no great motion, but Mr. Wrenn was inclined to let realism off easily in this feature of his voyage. At least there were undoubted life-preservers in the white racks overhead; and everywhere the world, to his certain witnessing, was turned to crusading, to setting forth in great ships as if it were again in the brisk morning of history when the joy of adventure possessed the Argonauts.

He wasn't excited over the liners they passed. He was so experienced in all of travel, save the traveling, as to have gained a calm interested knowledge. He knew the *Campagnia* three docks away, and explained to a Harlem grocer her fine points, speaking earnestly of stacks and sticks, tonnage and knots.

Not excited, but—where couldn't he go if he were pulling out for Arcady on the *Campagnia!* Gee! What were even the building-block towers of the Metropolitan and Singer buildings and the *Times's* cream-stick compared with some old shrine in a cathedral close that was misted with centuries!

All this he felt and hummed to himself, though not in words. He had never heard of Arcady, though for many years he had been a citizen of that demesne.

Sure, he declared to himself, he was on the liner now; he was sliding up the muddy Mersey (see the *W. S. Travel Notes* for the source of his visions); he was off to St. George's Square for an organ-recital (see the English Baedeker); then an express for London and—Gee!

The ferryboat was entering her slip. Mr. Wrenn trotted toward the bow to thrill over the bump of the boat's snub nose against the lofty swaying piles and the swash of the brown waves heaped before her as she sidled into place. He was carried by the herd on into the station.

He did not notice the individual people in his exultation as he heard the great chords of the station's paean. The vast roof roared as the iron coursers stamped titanic hoofs of scorn at the little stay-at-home.

That is a washed-out hint of how the poets might describe Mr. Wrenn's passion. What he said was "Gee!"

He strolled by the lists of destinations hung on the track gates. Chicago (the plains! the Rockies! sunset over mining-camps!), Washington, and the magic Southland—thither the iron horses would be galloping, their swarthy smoke manes whipped back by the whirlwind, pounding out with clamorous strong hoofs their sixty miles an hour. Very well. In time he also would mount upon the iron coursers and charge upon Chicago and the Southland; just as soon as he got ready.

Then he headed for Cortlandt Street; for Long Island, City. finally, the Navy Yard. Along his way were the docks of the tramp steamers where he might ship as steward in the all-promising Sometime. He had never done anything so reckless as actually to ask a skipper for the chance to go a-sailing, but he had once gone into a mission society's free shipping-office on West Street where a disapproving elder had grumped at him, "Are you a sailor? No? Can't do anything for you, my friend. Are you saved?" He wasn't going to risk another horror like that, yet when the golden morning of Sometime dawned he certainly was going to go cruising off to palm-bordered lagoons.

As he walked through Long Island City he contrived conversations with the sailors he passed. It would have surprised a Norwegian bos'un's mate to learn that he was really a gun-runner, and that, as a matter of fact, he was now telling yarns of the Spanish Main to the man who slid deprecatingly by him.

Mr. Wrenn envied the jackies on the training-ship and carelessly went to sea as the President's guest in the admiral's barge and was frightened by the stare of a sauntering shop-girl and arrived home before dusk, to Mrs. Zapp's straitened approval.

Dusk made incantations in his third-floor-front. Pleasantly fagged in those slight neat legs, after his walk, Mr. Wrenn sat in the wicker rocker by the window, patting his scrubby tan mustache and reviewing the day's wandering. When the gas was lighted he yearned over pictures in a geographical magazine for a happy hour, then yawned to himself, "Well-l-l, Willum, guess it's time to crawl into the downy."

He undressed and smoothed his ready-made suit on the rocking-chair back. Sitting on the edge of his bed, quaint in his cotton night-gown, like a rare little bird of dull plumage, he rubbed his head sleepily. Um-m-m-m-m! How tired he was! He went to open the window. Then his tamed heart leaped into a waltz, and he forgot third-floor-fronts and sleepiness.

Through the window came the chorus of fog-horns on North River. "Boom-m-m!" That must be a giant liner, battling up through the fog. (It was a ferry.) A liner! She'd be roaring just like that if she were off the Banks! If he were only off the Banks! "Toot! Toot!" That was a tug. "Whawn-n-n!" Another liner. The tumultuous chorus repeated to him all the adventures of the day.

He dropped upon the bed again and stared absently at his clothes. Out of the inside coat pocket stuck the unopened letter from Cousin John.

He read a paragraph of it. He sprang from the bed and danced a tarantella, pranced in his cottony nightgown like a drunken Yaqui. The letter announced that the flinty farm at Parthenon, left to Mr. Wrenn by his father, had been sold. Its location on a river bluff had made it valuable to the Parthenon Chautauqua Association. There was now to his credit in the Parthenon National Bank nine hundred and forty dollars!

He was wealthy, then. He had enough to stalk up and down the earth for many venturesome (but economical) months, till he should learn the trade of wandering, and its mysterious trick of living without a job or a salary.

He crushed his pillow with burrowing head and sobbed excitedly, with a terrible stomach-sinking and a chill shaking. Then he laughed and wanted to—but didn't—rush into the adjacent hall room and tell the total stranger there of this world-changing news. He listened in the hall to learn whether the Zapps were up, but heard nothing; returned and cantered up and down, gloating on a map of the world.

"Gee! It's happened. I could travel all the time. I guess I won't be—very much—afraid of wrecks and stuff. . . . Things like that. . . . Gee! If I don't get to bed I'll be late at the office in the morning!"

Mr. Wrenn lay awake till three o'clock. Monday morning he felt rather ashamed of having done so eccentric a thing. But he got to the office on time. He was worried with the cares of wealth, with having to decide when to leave for his world-wanderings, but he was also very much aware that office managers are disagreeable if one isn't on time. All morning he did nothing more reckless than balance his new fortune, plus his savings, against steamship fares on a waste half-sheet of paper.

The noon-hour was not The Job's, but his, for exploration of the parlous lands of romance that lie hard by Twenty-eighth Street and Sixth Avenue. But he had to go out to lunch with Charley Carpenter, the assistant bookkeeper, that he might tell the news. As for Charley, He needed frequently to have a confidant who knew personally the tyrannous ways of the office manager, Mr. Guilfogle.

Mr. Wrenn and Charley chose (that is to say, Charley chose) a table at Drubel's Eating House. Mr. Wrenn timidly hinted, "I've got some big news to tell you."

But Charley interrupted, "Say, did you hear old Goglefogle light into me this morning? I won't stand for it. Say, did you hear him—the old—"

"What was the trouble, Charley?"

"Trouble? Nothing was the trouble. Except with old Goglefogle. I made one little break in my accounts. Why, if old Gogie had to keep track of seventy-'leven accounts and watch every single last movement of a fool girl that can't even run the adding-machine, why, he'd get green around the gills. He'd never do anything *but* make mistakes! Well, I guess the old codger must have had a bum breakfast this morning. Wanted some exercise to digest it. Me, I was the exercise—I was the goat. He calls me in, and he calls me *down*, and me—well, just lemme tell you, Wrenn, I calls his bluff!"

Charley Carpenter stopped his rapid tirade, delivered with quick head-shakes like those of palsy, to raise his smelly cigarette to his mouth. Midway in this slow gesture the memory of his wrongs again overpowered him. He flung his right hand back on the table, scattering cigarette ashes, jerked back his head with the irritated patience of a nervous martyr, then waved both hands about spasmodically, while he snarled, with his cheaply handsome smooth face more flushed than usual:

"Sure! You can just bet your bottom dollar I let him see from the way I looked at him that I wasn't going to stand for no more monkey business. You bet I did!... I'll fix him, I will. You just *watch* me. (Hey, Drubel, got any lemon merang? Bring me a hunk, will yuh?) Why, Wrenn, that cross-eyed double-jointed fat old slob, I'll slam him in the slats so hard some day—I will, you just watch my smoke. If it wasn't for that messy wife of mine—I ought to desert her, and I will some day, and—"

"Yuh." Mr. Wrenn was curt for a second.... "I know how it is, Charley. But you'll get over it, honest you will. Say, I've got some news. Some land that my dad left me has sold for nearly a thousand plunks. By the way, this lunch is on me. Let me pay for it, Charley."

Charley promised to let him pay, quite readily. And, expanding, said:

"Great, Wrenn! Great! Lemme congratulate you. Don't know anybody I'd rather've had this happen to. You're a meek little baa-lamb, but you've got lots of stuff in you, old Wrennski. Oh say, by the way, could. you let me have fifty cents till Saturday? Thanks. I'll pay it back sure. By golly! you're the only man around the office that 'preciates what a double duck-lined old fiend old Goglefogle is, the old—"

"Aw, gee, Charley, I wish you wouldn't jump on Guilfogle so hard. He's always treated me square."

"Gogie—square? Yuh, he's square just like a hoop. You know it, too, Wrenn. Now that you've got enough money so's you don't need to be scared about the job you'll realize it, and you'll want to soak him, same's I do. *Say!*" The impulse of a great idea made him gleefully shake his fist sidewise. "Say! Why *don't* you soak him? They bank on you at the Souvenir Company. Darn' sight more than you realize, lemme tell you. Why, you do about half the stock-keeper's work, sides your own. Tell you what you do. You go to old Goglefogle and tell him you want a raise to twenty-five, and want it right now. Yes, by golly, *thirty!* You're worth that, or pretty darn' near it, but 'course old Goglefogle'll never give it to you. He'll threaten to fire you if you say a thing more about it. You can tell him to go ahead, and then where'll he be? Guess that'll call his bluff some!"

"Yes, but, Charley, then if Guilfogle feels he can't pay me that much—you know he's responsible to the directors; he can't do everything he wants to—why, he'll just have to fire me, after I've talked to him like that, whether he wants to or not. And that'd leave us—that'd leave them—without a sales clerk, right in the busy season."

"Why, sure, Wrenn; that's what we want to do. If you go it 'd leave 'em without just about *two* men. Bother 'em like the deuce. It 'd bother Mr. Mortimer X. Y. Guglefugle most of all, thank the Lord. He wouldn't know where he was at—trying to break in a man right in the busy season. Here's your chance. Come on, kid; don't pass it up."

"Oh gee, Charley, I can't do that. You wouldn't want me to try to *hurt* the Souvenir Company after being there for—lemme see, it must be seven years."

"Well, maybe you *like* to get your cute little nose rubbed on the grindstone! I suppose you'd like to stay on at nineteen per for the rest of your life."

"Aw, Charley, don't get sore; please don't! I'd like to get off, all right—like to go traveling, and stuff like that. Gee! I'd like to wander round. But I can't cut out right in the bus—"

"But can't you see, you poor nut, you won't be *leaving* 'em—they'll either pay you what they ought to or lose you."

"Oh, I don't know about that, Charley.

"Charley was making up for some uncertainty as to his own logic by beaming persuasiveness, and Mr. Wrenn was afraid of being hypnotized. "No, no!" he throbbed, rising.

"Well, all right!" snarled Charley, "if you like to be Gogie's goat.... Oh, you're all right, Wrennski. I suppose you had ought to stay, if you feel you got to.... Well, so long. I've got to beat it over and buy a pair of socks before I go back."

Mr. Wrenn crept out of Drubel's behind him, very melancholy. Even Charley admitted that he "had ought to stay," then; and what chance was there of persuading the dread Mr. Mortimer R. Guilfogle that he wished to be looked upon as one resigning? Where, then, any chance of globe-trotting; perhaps for months he would remain in slavery, and he had hoped just that morning— One dreadful quarter-hour with Mr. Guilfogle and he might be free. He grinned to himself as he admitted that this was like seeing Europe after merely swimming the mid-winter Atlantic.

Well, he had nine minutes more, by his two-dollar watch; nine minutes of vagabondage. He gazed across at a Greek restaurant with signs in real Greek letters like "ruins at—well, at Aythens." A Chinese chop-suey den with a red-and-yellow carved dragon, and at an upper window a squat Chinaman who might easily be carrying a *kris*, "or whatever them Chink knives are," as he observed for the hundredth time he had taken this journey. A rotisserie, before whose upright fender of scarlet coals whole ducks were happily roasting to a shiny brown. In a furrier's window were Siberian foxes' skins (Siberia! huts of "awful brave convicks"; the steely Northern Sea; guards in blouses, just as he'd seen them at an Academy of Music play) and a polar bear (meaning, to him, the Northern Lights, the long hike, and the *igloo* at night). And the florists! There were orchids that (though he only half knew it, and that all inarticulately) whispered to him of jungles where, in the hot hush, he saw the slumbering python and—"What was it in that poem, that, Mandalay, thing? *was* it about jungles? Anyway:

> "'Them garlicky smells,
> And the sunshine and the palms and the bells.'"

He had to hurry back to the office. He stopped only to pat the head of a florist's delivery horse that looked wistfully at him from the curb. "Poor old fella. What you thinking about? Want to be a circus horse and wander? Le's beat it together. You can't, eh? Poor old fella!"

At three-thirty, the time when it seems to office persons that the day's work never will end, even by a miracle, Mr. Wrenn was shaky about his duty to the firm. He was more so after an electrical interview with the manager, who spent a few minutes, which he happened to have free, in roaring "I want to know why" at Mr. Wrenn. There was no particular "why" that he wanted to know; he was merely getting scientific efficiency out of employees, a phrase which Mr. Guilfogle had taken from a business magazine that dilutes efficiency theories for inefficient employers.

At five-twenty the manager summoned him, complimented him on nothing in particular, and suggested that he stay late with Charley Carpenter and the stock-keeper to inventory a line of desk-clocks which they were closing out.

As Mr. Wrenn returned to his desk he stopped at a window on the corridor and coveted the bright late afternoon. The cornices of lofty buildings glistened; the sunset shone fierily through the glass-inclosed layer-like upper floors. He wanted to be out there in the streets with the shopping crowds. Old Goglefogle didn't consider him; why should he consider the firm?

CHAPTER II

HE WALKS WITH MISS THERESA

As he left the Souvenir Company building after working late at taking inventory and roamed down toward Fourteenth Street, Mr. Wrenn felt forlornly aimless. The worst of it all was that he could not go to the Nickelorion for moving pictures; not after having been cut by the ticket-taker. Then, there before him was the glaring sign of the Nickelorion tempting him; a bill with "Great Train Robbery Film Tonight" made his heart thump like stair-climbing—and he dashed at the ticket-booth with a nickel doughtily extended. He felt queer about the scalp as the cashier girl slid out a coupon. Why did she seem to be watching him so closely? As he dropped the ticket in the chopper he tried to glance away from the Brass-button Man. For one- nineteenth of a second he kept his head turned. It turned back of itself; he stared full at the man, half bowed—and received a hearty absent-minded nod and a "Fine evenin'." He sang to himself a monotonous song of great joy. When he stumbled over the feet of a large German in getting to a seat, he apologized as though he were accustomed to laugh easily with many friends.

The train-robbery film was—well, he kept repeating "Gee!" to himself pantingly. How the masked men did sneak, simply sneak and sneak, behind the bushes! Mr. Wrenn shrank as one of them leered out of the picture at him. How gallantly the train dashed toward the robbers, to the spirit-stirring roll of the snare-drum. The rush from the bushes followed; the battle with detectives concealed in the express-car. Mr. Wrenn was standing sturdily and shooting coolly with the slender hawk-faced Pinkerton man in puttees; with him he leaped to horse and followed the robbers through the forest. He stayed through the whole program twice to see the train robbery again.

As he started to go out he found the ticket-taker changing his long light-blue robe of state for a highly commonplace sack-coat without brass buttons. In his astonishment at seeing how a Highness could be transformed into an every-day man, Mr. Wrenn stopped, and, having stopped, spoke:

"Uh—that was quite a—quite a picture—that train robbery. Wasn't it."

"Yuh, I guess—Now where's the devil and his wife flew away to with my hat? Them guys is always swiping it. Picture, mister? Why, I didn't see it no more 'n—Say you, Pink Eye, say you crab-footed usher, did you swipe my hat? Ain't he the cut-up, mister! Ain't both them ushers the jingling sheepsheads, though! Being cute and hiding my hat in the box-office. *Picture?* I don't get no chance to see any of 'em. Funny, ain't it?—me barking for 'em like I was the grandmother of the guy that invented 'em, and not knowing whether the train robbery—Now who stole my going-home shoes?... Why, I don't know whether the train did any robbing or not!"

He slapped Mr. Wrenn on the back, and the sales clerk's heart bounded in comradeship. He was surprised into declaring:

"Say—uh—I bowed to you the other night and you—well, honestly, you acted like you never saw me."

"Well, well, now, and that's what happens to me for being the dad of five kids and a she-girl and a tom-cat. Sure, I couldn't 've seen you. Me, I was probably that busy with fambly cares—I was probably thinking who was it et the lemon pie on me—was it Pete or Johnny, or shall I lick 'em both together, or just bite me wife."

Mr. Wrenn knew that the ticket-taker had never, never really considered biting his wife. *He* knew! His nod and grin and "That's the idea!" were urbanely sophisticated. He urged:

"Oh yes, I'm sure you didn't intend to hand me the icy mitt. Say! I'm thirsty. Come on over to Moje's and I'll buy you a drink."

He was aghast at this abyss of money-spending into which he had leaped, and the Brass-button Man was suspiciously wondering what this person wanted of him; but they crossed to the adjacent saloon, a New York corner saloon, which of course "glittered" with a large mirror, heaped glasses, and a long shining foot-rail on which, in bravado, Mr. Wrenn placed his Cum-Fee-Best shoe.

"Uh?" said the bartender.

"Rye, Jimmy," said the Brass-button Man.

"Uh-h-h-h-h," said Mr. Wrenn, in a frightened diminuendo, now that—wealthy citizen though he had become—he was in danger of exposure as a mollycoddle who couldn't choose his drink properly. "Stummick been hurting me. Guess I'd better just take a lemonade."

"You're the brother-in-law to a wise one," commented the Brass-button Man. "Me, I ain't never got the sense to do the traffic cop on the booze. The old woman she says to me, 'Mory,' she says, 'if you was in heaven and there was a pail of beer on one side and a gold harp on the other,' she says, 'and you was to have your pick, which would you take?' And what 'd yuh think I answers her?"

"The beer," said the bartender. "She had your number, all right."

"Not on your tin-type," declared the ticket-taker.

"'Me?' I says to her. 'Me? I'd pinch the harp and pawn it for ten growlers of Dutch beer and some man-sized rum!'"

"Hee, hee hee!" grinned Mr. Wrenn.

"Ha, ha, ha!" grumbled the bartender.

"Well-l-l," yawned the ticket-taker, "the old woman'll be chasing me best pants around the flat, if she don't have me to chase, pretty soon. Guess I'd better beat it. Much obliged for the drink, Mr. Uh. So long, Jimmy."

Mr. Wrenn set off for home in a high state of exhilaration which, he noticed, exactly resembled driving an aeroplane, and went briskly up the steps of the Zapps' genteel but unexciting residence. He was much nearer to heaven than West Sixteenth Street appears to be to the outsider. For he was an explorer of the Arctic, a trusted man on the job, an associate of witty Bohemians. He was an army lieutenant who had, with his friend the hawk-faced Pinkerton man, stood off bandits in an attack on a train. He opened and closed the door gaily.

He was an apologetic little Mr. Wrenn. His landlady stood on the bottom step of the hall stairs in a bunchy Mother Hubbard, groaning:

"Mist' Wrenn, if you got to come in so late, Ah wish you wouldn't just make all the noise you can. Ah don't see why Ah should have to be kept awake all night. Ah suppose it's the will of the Lord that whenever Ah go out to see Mrs. Muzzy and just drink a drop of coffee Ah must get insomina, but Ah don't see why anybody that tries to be a gennulman should have to go and bang the door and just rack mah nerves."

He slunk up-stairs behind Mrs. Zapp's lumbering gloom.

"There's something I wanted to tell you, Mrs. Zapp—something that's happened to me. That's why I was out celebrating last evening and got in so late." Mr. Wrenn was diffidently sitting in the basement.

"Yes," dryly, "Ah noticed you was out late, Mist' Wrenn."

"You see, Mrs. Zapp, I—uh—my father left me some land, and it's been sold for about one thousand plunks."

" Ah'm awful' glad, Mist' Wrenn," she said, funereally. "Maybe you'd like to take that hall room beside yours now. The two rooms'd make a nice apartment." (She really said "nahs 'pahtmun', "you understand.)

"Why, I hadn't thought much about that yet." He felt guilty, and was profusely cordial to Lee Theresa Zapp, the factory forewoman, who had just thumped down-stairs.

Miss Theresa was a large young lady with a bust, much black hair, and a handsome disdainful discontented face. She waited till he had finished greeting her, then sniffed, and at her mother she snarled:

"Ma, they went and kept us late again to-night. I'm getting just about tired of having a bunch of Jews and Yankees think I'm a nigger. Uff! I hate them!"

"T'resa, Mist' Wrenn's just inherited two thousand dollars, and he's going to take that upper hall room." Mrs. Zapp beamed with maternal fondness at the timid lodger.

But the gallant friend of Pinkertons faced her—for the first time. "Waste his travel-money?" he was inwardly exclaiming as he said:

"But I thought you had some one in that room. I heard som—"

"That fellow! Oh, he ain't going to be perm'nent. And he promised me—So you can have—"

"I'm *awful* sorry, Mrs. Zapp, but I'm afraid I can't take it. Fact is, I may go traveling for a while."

"Co'se you'll keep your room if you do, Mist' Wrenn?"

"Why, I'm afraid I'll have to give it up, but—Oh, I may not be going for a long long while yet; and of course I'll be glad to come—I'll want to come back here when I get back to New York. I won't be gone for more than, oh, probably not more than a year anyway, and—"

"And Ah thought you said you was going to be perm'nent!" Mrs. Zapp began quietly, prefatory to working herself up into hysterics. "And here Ah've gone and had your room fixed up just for you, and new paper put in, and you've always been talking such a lot about how you wanted your furniture arranged, and Ah've gone and made all mah plans—"

Mr. Wrenn had been a shyly paying guest of the Zapps for four years. That famous new paper had been put up two years before. So he spluttered: "Oh, I'm *awfully* sorry. I wish—uh—I don't—"

"Ah'd *thank* you, Mist' Wrenn, if you could *conveniently* let me *know* before you go running off and leaving me with empty rooms, with the landlord after the rent, and me turning away people that 'd pay more for the room, because Ah wanted to keep it for you. And people always coming to see you and making me answer the door and—"

Even the rooming-house worm was making small worm-like sounds that presaged turning. Lee Theresa snapped just in time, "Oh, cut it out, Ma, will you!" She had been staring at the worm, for he had suddenly become interesting and adorable and, incidentally, an heir. "I don't see why Mr. Wrenn ain't giving us all the notice we can expect. He said he mightn't be going for a long time."

"Oh!" grunted Mrs. Zapp. "So mah own flesh and blood is going to turn against me!"

She rose. Her appearance of majesty was somewhat lessened by the creak of stays, but her instinct for unpleasantness was always good. She said nothing as she left them, and she plodded up-stairs with a train of sighs.

Mr. Wrenn looked as though sudden illness had overpowered him. But Theresa laughed, and remarked: "You don't want to let Ma get on her high horse, Mr. Wrenn. She's a bluff."

With much billowing of the lower, less stiff part of her garments, she sailed to the cloudy mirror over the magazine-filled bookcase and inspected her cap of false curls, with many prods of her large firm hands which flashed with Brazilian diamonds. Though he had heard the word "puffs," he did not know that half her hair was false. He stared at it. Though in disgrace, he felt the honor of knowing so ample and rustling a woman as Miss Lee Theresa.

"But, say, I wish I could 've let her know I was going earlier, Miss Zapp. I didn't know it myself, but it does seem like a mean trick. I s'pose I ought to pay her something extra."

"Why, child, you won't do anything of the sort. Ma hasn't got a bit of kick coming. You've always been awful nice, far as I can see." She smiled lavishly. "I went for a walk to-night.... I wish all those men wouldn't stare at a girl so. I'm sure I don't see why they should stare at me."

Mr. Wrenn nodded, but that didn't seem to be the right comment, so he shook his head, then looked frightfully embarrassed.

"I went by that Armenian restaurant you were telling me about, Mr. Wrenn. Some time I believe I'll go dine there." Again she paused.

He said only, "Yes, it is a nice place."

Remarking to herself that there was no question about it, after all, he *was* a little fool, Theresa continued the siege. "Do you dine there often?"

"Oh yes. It is a nice place."

"Could a lady go there?"

"Why, yes, I—"

"Yes!"

"I should think so," he finished.

"Oh!... I do get so awfully tired of the greasy stuff Ma and Goaty dish up. They think a big stew that tastes like dish-water is a dinner, and if they do have anything I like they keep on having the same thing every day till I throw it in the sink. I wish I could go to a restaurant once in a while for a change, but of course—I dunno's it would be proper for a lady to go alone even there. What do you think? Oh dear!" She sat brooding sadly.

He had an inspiration. Perhaps Miss Theresa could be persuaded to go out to dinner with him some time. He begged:

"Gee, I wish you'd let me take you up there some evening, Miss Zapp."

"Now, didn't I tell you to call me `Miss Theresa'? Well, I suppose you just don't want to be friends with me. Nobody does." She brooded again.

"Oh, I didn't mean to hurt your feelings. Honest I didn't. I've always thought you'd think I was fresh if I called you `Miss Theresa,' and so I—"

"Why, I guess I could go up to the Armenian with you, perhaps. When would you like to go? You know I've always got lots of dates but I—um—let's see, I think I could go to-morrow evening."

"Let's do it! Shall I call for you, Miss—uh—Theresa?"

"Yes, you may if you'll be a good boy. Good night." She departed with an air of intimacy.

Mr. Wrenn scuttled to the Nickelorion, and admitted to the Brass-button Man that he was "feeling pretty good 's evening."

He had never supposed that a handsome creature like Miss Theresa could ever endure such a "slow fellow" as himself. For about one minute he considered with a chill the question of whether she was agreeable because of his new wealth, but reproved the fiend who was making the suggestion; for had he not heard her mention with great scorn a second cousin who had married an old Yankee for his money? That just settled *that*, he assured himself, and scowled at a passing messenger-boy for having thus hinted, but hastily grimaced as the youngster showed signs of loud displeasure.

The Armenian restaurant is peculiar, for it has foreign food at low prices, and is below Thirtieth Street, yet it has not become Bohemian. Consequently it has no bad music and no crowd of persons from Missouri whose women risk salvation for an evening by smoking cigarettes. Here prosperous Oriental merchants, of mild natures and bandit faces, drink semi-liquid Turkish coffee and discuss rugs and revolutions.

In fact, the place seemed so unartificial that Theresa, facing Mr. Wrenn, was bored. And the menu was foreign without being Society viands. It suggested rats' tails and birds' nests, she was quite sure. She would gladly have experimented with *pate de foie gras* or alligator-pears, but what social prestige was there to be gained at the factory by remarking that she "always did like *pahklava*"? Mr. Wrenn did not see that she was glancing about discontentedly, for he was delightedly listening to a lanky young man at the next table who was remarking to his *vis-a-vis*, a pale slithey lady in black, with the lines of a torpedo-boat: "Try some of the stuffed vine-leaves, child of the angels, and some wheat *pilaf* and some *bourma*. Your wheat *pilaf* is a comfortable food and cheering to the stomach of man. Simply *won*-derful. As for the *bourma*, he is a merry beast, a brown rose of pastry with honey cunningly secreted between his petals and—Here! Waiter! Stuffed vine-leaves, wheat *p'laf, bourm'*—twice on the order and hustle it."

"When you get through listening to that man—he talks like a bar of soap—tell me what there is on this bill of fare that's safe to eat," snorted Theresa.

"I thought he was real funny," insisted Mr. Wrenn.... "I'm sure you'll like *shish kebab* and s—"

"*Shish kibub!* Who ever heard of such a thing! Haven't they any—oh, I thought they'd have stuff they call `Turkish Delight' and things like that."

"`Turkish Delights' is cigarettes, I think."

"Well, I know it isn't, because I read about it in a story in a magazine. And they were eating it. On the terrace.... What is that *shish kibub*?"

"*Kebab*.... It's lamb roasted on skewers. I know you'll like it."

"Well, I'm not going to trust any heathens to cook my meat. I'll take some eggs and some of that—what was it the idiot was talking about—*berma*?"

"*Bourma*.... That's awful nice. With honey. And do try some of the stuffed peppers and rice."

"All right," said Theresa, gloomily.

Somehow Mr. Wrenn wasn't vastly transformed even by the possession of the two thousand dollars her mother had reported. He was still "funny and sort of scary," not like the overpowering Southern gentlemen she supposed she remembered. Also, she was hungry. She listened with stolid glumness to Mr. Wrenn's observation that that was "an awful big hat the lady with the funny guy had on."

He was chilled into quietness till Papa Gouroff, the owner of the restaurant, arrived from above-stairs. Papa Gouroff was a Russian Jew who had been a police spy in Poland and a hotel proprietor in Mogador, where he called himself Turkish and married a renegade Armenian. He had a nose like a sickle and a neck like a blue-gum nigger. He hoped that the place would degenerate into a Bohemian restaurant where liberal clergymen would think they were slumming, and barbers would think they were entering society, so he always wore a *fez* and talked bad Arabic. He was local color, atmosphere, Bohemian flavor. Mr. Wrenn murmured to Theresa:

"Say, do you see that man? He's Signor Gouroff, the owner. I've talked to him a lot of times. Ain't he great! Golly! look at that beak of his. Don't he make you think of *kiosks* and *hyrems* and stuff? Gee! What does he make you think—"

"He's got on a dirty collar…. That waiter's awful slow…. Would you please be so kind and pour me another glass of water?"

But when she reached the honied *bourma* she grew tolerant toward Mr. Wrenn. She had two cups of cocoa and felt fat about the eyes and affectionate. She had mentioned that there were good shows in town. Now she resumed:

"Have you been to `The Gold Brick' yet?"

"No, I—uh—I don't go to the theater much."

"Gwendolyn Muzzy was telling me that this was the funniest show she'd ever seen. Tells how two confidence men fooled one of those terrible little jay towns. Shows all the funny people, you know, like they have in jay towns…. I wish I could go to it, but of course I have to help out the folks at home, so— Well…. Oh dear."

"Say! I'd like to take you, if I could. Let's go—this evening!" He quivered with the adventure of it.

"Why, I don't know; I didn't tell Ma I was going to be out. But—oh, I guess it would be all right if I was with you."

"Let's go right up and get some tickets."

"All right." Her assent was too eager, but she immediately corrected that error by yawning, "I don't suppose I'd ought to go, but if you want to—"

They were a very lively couple as they walked up. He trickled sympathy when she told of the selfishness of the factory girls under her and the meanness of the superintendent over her, and he laughed several times as she remarked that the superintendent "ought to be boiled alive—that's what *all* lobsters ought to be," so she repeated the epigram with such increased jollity that they swung up to the theater in a gale; and, once facing the ennuied ticket-seller, he demanded dollar seats just as though he had not been doing sums all the way up to prove that seventy-five-cent seats were the best he could afford.

The play was a glorification of Yankee smartness. Mr. Wrenn was disturbed by the fact that the swindler heroes robbed quite all the others, but he was stirred by the brisk romance of money-making. The swindlers were supermen—blonde beasts with card indices and options instead of clubs. Not that Mr. Wrenn made any observations regarding supermen. But when, by way of commercial genius, the swindler robbed a young night clerk Mr. Wrenn whispered to Theresa, "Gee! he certainly does know how to jolly them, heh?"

"Sh-h-h-h-h-h!" said Theresa.

Every one made millions, victims and all, in the last act, as a proof of the social value of being a live American business man. As they oozed along with the departing audience Mr. Wrenn gurgled:

"That makes me feel just like I'd been making a million dollars." Masterfully, he proposed, "Say, let's go some place and have something to eat."

"All right."

"Let's—I almost feel as if I could afford Rector's, after that play; but, anyway, let's go to Allaire's."

Though he was ashamed of himself for it afterward, he was almost haughty toward his waiter, and ordered Welsh rabbits and beer quite as though he usually breakfasted on them. He may even have strutted a little as he hailed a car with an imaginary walking-stick. His parting with Miss Theresa was intimate; he shook her hand warmly.

As he undressed he hoped that he had not been too abrupt with the waiter, "poor cuss." But he lay awake to think of Theresa's hair and hand-clasp; of polished desks and florid gentlemen who curtly summoned bank-presidents and who had—he tossed the bedclothes about in his struggle to get the word—who had a *punch!*

He would do that Great Traveling of his in the land of Big Business!

The five thousand princes of New York to protect themselves against the four million ungrateful slaves had devised the sacred symbols of dress-coats, large houses, and automobiles as the outward and visible signs of the virtue of making money, to lure rebels into respectability and teach them the social value of getting a dollar away from that inhuman, socially injurious fiend, Some One Else. That Our Mr. Wrenn should dream for dreaming's sake was catastrophic; he might do things because he wanted to, not because they were fashionable; whereupon, police forces and the clergy would disband, Wall Street and Fifth Avenue would go thundering down. Hence, for him were provided those Y. M. C. A. night book-keeping classes administered by solemn earnest men of thirty for solemn credulous youths of twenty-nine; those sermons on content; articles on "building up the rundown store by live advertising"; Kiplingesque stories about playing the game; and correspondence-school advertisements that shrieked, "Mount the ladder to thorough knowledge—the path to power and to the fuller pay-envelope."

To all these Mr. Wrenn had been indifferent, for they showed no imagination. But when he saw Big Business glorified by a humorous melodrama, then The Job appeared to him as picaresque adventure, and he was in peril of his imagination.

The eight-o'clock sun, which usually found a wildly shaving Mr. Wrenn, discovered him dreaming that he was the manager of the Souvenir Company. But that was a complete misunderstanding of the case. The manager of the Souvenir Company was Mr. Mortimer R. Guilfogle, and he called Mr. Wrenn in to acquaint him with that fact when the new magnate started his career in Big Business by arriving at the office one hour late.

What made it worse, considered Mr. Guilfogle, was that this Wrenn had a higher average of punctuality than any one else in the office, which proved that he knew better. Worst of all, the Guilfogle family eggs had not been scrambled right at breakfast; they had been anemic. Mr. Guilfogle punched the buzzer and set his face toward the door, with a scowl prepared.

Mr. Wrenn seemed weary, and not so intimidated as usual.

"Look here, Wrenn; you were just about two hours late this morning. What do you think this office is? A club or a reading-room for hoboes? Ever occur to you we'd like to have you favor us with a call now and then so's we can learn how you're getting along at golf or whatever you're doing these days?"

There was a sample baby-shoe office pin-cushion on the manager's desk. Mr. Wrenn eyed this, and said nothing. The manager:

"Hear what I said? D'yuh think I'm talking to give my throat exercise?"

Mr. Wrenn was stubborn. "I couldn't help it."

"Couldn't help—! And you call that an explanation! I know just exactly what you're thinking, Wrenn; you're thinking that because I've let you have a lot of chances to really work into the business lately you're necessary to us, and not simply an expense—"

"Oh no, Mr. Guilfogle; honest, I didn't think—"

"Well, hang it, man, you *want* to think. What do you suppose we pay you a salary for? And just let me tell you, Wrenn, right here and now, that if you can't condescend to spare us some of your valuable time, now and then, we can good and plenty get along without you."

An old tale, oft told and never believed; but it interested Mr. Wrenn just now.

"I'm real glad you can get along without me. I've just inherited a big wad of money! I think I'll resign! Right now!"

Whether he or Mr. Mortimer R. Guilfogle was the more aghast at hearing him bawl this no one knows. The manager was so worried at the thought of breaking in a new man that his eye-glasses slipped off his poor perspiring nose. He begged, in sudden tones of old friendship:

"Why, you can't be thinking of leaving us! Why, we expect to make a big man of you, Wrenn. I was joking about firing you. You ought to know that, after the talk we had at Mouquin's the other night. You can't be thinking of leaving us! There's no end of possibilities here."

"Sorry," said the dogged soldier of dreams.

"Why—" wailed that hurt and astonished victim of ingratitude, Mr. Guilfogle.

"I'll leave the middle of June. That's plenty of notice," chirruped Mr. Wrenn.

At five that evening Mr. Wrenn dashed up to the Brass-button Man at his station before the Nickelorion, crying:

"Say! You come from Ireland, don't you?"

"Now what would you think? Me—oh no; I'm a Chinaman from Oshkosh!"

"No, honest, straight, tell me. I've got a chance to travel. What d'yuh think of that? Ain't it great! And I'm going right away. What I wanted to ask you was, what's the best place in Ireland to see?"

"Donegal, o' course. I was born there."

Hauling from his pocket a pencil and a worn envelope, Mr. Wrenn joyously added the new point of interest to a list ranging from Delagoa Bay to Denver.

He skipped up-town, looking at the stars. He shouted as he saw the stacks of a big Cunarder bulking up at the end of Fourteenth Street. He stopped to chuckle over a lithograph of the Parthenon at the window of a Greek bootblack's stand. Stars—steamer—temples, all these were his. He owned them now. He was free.

Lee Theresa sat waiting for him in the basement livingroom till ten-thirty while he was flirting with trainboards at the Grand Central. Then she went to bed, and, though he knew it not, that prince of wealthy suitors, Mr. Wrenn, had entirely lost the heart and hand of Miss Zapp of the F. F. V.

He stood before the manager's god-like desk on June 14, 1910. Sadly:

"Good-by, Mr. Guilfogle. Leaving to-day. I wish—Gee! I wish I could tell you, you know—about how much I appreciate—"

The manager moved a wire basket of carbon copies of letters from the left side of his desk to the right, staring at them thoughtfully; rearranged his pencils in a pile before his ink-well; glanced at the point of an indelible pencil with a manner of startled examination; tapped his desk-blotter with his knuckles; then raised his eyes. He studied Mr. Wrenn, smiled, put on the look he used when inviting him out for a drink. Mr. Guilfogle was essentially an honest fellow, harshened by The Job; a well-satisfied victim, with the imagination clean gone out of him, so that he took follow-up letters and the celerity of office-boys as the only serious things in the world. He was strong, alive, not at all a bad chap, merely efficient.

"Well, Wrenn, I suppose there's no use of rubbing it in. Course you know what I think about the whole thing. It strikes me you're a fool to leave a good job. But, after all, that's your business, not ours. We like you, and when you get tired of being just a bum, why, come back; we'll always try to have a job open for you. Meanwhile I hope you'll have a mighty good time, old man. Where you going? When d'yuh start out?"

"Why, first I'm going to just kind of wander round generally. Lots of things I'd like to do. I think I'll get away real soon now…. Thank you awfully, Mr. Guilfogle, or keeping a place open for me. Course I prob'ly won't need it, but gee! I sure do appreciate it."

"Say, I don't believe you're so plumb crazy about leaving us, after all, now that the cards are all dole out. Straight now, are you?"

"Yes, sir, it does make me feel a little blue—been here so long. But it'll be awful good to get out at sea."

"Yuh, I know, Wrenn. I'd like to go traveling myself—I suppose you fellows think I wouldn't care to go bumming around like you do and never have to worry about how the firm's going to break even. But—Well, good-by, old man, and don't forget us. Drop me a line now and then and let me know how you're getting along. Oh say, if you happen to see any novelties that look good let us hear about them. But drop me a line, anyway. We'll always be glad to hear from you. Well, good-by and good luck. Sure and drop me a line."

In the corner which had been his home for eight years Mr. Wrenn could not devise any new and yet more improved arrangement of the wire baskets and clips and desk reminders, so he cleaned a pen, blew some gray eraser-dust from under his iron ink-well standard, and decided that his desk was in order; reflecting:

He'd been there a long time. Now he could never come back to it, no matter how much he wanted to…. How good the manager had been to him. Gee! he hadn't appreciated how considerut Guilfogle was!

He started down the corridor on a round of farewells to the boys. "Too bad he hadn't never got better acquainted with them, but it was too late now. Anyway, they were such fine jolly sports; they'd never miss a stupid guy like him."

Just then he met them in the corridor, all of them except Guilfogle, headed by Rabin, the traveling salesman, and Charley Carpenter, who was bearing a box of handkerchiefs with a large green-and-crimson-paper label.

"Gov'nor Wrenn," orated Charley, "upon this suspicious occasion we have the pleasure of showing by this small token of our esteem our 'preciation of your untiring efforts in the investigation of Mortimer R. Gugglegiggle of the Graft Trust and—

"Say, old man, joking aside, we're mighty sorry you're going and—uh—well, we'd like to give you something to show we're—uh—mighty sorry you're going. We thought of a box of cigars, but you don't smoke much; anyway, these han'k'chiefs'll help to show—Three cheers for Wrenn, fellows!"

Afterward, by his desk, alone, holding the box of handkerchiefs with the resplendent red-and-green label, Mr. Wrenn began to cry.

He was lying abed at eight-thirty on a morning of late June, two weeks after leaving the Souvenir Company, deliberately hunting over his pillow for cool spots, very hot and restless in the legs and enormously depressed in the soul. He would have got up had there been anything to get up for. There was nothing, yet he felt uneasily guilty. For two weeks he had been afraid of losing, by neglect, the job he had already voluntarily given up. So there are men whom the fear of death has driven to suicide.

Nearly every morning he had driven himself from bed and had finished shaving before he was quite satisfied that he didn't have to get to the office on time. As he wandered about during the day he remarked with frequency, "I'm scared as teacher's pet playing hookey for the first time, like what we used to do in Parthenon." All proper persons were at work of a week-day afternoon. What, then, was he doing walking along the street when all morality demanded his sitting at a desk at the Souvenir Company, being a little more careful, to win the divine favor of Mortimer R. Guilfogle?

He was sure that if he were already out on the Great Traveling he would be able to "push the buzzer on himself and get up his nerve." But he did not know where to go. He had planned so many trips these years that now he couldn't keep any one of them finally decided on for more than an hour. It rather stretched his short arms to embrace at once a gay old dream of seeing Venice and the stern civic duty of hunting abominably dangerous beasts in the Guatemala bush.

The expense bothered him, too. He had through many years so persistently saved money for the Great Traveling that he begrudged money for that Traveling itself. Indeed, he planned to spend not more than $300 of the $1,235.80 he had now accumulated, on his first venture, during which he hoped to learn the trade of wandering.

He was always influenced by a sentence he had read somewhere about "one of those globe-trotters you meet carrying a monkey-wrench in Calcutta, then in raiment and a monocle at the Athenaeum." He would learn some Kiplingy trade that would teach him the use of astonishingly technical tools, also daring and the location of smugglers' haunts, copra islands, and whaling-stations with curious names.

He pictured himself shipping as third engineer at the Manihiki Islands or engaged for taking moving pictures of an aeroplane flight in Algiers. He *had* to get away from Zappism. He had to be out on the iron seas, where the battle-ships and liners went by like a marching military band. But he couldn't get started.

Once beyond Sandy Hook, he would immediately know all about engines and fighting. It would help, he was certain, to be shanghaied. But no matter how wistfully, no matter how late at night he timorously forced himself to loiter among unwashed English stokers on West Street, he couldn't get himself molested except by glib persons wishing ten cents "for a place to sleep."

When he had dallied through breakfast that particular morning he sat about. Once he had pictured sitting about reading travel-books as a perfect occupation. But it concealed no exciting little surprises when he could be a Sunday loafer on any plain Monday. Furthermore, Goaty never made his bed till noon, and the gray-and-brown-patched coverlet seemed to trail all about the disordered room.

Midway in a paragraph he rose, threw *One Hundred Ways to See California* on the tumbled bed, and ran away from Our Mr. Wrenn. But Our Mr. Wrenn pursued him along the wharves, where the sun glared on oily water. He had seen the wharves twelve times that fortnight. In fact, he even cried viciously that "he had seen too blame much of the blame wharves."

Early in the afternoon he went to a moving-picture show, but the first sight of the white giant figures bulking against the gray background was wearily unreal; and when the inevitable large-eyed black-braided Indian maiden met the canonical cow-puncher he threshed about in his seat, was irritated by the nervous click of the machine and the hot stuffiness of the room, and ran away just at the exciting moment when the Indian chief dashed into camp and summoned his braves to the war-path.

Perhaps he could hide from thought at home.

As he came into his room he stood at gaze like a kitten of good family beholding a mangy mongrel asleep in its pink basket. For on his bed was Mrs. Zapp, her rotund curves stretching behind her large flat feet, whose soles were toward him. She was noisily somnolent; her stays creaked regularly as she breathed, except when she moved slightly and groaned.

Guiltily he tiptoed down-stairs and went snuffling along the dusty unvaried brick side streets, wondering where in all New York he could go. He read minutely a placard advertising an excursion to the Catskills, to start that evening. For an exhilarated moment he resolved to go, but—" oh, there was a lot of them rich society folks up there." He bought a morning *American* and, sitting in Union Square, gravely studied the humorous drawings.

He casually noticed the "Help Wanted" advertisements.

They suggested an uninteresting idea that somehow he might find it economical to go venturing as a waiter or farm-hand.

And so he came to the gate of paradise:

> MEN WANTED. Free passage on cattle-boats to Liverpool feeding cattle. Low fee. Easy work. Fast boats. Apply International and Atlantic Employment Bureau,—Greenwich Street.

"Gee!" he cried, "I guess Providence has picked out my first hike for me."

CHAPTER III

HE STARTS FOR THE LAND OF ELSEWHERE

The International and Atlantic Employment Bureau is a long dirty room with the plaster cracked like the outlines on a map, hung with steamship posters and the laws of New York regarding employment offices, which are regarded as humorous by the proprietor, M. Baraieff, a short slender ejaculatory person with a nervous black beard, lively blandness, and a knowledge of all the incorrect usages of nine languages. Mr. Wrenn edged into this junk-heap of nationalities with interested wonder. M. Baraieff rubbed his smooth wicked hands together and bowed a number of times.

Confidentially leaning across the counter, Mr. Wrenn murmured: "Say, I read your ad. about wanting cattlemen. I want to make a trip to Europe. How—?"

"Yes, yes, yes, yes, Mistaire. I feex you up right away. Ten dollars pleas-s-s."

"Well, what does that entitle me to?"

"I tole you I feex you up. Ha! Ha! I know it; you are a gentleman; you want a nice leetle trip on Europe. Sure. I feex you right up. I send you off on a nice easy cattleboat where you won't have to work much hardly any. Right away it goes. Ten dollars pleas-s-s."

"But when does the boat start? Where does it start from?" Mr. Wrenn was a bit confused. He had never met a man who grimaced so politely and so rapidly.

"Next Tuesday I send you right off."

Mr. Wrenn regretfully exchanged ten dollars for a card informing Trubiggs, Atlantic Avenue, Boston, that Mr. "Ren" was to be "ship 1st poss. catel boat right away and charge my acct. fee paid Baraieff." Brightly declaring "I geef you a fine ship," M. Baraieff added, on the margin of the card, in copper-plate script, "Best ship, easy work." He caroled, "Come early next Tuesday morning, "and bowed out Mr. Wrenn like a Parisian shopkeeper. The row of waiting servant-girls curtsied as though they were a hedge swayed by the wind, while Mr. Wrenn self-consciously hurried to get past them.

He was too excited to worry over the patient and quiet suffering with which Mrs. Zapp heard the announcement that he was going. That Theresa laughed at him for a cattleman, while Goaty, in the kitchen, audibly observed that "nobody but a Yankee would travel in a pig-pen, "merely increased his joy in moving his belongings to a storage warehouse.

Tuesday morning, clad in a sweater-jacket, tennis-shoes, an old felt hat, a khaki shirt and corduroys, carrying a suit-case packed to bursting with clothes and Baedekers, with one hundred and fifty dollars in express-company drafts craftily concealed, he dashed down to Baraieff's hole. Though it was only eight-thirty, he was afraid he was going to be late.

Till 2 P.M. he sat waiting, then was sent to the Joy Steamship Line wharf with a ticket to Boston and a letter to Trubiggs's shipping-office: "Give bearer Ren as per inclosed receet one trip England catel boat charge my acct. SYLVESTRE BARAIEFF, N. Y."

Standing on the hurricane-deck of the Joy Line boat, with his suit-case guardedly beside him, he crooned to himself tuneless chants with the refrain, "Free, free, out to sea. Free, free, that's *me!*" He had persuaded himself that there was practically no danger of the boat's sinking or catching fire. Anyway, he just wasn't going to be scared. As the steamer trudged up East River he watched the late afternoon sun brighten the Manhattan factories and make soft the stretches of Westchester fields. (Of course, he "thrilled.")

He had no state-room, but was entitled to a place in a twelve-berth room in the hold. Here large farmers without their shoes were grumpily talking all at once, so he returned to the deck; and the rest of the night, while the other passengers snored, he sat modestly on a canvas stool, unblinkingly gloating over a sea-fabric of frosty blue that was shot through with golden threads when they passed lighthouses or ships. At dawn he was weary, peppery-eyed, but he viewed the flooding light with approval.

At last, Boston.

The front part of the shipping-office on Atlantic Avenue was a glass-inclosed room littered with chairs, piles of circulars, old pictures of Cunarders, older calendars, and directories to be ranked as antiques. In the midst of these remains a red-headed Yankee of forty, smoking a Pittsburg stogie, sat tilted back in a kitchen chair, reading the Boston *American*. Mr. Wrenn delivered M. Baraieff's letter and stood waiting, holding his suit-case, ready to skip out and go aboard a cattle-boat immediately.

The shipping-agent glanced through the letter, then snapped:

"Bryff's crazy. Always sends 'em too early. Wrenn, you ought to come to me first. What j'yuh go to that Jew first for? Here he goes and sends you a day late— or couple days too early. 'F you'd got here last night I could 've sent you off this morning on a Dominion Line boat. All I got now is a Leyland boat that starts from Portland Saturday. Le's see; this is Wednesday. Thursday, Friday—you'll have to wait three days. Now you want me to fix you up, don't you? I might not be able to get you off till a week from now, but you'd like to get off on a good boat Saturday instead, wouldn't you?"

"Oh yes; I *would*. I—"

"Well, I'll try to fix it. You can see for yourself; boats ain't leaving every minute just to please Bryff. And it's the busy season. Bunches of rah-rah boys wanting to cross, and Canadians wanting to get back to England, and Jews beating it to Poland—to sling bombs at the Czar, I guess. And lemme tell you, them Jews is all right. They're willing to pay for a man's time and trouble in getting 'em fixed up, and so—"

With dignity Mr. William Wrenn stated, "Of course I'll be glad to—uh—make it worth your while."

"I *thought* you was a gentleman. Hey, Al! *Al!*" An underfed boy with few teeth, dusty and grown out of his trousers, appeared. "Clear off a chair for the gentleman. Stick that valise on top my desk.... Sit down, Mr. Wrenn. You see, it's like this: I'll tell you in confidence, you understand. This letter from Bryff ain't worth the paper it's written on. He ain't got any right to be sending out men for cattle-boats. Me, I'm running that. I deal direct with all the Boston and Portland lines. If you don't believe it just go out in the back room and ask any of the cattlemen out there."

"Yes, I see," Mr. Wrenn observed, as though he were ill, and toed an old almanac about the floor. "Uh—Mr.—Trubiggs, is it?"

"Yump. Yump, my boy. Trubiggs. Tru by name and true by nature. Heh?"

This last was said quite without conviction. It was evidently a joke which had come down from earlier years. Mr. Wrenn ignored it and declared, as stoutly as he could:

"You see, Mr. Trubiggs, I'd be willing to pay you—"

"I'll tell you just how it is, Mr. Wrenn. I ain't one of these Sheeny employment bureaus; I'm an American; I like to look out for Americans. Even if you *didn't* come to me first I'll watch out for your interests, same's if they was mine. Now, do you want to get fixed up with a nice fast boat that leaves Portland next Saturday, just a couple of days' wait?"

"Oh yes, I *do*, Mr. Trubiggs."

"Well, my list is really full—men waiting, too—but if it 'd be worth five dollars to you to—"

"Here's the five dollars."

The shipping-agent was disgusted. He had estimated from Mr. Wrenn's cheap sweater-jacket and tennis-shoes that he would be able to squeeze out only three or four dollars, and here he might have made ten. More in sorrow than in anger:

"Of course you understand I may have a lot of trouble working you in on the *next* boat, you coming as late as this. Course five dollars is less 'n what I usually get." He contemptuously tossed the bill on his desk. "If you want me to slip a little something extra to the agents—"

Mr. Wrenn was too head-achy to be customarily timid. "Let's see that. Did I give you only five dollars?" Receiving the bill, he folded it with much primness, tucked it into the pocket of his shirt, and remarked:

"Now, you said you'd fix me up for five dollars. Besides, that letter from Baraieff is a form with your name printed on it; so I know you do business with him

ight along. If five dollars ain't enough, why, then you can just go to hell, Mr. Trubiggs; yes, sir, that's what you can do. I'm just getting tired of monkeying around.
f five *is* enough I'll give this back to you Friday, when you send me off to Portland,
f you give me a receipt. There!" He almost snarled, so weary and discouraged was
ne.

Now, Trubiggs was a warm-hearted rogue, and he liked the society of what
ne called "white people." He laughed, poked a Pittsburg stogie at Mr. Wrenn, and
consented:

"All right. I'll fix you up. Have a smoke. Pay me the five Friday, or pay it to my
foreman when he puts you on the cattle-boat. I don't care a rap which. You're all
right. Can't bluff you, eh?"

And, further bluffing Mr. Wrenn, he suggested to him a lodging-house for his
two nights in Boston. "Tell the clerk that red-headed Trubiggs sent you, and he'll
give you the best in the house. Tell him you're a friend of mine."

When Mr. Wrenn had gone Mr. Trubiggs remarked to some one, by telephone,
"'Nother sucker coming, Blaugeld. Now don't try to do me out of my bit or I'll cap
for some other joint, understand? Huh? Yuh, stick him for a thirty-five-cent bed.
S' long."

The caravan of Trubiggs's cattlemen who left for Portland by night steamer,
Friday, was headed by a bulky-shouldered boss, who wore no coat and whose
corduroy vest swung cheerfully open. A motley troupe were the cattlemen—Jews
with small trunks, large imitation-leather valises and assorted bundles, a stolid
prophet-bearded procession of weary men in tattered derbies and sweat-shop
clothes.

There were Englishmen with rope-bound pine chests. A lewd-mouthed American named Tim, who said he was a hatter out of work, and a loud-talking tough
called Pete mingled with a straggle of hoboes.

The boss counted the group and selected his confidants for the trip to Portland—Mr. Wrenn and a youth named Morton.

Morton was a square heavy-fleshed young man with stubby hands, who, up
to his eyes, was stolid and solid as a granite monument, but merry of eye and hint-
ing friendliness in his tousled soft-brown hair. He was always wielding a pipe and
artfully blowing smoke through his nostrils.

Mr. Wrenn and he smiled at each other searchingly as the Portland boat pulled
out, and a wind swept straight from the Land of Elsewhere.

After dinner Morton, smoking a pipe shaped somewhat like a golf-stick head
and somewhat like a toad, at the rail of the steamer, turned to Mr. Wrenn with:

"Classy bunch of cattlemen we've got to go with. Not!... My name's Morton."

"I'm awful glad to meet you, Mr. Morton. My name's Wrenn."

"Glad to be off at last, ain't you?"

"Golly! I should say I *am!*"

"So'm I. Been waiting for this for years. I'm a clerk for the P. R. R. in N' York."

"I come from New York, too."

"So? Lived there long?"

"Uh-huh, I—" began Mr. Wrenn.

"Well, I been working for the Penn. for seven years now. Now I've got a vacation of three months. On me. Gives me a chance to travel a little. Got ten plunks and a second-class ticket back from Glasgow. But I'm going to see England and France just the same. Prob'ly Germany, too."

"Second class? Why don't you go steerage, and save?"

"Oh, got to come back like a gentleman. You know. You're from New York, too, eh?"

"Yes, I'm with an art-novelty company on Twenty-eighth Street. I been wanting to get away for quite some time, too…. How are you going to travel on ten dollars?"

"Oh, work m' way. Cinch. Always land on my feet. Not on my uppers, at that. I'm only twenty-eight, but I've been on my own, like the English fellow says, since I was twelve…. Well, how about you? Traveling or going somewhere?"

"Just traveling. I'm glad we're going together, Mr. Morton. I don't think most of these cattlemen are very nice. Except for the old Jews. They seem to be fine old coots. They make you think of—oh—you know—prophets and stuff. Watch 'em, over there, making tea. I suppose the steamer grub ain't kosher. I seen one on the Joy Line saying his prayers—I suppose he was—in a kind of shawl."

"Well, well! You don't say so!"

Distinctly, Mr. Wrenn felt that he was one of the gentlemen who, in Kipling, stand at steamer rails exchanging observations on strange lands. He uttered, cosmopolitanly:

"Gee! Look at that sunset. Ain't that grand!"

"Holy smoke! it sure is. I don't see how anybody could believe in religion after looking at that."

Shocked and confused at such a theory, yet excited at finding that Morton apparently had thoughts, Mr. Wrenn piped: "Honestly, I don't see that at *all*. I don't see how anybody could disbelieve anything after a sunset like that. Makes me believe all sorts of thing—gets me going—I imagine I'm all sorts of places—on the Nile and so on."

"Sure! That's just it. Everything's so peaceful and natural. Just *is*. Gives the imagination enough to do, even by itself, without having to have religion."

"Well," reflected Mr. Wrenn, "I don't hardly ever go to church. I don't believe much in all them highbrow sermons that don't come down to brass tacks—ain't got nothing to do with real folks. But just the same, I love to go up to St. Patrick's Cathedral. Why, I get real *thrilled*—I hope you won't think I'm trying to get highbrowed, Mr. Morton."

"Why, no. Cer'nly not. I understand. Gwan."

"It gets me going when I look down the aisle at the altar and see the arches and so on. And the priests in their robes—they look so—so way up—oh, I dunno just how to say it—so kind of *uplifted*."

"Sure, I know. Just the esthetic end of the game. Esthetic, you know—the beauty part of it."

"Yuh, sure, that's the word. 'Sthetic, that's what it is. Yes, 'sthetic. But, just the same, it makes me feel's though I believed in all sorts of things."

"Tell you what I believe may happen, though," exulted Morton. "This socialism, and maybe even these here International Workers of the World, may pan out as a new kind of religion. I don't know much about it, I got to admit. But looks as though it might be that way. It's dead certain the old political parties are just gangs—don't stand for anything except the name. But this comrade business— good stunt. Brotherhood of man—real brotherhood. My idea of religion. One that is because it's got to be, not just because it always has been. Yessir, me for a religion of guys working together to make things easier for each other."

"You bet!" commented Mr. Wrenn, and they smote each other upon the shoulder and laughed together in a fine flame of shared hope.

"I wish I knew something about this socialism stuff," mused Mr. Wrenn, with tilted head, examining the burnt-umber edges of the sunset.

"Great stuff. Not working for some lazy cuss that's inherited the right to boss you. And *international* brotherhood, not just neighborhoods. New thing."

"Gee! I surely would like that, awfully," sighed Mr. Wrenn.

He saw the processional of world brotherhood tramp steadily through the paling sunset; saffron-vestured Mandarin marching by flax-faced Norseman and languid South Sea Islander—the diverse peoples toward whom he had always yearned.

"But I don't care so much for some of these ranting street-corner socialists, though," mused Morton. "The kind that holler `Come get saved *our* way or go to hell! Keep off scab guides to prosperity.'"

"Yuh, sure. Ha! ha! ha!"

"Huh! huh!"

Morton soon had another thought. "Still, same time, us guys that do the work have got to work out something for ourselves. We can't bank on the rah-rah boys that wear eye-glasses and condescend to like us, cause they think we ain't entirely too dirty for 'em to associate with, and all these writer guys and so on. That's where you got to hand it to the street-corner shouters."

"Yes, that's *so*. Y' right there, I guess, all right."

They looked at each other and laughed again; initiated friends; tasting each other's souls. They shared sandwiches and confessions. When the other passengers had gone to bed and the sailors on watch seemed lonely the two men were still declaring, shyly but delightedly, that "things is curious."

In the damp discomfort of early morning the cattlemen shuffled from the steamer at Portland and were herded to a lunch-room by the boss, who cheerfully smoked his corn-cob and ejaculated to Mr. Wrenn and Morton such interesting facts as:

"Trubiggs is a lobster. You don't want to let the bosses bluff you aboard the *Merian*. They'll try to chase you in where the steers'll gore you. The grub'll be—"

"What grub do you get?"

"Scouse and bread. And water."

"What's scouse?"

"Beef stew without the beef. Oh, the grub'll be rotten. Trubiggs is a lobster. He wouldn't be nowhere if 't wa'n't for me."

Mr. Wrenn appreciated England's need of roast beef, but he timidly desired not to be gored by steers, which seemed imminent, before breakfast coffee. The streets were coldly empty, and he was sleepy, and Morton was silent. At the restaurant, sitting on a high stool before a pine counter, he choked over an egg sandwich made with thick crumby slices of a bread that had no personality to it. He roved forlornly about Portland, beside the gloomy pipe-valiant Morton, fighting two fears: the company might not need all of them this trip, and he might have to wait; secondly, if he incredibly did get shipped and started for England the steers might prove dreadfully dangerous. After intense thinking he ejaculated, "Gee! it's be bored or get gored." Which was much too good not to tell Morton, so they laughed very much, and at ten o'clock were signed on for the trip and led, whooping, to the deck of the S.S. *Merian*.

Cattle were still struggling down the chutes from the dock. The dirty decks were confusingly littered with cordage and the cattlemen's luggage. The Jewish elders stared sepulchrally at the wilderness of open hatches and rude passageways, as though they were prophesying death.

But Mr. Wrenn, standing sturdily beside his suit-case to guard it, fawned with romantic love upon the rusty iron sides of their pilgrims' caravel; and as the *Merian* left the wharf with no more handkerchief-waving or tears than attends a ferry's leaving he mumbled:

"Free, free, out to sea. Free, free, that's *me!*"

Then, "Gee!… Gee whittakers!"

CHAPTER IV

HE BECOMES THE GREAT LITTLE BILL WRENN

When the *Merian* was three days out from Portland the frightened cattleman stiff known as "Wrennie" wanted to die, for he was now sure that the smell of the fo'c'sle, in which he was lying on a thin mattress of straw covered with damp gunny-sacking, both could and would become daily a thicker smell, a stronger smell, a smell increasingly diverse and deadly.

Though it was so late as eight bells of the evening, Pete, the tough factory hand, and Tim, the down-and-out hatter, were still playing seven-up at the dirty fo'c'sle table, while McGarver, under-boss of the Morris cattle gang, lay in his berth, heavily studying the game and blowing sulphurous fumes of Lunch Pail Plug Cut tobacco up toward Wrennie.

Pete, the tough, was very evil. He sneered. He stole. He bullied. He was a drunkard and a person without cleanliness of speech. Tim, the hatter, was a loud-talking weakling, under Pete's domination. Tim wore a dirty rubber collar without a tie, and his soul was like his neckware.

McGarver, the under-boss, was a good shepherd among the men, though he had recently lost the head foremanship by a spree complicated with language and violence. He looked like one of the *Merian* bulls, with broad short neck and short curly hair above a thick-skinned deeply wrinkled low forehead. He never undressed, but was always seen, as now, in heavy shoes and blue-gray woolen socks tucked over the bottoms of his overalls. He was gruff and kind and tyrannical and honest.

Wrennie shook and drew his breath sharply as the foghorn yawped out its "Whawn-n-n-n" again, reminding him that they were still in the Bank fog; that at any moment they were likely to be stunned by a heart-stopping crash as some liner's bow burst through the fo'c'sle's walls in a collision. Bow-plates buckling in and shredding, the in-thrust of an enormous black bow, water flooding in, cries and—However, the horn did at least show that They were awake up there on the bridge to steer him through the fog; and weren't They experienced seamen? Hadn't They made this trip ever so many times and never got killed? Wouldn't They take all sorts of pains on Their own account as well as on his?

But—just the same, would he really ever get to England alive? And if he did, would he have to go on holding his breath in terror for nine more days? Would the fo'c'sle always keep heaving up—up—up, like this, then down—down—down, as though it were going to sink?

"How do yuh like de fog-horn, Wrennie?"

Pete, the tough, spit the question up at him from a corner of his mouth. "Hope we don't run into no ships."

He winked at Tim, the weakling hatter, who took the cue and mourned:

"I'm kinda afraid we're going to, ain't you, Pete? The mate was telling me he was scared we would."

"Sures' t'ing you know. Hey, Wrennie, wait till youse have to beat it down-stairs and tie up a bull in a storm. Hully gee! Youse'll last quick on de game, Bird-ie!"

"Oh, shut up," snapped Wrennie's friend Morton.

But Morton was seasick; and Pete, not heeding him, outlined other dangers which he was happily sure were threatening them. Wrennie shivered to hear that the "grub 'd git worse." He writhed under Pete's loud questions about his loss, in some cattle-pen, of the gray-and-scarlet sweater-jacket which he had proudly and gaily purchased in New York for his work on the ship. And the card-players as-sured him that his suit-case, which he had intrusted to the Croac ship's carpenter, would probably be stolen by "Satan."

Satan! Wrennie shuddered still more. For Satan, the gaunt-jawed hook-nosed rail-faced head foreman, diabolically smiling when angry, sardonically sneering when calm, was a lean human whip-lash. Pete sniggered. He dilated upon Satan's wrath at Wrennie for not "coming across" with ten dollars for a bribe as he, Pete, had done.

(He lied, of course. And his words have not been given literally. They were not beautiful words.)

McGarver, the straw-boss, would always lie awake to enjoy a good brisk inde-cent story, but he liked Wrennie's admiration of him, so, lunging with his bull-like head out of his berth, he snorted:

"Hey, you, Pete, it's time to pound your ear. Cut it out."

Wrennie called down, sternly, "I ain't no theological student, Pete, and I don't mind profanity, but I wish you wouldn't talk like a garbage-scow."

"Hey, Poicy, did yuh bring your dictionary?" Pete bellowed to Tim, two feet distant from him. To Wrennie, "Say, Gladys, ain't you afraid one of them long woids like, t'eological, will turn around and bite you right on the wrist?"

"Dry up!" irritatedly snapped a Canadian.

"Aw, cut it out, you —," groaned another.

"Shut up," added McGarver, the straw-boss. "Both of you." Raging: "Gwan to bed, Pete, or I'll beat your block clean off. I mean it, see? *Hear me?*"

Yes, Pete heard him. Doubtless the first officer on the bridge heard, too, and perhaps the inhabitants of Newfoundland. But Pete took his time in scratching the back of his neck and stretching before he crawled into his berth. For half an hour he talked softly to Tim, for Wrennie's benefit, stating his belief that Satan, the head boss, had once thrown overboard a Jew much like Wrennie, and was likely thus to serve Wrennie, too. Tim pictured the result when, after the capsizing of the steamer which would undoubtedly occur if this long sickening motion kept up, Wrennie had to take to a boat with Satan.

The fingers of Wrennie curled into shape for strangling some one.

When Pete was asleep he worried off into thin slumber.

Then, there was Satan, the head boss, jerking him out of his berth, stirring his cramped joints to another dawn of drudgery—two hours of work and two of waiting before the daily eight-o'clock insult called breakfast. He tugged on his shoes, marveling at Mr. Wrenn's really being there, at his sitting in cramped stoop on the side of a berth in a dark filthy place that went up and down like a freight elevator, subject to the orders of persons whom he did not in the least like.

Through the damp gray sea-air he staggered hungrily along the gangway to the hatch amidships, and trembled down the iron ladder to McGarver's crew 'tween-decks.

First, watering the steers. Sickened by walking backward with pails of water he carried till he could see and think of nothing in the world save the water-butt, the puddle in front of it, and the cattlemen mercilessly dipping out pails there, through centuries that would never end. How those steers did drink!

McGarver's favorite bull, which he called "the Grenadier," took ten pails and still persisted in leering with dripping gray mouth beyond the headboard, trying to reach more. As Wrennie was carrying a pail to the heifers beyond, the Grenadier's horn caught and tore his overalls. The boat lurched. The pail whirled out of his hand. He grasped an iron stanchion and kicked the Grenadier in the jaw till the steer backed off, a reformed character.

McGarver cheered, for such kicks were a rule of the game.

"Good work," ironically remarked Tim, the weakling hatter.

"You go to hell," snapped Wrennie, and Tim looked much more respectful.

But Wrennie lost this credit before they had finished feeding out the hay, for he grew too dizzy to resent Tim's remarks.

Straining to pitch forkfuls into the pens while the boat rolled, slopping along the wet gangway, down by the bunkers of coal, where the heat seemed a close-wound choking shroud and the darkness was made only a little pale by light coming through dust-caked port-holes, he sneezed and coughed and grunted till he was exhausted. The floating bits of hay-dust were a thousand impish hands with poisoned nails scratching at the roof of his mouth. His skin prickled all over. He constantly discovered new and aching muscles. But he wabbled on until he finished the work, fifteen minutes after Tim had given out.

He crawled up to the main deck and huddled in the shelter of a pile of hay-bales where Pete was declaring to Tim and the rest that Satan "couldn't never get nothing on him."

Morton broke into Pete's publicity with the question, "Say, is it straight what they say, Pete, that you're the guy that owns the Leyland Line and that's why you know so much more than the rest of us poor lollops? Watson, the needle, quick!" [Applause and laughter.]

Wrennie felt personally grateful to Morton for this, but he went up to the aft top deck, where he could lie alone on a pile of tarpaulins. He made himself observe the sea which, as Kipling and Jack London had specifically promised him in their stories, surrounded him, everywhere shining free; but he glanced at it only once. To the north was a liner bound for home.

Home! Gee! That *was* rubbing it in! While at work, whether he was sick or not, he could forget—things. But the liner, fleeting on with bright ease, made the cattle-boat seem about as romantic as Mrs. Zapp's kitchen sink.

Why, he wondered—"why had he been a chump? Him a wanderer? No; he was a hired man on a sea-going dairy-farm. Well, he'd get onto this confounded job before he was through with it, but then—gee! back to God's Country!"

While the *Merian*, eleven days out, pleasantly rocked through the Irish Sea, with the moon revealing the coast of Anglesey, one Bill Wrenn lay on the after-deck, condescending to the heavens. It was so warm that they did not need to sleep below, and half a dozen of the cattlemen had brought their mattresses up on deck. Beside Bill Wrenn lay the man who had given him that name—Tim, the hatter, who had become weakly alarmed and admiring as Wrennie learned to rise feeling like a boy in early vacation-time, and to find shouting exhilaration in sending a forkful of hay fifteen good feet.

Morton, who lay near by, had also adopted the name "Bill Wrenn." Most of the trip Morton had discussed Pete and Tim instead of the fact that "things is curious." Mr. Wrenn had been jealous at first, but when he learned from Morton the theory that even a Pete was a "victim of 'vironment'" he went out for knowing him quite systematically.

To McGarver he had been "Bill Wrenn" since the fifth day, when he had kept a hay-bale from slipping back into the hold on the boss's head. Satan and Pete still called him "Wrennie," but he was not thinking about them just now with Tim listening admiringly to his observations on socialism.

Tim fell asleep. Bill Wrenn lay quiet and let memory color the sky above him. He recalled the gardens of water which had flowered in foam for him, strange ships and nomadic gulls, and the schools of sleekly black porpoises that, for him, had whisked through violet waves. Most of all, he brought back the yesterday's long excitement and delight of seeing the Irish coast hills—his first foreign land—whose faint sky fresco had seemed magical with the elfin lore of Ireland, a country that had ever been to him the haunt not of potatoes and politicians, but of fays. He had wanted fays. They were not common on the asphalt of West Sixteenth Street. But now he had seen them beckoning in Wanderland.

He was falling asleep under the dancing dome of the sky, a happy Mr. Wrenn, when he was aroused as a furious Bill, the cattleman. Pete was clogging near by, singing hoarsely, "Dey was a skoit and 'er name was Goity."

"You shut up!" commanded Bill Wrenn.

"Say, be careful!" the awakened Tim implored of him. Pete snorted: "Who says to 'shut up,' hey? Who was it, Satan?"

From the capstan, where he was still smoking, the head foreman muttered: "What's the odds? The little man won't say it again."

Pete stood by Bill Wrenn's mattress. "Who said 'shut up'?" sounded ominously.

Bill popped out of bed with what he regarded as a vicious fighting-crouch. For he was too sleepy to be afraid. "I did! What you going to do about it?" More mildly, as a fear of his own courage began to form, "I want to sleep."

"Oh! You want to sleep. Little mollycoddle wants to sleep, does he? Come here!"

The tough grabbed at Bill's shirt-collar across the mattress. Bill ducked, stuck out his arm wildly, and struck Pete, half by accident. Roaring, Pete bunted him, and he went down, with Pete kneeling on his stomach and pounding him.

Morton and honest McGarver, the straw-boss, sprang to drag off Pete, while Satan, the panther, with the first interest they had ever seen in his eyes, snarled: "Let 'em fight fair. Rounds. You're a' right, Bill."

"Right," commended Morton.

Armored with Satan's praise, firm but fearful in his rubber sneakers, surprised and shocked to find himself here doing this, Bill Wrenn squared at the rowdy. The moon touched sadly the lightly sketched Anglesey coast and the rippling wake, but Bill Wrenn, oblivious of dream moon and headland, faced his fellow-bruiser.

They circled. Pete stuck out his foot gently. Morton sprang in, bawling furiously, "None o' them rough-and-tumble tricks."

"Right-o," added McGarver.

Pete scowled. He was left powerless. He puffed and grew dizzy as Bill Wrenn danced delicately about him, for he could do nothing without back-street tactics. He did bloody the nose of Bill and pummel his ribs, but many cigarettes and much whisky told, and he was ready to laugh foolishly and make peace when, at the end of the sixth round, he felt Bill's neat little fist in a straight—and entirely accidental—rip to the point of his jaw.

Pete sent his opponent spinning with a back-hander which awoke all the cruelty of the terrible Bill. Silently Bill Wrenn plunged in with a smash! smash! smash! like a murderous savage, using every grain of his strength.

Let us turn from the lamentable luck of Pete. He had now got the idea that his supposed victim could really fight. Dismayed, shocked, disgusted, he stumbled and sought to flee, and was sent flat.

This time it was the great little Bill who had to be dragged off. McGarver held him, kicking and yammering, his mild mustache bristling like a battling cat's, till the next round, when Pete was knocked out by a clumsy whirlwind of fists.

He lay on the deck, with Bill standing over him and demanding, "What's my name, *heh?*"

"I t'ink it's Bill now, all right, Wrennie, old hoss—Bill, old hoss," groaned Pete.

He was permitted to sneak off into oblivion.

Bill Wrenn went below. In the dark passage by the fidley he fell to tremorous weeping. But the brackish hydrant water that stopped his nose-bleed saved him from hysterics. He climbed to the top deck, and now he could again see his brother pilgrim, the moon.

The stiffs and bosses were talking excitedly of the fight. Tim rushed up to gurgle: "Great, Bill, old man! You done just what I'd 'a' done if he'd cussed me. I told you Pete was a bluffer."

"Git out," said Satan.

Tim fled.

Morton came up, looked at Bill Wrenn, pounded him on the shoulder, and went off to his mattress. The other stiffs slouched away, but McGarver and Satan were still discussing the fight.

Snuggling on the hard black pile of tarpaulins, Bill talked to them, warmed to them, and became Mr. Wrenn. He announced his determination to wander adown every shining road of Europe.

"Nice work." "Sure." "You'll make a snappy little ole globe-trotter." "Sure; ought to be able to get the slickest kind of grub for four bits a day." "Nice work," Satan interjected from time to time, with smooth irony. "Sure. Go ahead. Like to hear your plans."

McGarver broke in: "Cut that out, Marvin. You're a 'Satan' all right. Quit your kidding the little man. He's all right. And he done fine on the job last three-four days."

Lying on his mattress, Bill stared at the network of the ratlines against the brilliant sky. The crisscross lines made him think of the ruled order-blanks of the Souvenir Company.

"Gee!" he mused, "I'd like to know if Jake is handling my work the way we—they—like it. I'd like to see the old office again, and Charley Carpenter, just for a couple of minutes. Gee! I wish they could have seen me put it all over Pete to-night! That's what I'm going to do to the blooming Englishmen if they don't like me."

The S.S. *Merian* panted softly beside the landing-stage at Birkenhead, Liverpool's Jersey City, resting in the sunshine after her voyage, while the cattle were unloaded. They had encountered fog-banks at the mouth of the Mersey River. Mr. Wrenn had ecstatically watched the shores of England—*England!*—ride at him through the fog, and had panted over the lines of English villas among the dunes. It was like a dream, yet the shore had such amazingly safe solid colors, real red and green and yellow, when contrasted with the fog-wet deck unearthily glancing with mist-lights.

Now he was seeing his first foreign city, and to Morton, stolidly curious beside him, he could say nothing save "Gee!" With church-tower and swarthy dome behind dome, Liverpool lay across the Mersey. Up through the Liverpool streets that ran down to the river, as though through peep-holes slashed straight back into the Middle Ages, his vision plunged, and it wandered unchecked through each street while he hummed:

"Free, free, in Eu-ro-pee, that's *me!*"

The cattlemen were called to help unload the remaining hay. They made a game of it. Even Satan smiled, even the Jewish elders were lightly affable as they made pretendedly fierce gestures at the squat patient hay-bales. Tim, the hatter, danced a limber foolish jig upon the deck, and McGarver bellowed, "The bon-nee bon-nee banks of Loch Lo-o-o-o-mond."

The crowd bawled: "Come on, Bill Wrenn; your turn. Hustle up with that bale, Pete, or we'll sic Bill on you."

Bill Wrenn, standing very dignified, piped: "I'm Colonel Armour. I own all these cattle, 'cept the Morris uns, see? Gotta do what I say, savvy? Tim, walk on your ear."

The hatter laid his head on the deck and waved his anemic legs in accordance with directions from Colonel Armour (late Wrenn).

The hay was off. The *Merian* tooted and headed across the Mersey to the Huskinson Dock, in Liverpool, while the cattlemen played tag about the deck. Whooping and laughing, they made last splashy toilets at the water-butts, dragged out their luggage, and descended to the dock-house.

As the cattlemen passed Bill Wrenn and Morton, shouting affectionate goodbys in English or courteous Yiddish, Bill commented profanely to Morton on the fact that the solid stone floor of the great shed seemed to have enough sea-motion to "make a guy sick." It was nearly his last utterance as Bill Wrenn. He became Mr. Wrenn, absolute Mr. Wrenn, on the street, as he saw a real English bobby, a real English carter, and the sign, "Cocoa House. Tea *Id.*"

England!

"Now for some real grub!" cried Morton. "No more scouse and willow-leaf tea."

Stretching out their legs under a table glorified with toasted Sally Lunns and Melton Mowbrays, served by a waitress who said "Thank *you*" with a rising inflection, they gazed at the line of mirrors running Britishly all around the room over the long lounge seat, and smiled with the triumphant content which comes to him whose hunger for dreams and hunger for meat-pies are satisfied together.

CHAPTER V

HE FINDS MUCH QUAINT ENGLISH FLAVOR

Big wharves, all right. England sure is queen of the sea, heh? Busy town, Liverpool. But, say, there is a quaint English flavor to these shops.... Look at that: 'Red Lion Inn.'... 'Overhead trams' they call the elevated. Real flavor, all right. English as can be.... I sure like to wander around these little shops. Street crowd. That's where you get the real quaint flavor."

Thus Morton, to the glowing Mr. Wrenn, as they turned into St. George's Square, noting the Lipton's Tea establishment. *Sir* Thomas Lipton—wasn't he a friend of the king? Anyway, he was some kind of a lord, and he owned big society racing-yachts.

In the grandiose square Mr. Wrenn prayerfully remarked, "Gee!"

"Greek temple. Fine," agreed Morton.

"That's St. George's Hall, where they have big organ concerts," explained Mr. Wrenn. "And there's the art-gallery across the Square, and here's the Lime Street Station." He had studied his Baedeker as club women study the cyclopedia. "Let's go over and look at the trains."

"Funny little boxes, ain't they, Wrenn, them cars! Quaint things. What is it they call 'em—carriages? First, second, third class...."

"Just like in books."

"Booking-office. That's tickets.... Funny, eh?"

Mr. Wrenn insisted on paying for both their high teas at the cheap restaurant, timidly but earnestly. Morton was troubled. As they sat on a park bench, smoking those most Anglican cigarettes, "Dainty Bits," Mr. Wrenn begged:

"What's the matter, old man?"

"Oh, nothing. Just thinking." Morton smiled artificially. He added, presently: "Well, old Bill, got to make the break. Can't go on living on you this way."

"Aw, thunder! You ain't living on me. Besides, I want you to. Honest I do. We can have a whole lot better time together, Morty."

"Yes, but—Nope; I can't do it. Nice of you. Can't do it, though. Got to go on my own, like the fellow says."

"Aw, come on. Look here; it's my money, ain't it? I got a right to spend it the way I want to, haven't I? Aw, come on. We'll bum along together, and then when he money is gone we'll get some kind of job together. Honest, I want you to."

"Hunka. Don't believe you'd care for the kind of knockabout jobs I'll have to get."

"Sure I would. Aw, come on, Morty. I—"

"You're too level-headed to like to bum around like a fool hobo. You'd dam soon get tired of it."

"What if I did? Morty, look here. I've been learning something on this trip. I've always wanted to just do one thing—see foreign places. Well, I want to do that just as much as ever. But there's something that's a whole lot more important. Somehow, I ain't ever had many friends. Some ways you're about the best friend I've ever had—you ain't neither too highbrow or too lowbrow. And this friendship business—it means such an awful lot. It's like what I was reading about—something by Elbert Hubbard or—thunder, I can't remember his name, but, anyway, it's one of those poet guys that writes for the back page of the *Journal*—something about a *joyous adventure*. That's what being friends is. Course you understand I wouldn't want to say this to most people, but you'll understand how I mean. It's—this friendship business is just like those old crusaders— you know—they'd start out on a fine morning—you know; armor shining, all that stuff. It wouldn't make any dif. what they met as long as they was fighting together. Rainy nights with folks sneaking through the rain to get at 'em, and all sorts of things— ready for anything, long as they just stuck together. That's the way this friendship business is, I b'lieve. Just like it said in the *Journal*. Yump, sure is. Gee! it's—Chance to tell folks what you think and really get some fun out of seeing places together. And I ain't ever done it much. Course I don't mean to say I've been living off on any blooming desert island all my life, but, just the same, I've always been kind of alone—not knowing many folks. You know how it is in a New York rooming-house. So now—Aw, don't slip up on me, Morty. Honestly, I don't care what kind of work we do as long as we can stick together; I don't care a hang if we don't get anything better to do than scrub floors!"

Morton patted his arm and did not answer for a while. Then:

"Yuh, I know how you mean. And it's good of you to like beating it around with me. But you sure got the exaggerated idee of me. And you'd get sick of the holes I'm likely to land in."

There was a certain pride which seemed dreadfully to shut Mr. Wrenn out as Morton added:

"Why, man, I'm going to do all of Europe. From the Turkish jails to—oh, St. Petersburg…. You made good on the *Merian*, all right. But you do like things ship-shape."

"Oh, I'd—"

"We might stay friends if we busted up now and met in New York again. But not if you get into all sorts of bum places w—"

"Why, look here, Morty—"

"—with me…. However, I'll think it over. Let's not talk about it till to-morrow."

"Oh, please do think it over, Morty, old man, won't you? And to-night you'll let me take you to a music-hall, won't you?"

"Uh—yes," Morton hesitated.

A music-hall—not mere vaudeville! Mr. Wrenn could hardly keep his feet on the pavement as they scampered to it and got ninepenny seats. He would have thought it absurd to pay eighteen cents for a ticket, but pence—They were out at nine-thirty. Happily tired, Mr. Wrenn suggested that they go to a temperance hotel at his expense, for he had read in Baedeker that temperance hotels were respectable—also cheap.

"No, no!" frowned Morton. "Tell you what you do, Bill. You go to a hotel, and I'll beat it down to a lodging-house on Duke Street…. Juke Street!… Remember how I ran onto Pete on the street? He told me you could get a cot down there for fourpence."

"Aw, come on to a hotel. Please do! It 'd just hurt me to think of you sleeping in one of them holes. I wouldn't sleep a bit if—"

"Say, for the love of Mike, Wrenn, get wise! Get wise, son! I'm not going to sponge on you, and that's all there is to it."

Bill Wrenn strode into their company for a minute, and quoth the terrible Bill:

"Well, you don't need to get so sore about it. I don't go around asking folks can I give 'em a meal ticket all the time, let me tell you, and when I do—Oh rats! Say, I didn't mean to get huffy, Morty. But, doggone you, old man, you can't shake me this easy. I sye, old top, I'm peeved; yessir. We'll go Dutch to a lodging-house, or even walk the streets."

"All right, sir; all right. I'll take you up on that. We'll sleep in an areaway some place."

They walked to the outskirts of Liverpool, questing the desirable dark alley. Awed by the solid quietude and semigrandeur of the large private estates, through narrow streets where dim trees leaned over high walls whose long silent stretches were broken only by mysterious little doors, they tramped bashfully, inspecting, but always rejecting, nooks by lodge gates.

They came to a stone church with a porch easily reached from the street, a large and airy stone porch, just suited, Morton declared, "to a couple of hoboes like us. If a bobby butts in, why, we'll just slide under them seats. Then the bobby can go soak his head."

Mr. Wrenn had never so far defied society as to steal a place for sleeping. He felt very uneasy, like a man left naked on the street by robbers, as he rolled up his coat for a pillow and removed his shoes in a place that was perfectly open to the street. The paved floor was cold to his bare feet, and, as he tried to go to sleep, it kept getting colder and colder to his back. Reaching out his hand, he fretfully rubbed the cracks between stones. He scowled up at the ceiling of the porch. He couldn't bear to look out through the door, for it framed the vicar's house, with lamplight bodying forth latticed windows, suggesting soft beds and laughter and comfortable books. All the while his chilled back was aching in new places.

He sprang up, put on his shoes, and paced the churchyard. It seemed a great waste of educational advantages not to study the tower of this foreign church, but he thought much more about his aching shoulder-blades.

Morton came from the porch stiff but grinning. "Didn't like it much, eh, Bill? Afraid you wouldn't. Must say I didn't either, though. Well, come on. Let's beat it around and see if we can't find a better place."

In a vacant lot they discovered a pile of hay. Mr. Wrenn hardly winced at the hearty slap Morton gave his back, and he pronounced, "Some Waldorf-Astoria, that stack!" as they sneaked into the lot. They had laid loving hands upon the hay, remarking, "Well, I *guess!*" when they heard from a low stable at the very back of the lot:

"I say, you chaps, what are you doing there?"

A reflective carter, who had been twisting two straws, ambled out of the shadow of the stable and prepared to do battle.

"Say, old man, can't we sleep in your hay just to-night?" argued Morton. "We're Americans. Came over on a cattle-boat. We ain't got only enough money to last us for food," while Mr. Wrenn begged, "Aw, please let us."

"Oh! You're Americans, are you? You seem decent enough. I've got a brother in the States. He used to own this stable with me. In St. Cloud, Minnesota, he is, you know. Minnesota's some kind of a shire. Either of you chaps been in Minnesota?"

"Sure," lied Morton; "I've hunted bear there."

"Oh, I say, bear now! My brother's never written m —"

"Oh, that was way up in the northern part, in the Big Woods. I've had some narrow escapes."

Then Morton, who had never been west of Pittsburg, sang somewhat in this wise the epic of the hunting he had never done:

Alone. Among the pines. Dead o' winter. Only one shell in his rifle. Cold of winter. Snow — deep snow. Snow-shoes. Hiking along — reg'lar mushing — packing grub to the lumber-camp. Way up near the Canadian border. Cold, terrible cold. Stars looked like little bits of steel.

Mr. Wrenn thought he remembered the story. He had read it in a magazine. Morton was continuing:

Snow stretched out among the pines. He was wearing a Mackinaw and shoe-packs. Saw a bear loping along. He had — Morton had — a .44-.40 Marlin, but only one shell. Thrust the muzzle of his rifle right into the bear's mouth. Scared for a minute. Almost fell off his snow-shoes. Hardest thing he ever did, to pull that trigger. Fired. Bear sort of jumped at him, then rolled over, clawing. Great place, those Minnesota Big—

"What's a shoe-pack?" the Englishman stolidly interjected.

"Kind of a moccasin.... Great place, those woods. Hope your brother gets the chance to get up there."

"I say, I wonder did you ever meet him? Scrabble is his name, Jock Scrabble."

"Jock Scrabble—no, but *say!* By golly, there was a fellow up in the Big Woods that came from St. Cl—St. Cloud? Yes, that was it. He was telling us about the town. I remember he said your brother had great chances there."

The Englishman meditatively accepted a bad cigar from Mr. Wrenn. Suddenly: "You chaps can sleep in the stable-loft if you'd like. But you must blooming well stop smoking."

So in the dark odorous hay-mow Mr. Wrenn stretched out his legs with an affectionate "good night" to Morton. He slept nine hours. When he awoke, at the sound of a chain clanking in the stable below, Morton was gone. This note was pinned to his sleeve:

> DEAR OLD MAN,—I still feel sure that you will not enjoy the hiking. Bumming is not much fun for most people, I don't think, even if they say it is. I do not want to live on you. I always did hate to graft on people. So I am going to beat it off alone. But I hope I will see you in N Y & we will enjoy many a good laugh together over our trip. If you will phone the P. R. R. you can find out when I get back & so on. As I do not know what your address will be. Please look me up & I hope you will have a good trip.
>
> Yours truly,
> HARRY P. MORTON.

Mr. Wrenn lay listening to the unfriendly rattling of the chain harness below for a long time. When he crawled languidly down from the hay-loft he glowered in a manner which was decidedly surly even for Bill Wrenn at a middle-aged English stranger who was stooping over a cow's hoof in a stall facing the ladder.

"Wot you doing here?" asked the Englishman, raising his head and regarding Mr. Wrenn as a housewife does a cockroach in the salad-bowl.

Mr. Wrenn was bored. This seemed a very poor sort of man; a bloated Cockney, with a dirty neck-cloth, vile cuffs of grayish black, and a waistcoat cut foolishly high.

"The owner said I could sleep here," he snapped.

"Ow. 'E did, did 'e? 'E ayn't been giving you any of the perishin' 'osses, too, 'as 'e?"

It was sturdy old Bill Wrenn who snarled, "Oh, shut up!" Bill didn't feel like standing much just then. He'd punch this fellow as he'd punched Pete, as soon as not—or even sooner.

"Ow.... It's shut up, is it?... I've 'arf a mind to set the 'tecs on you, but I'm lyte.

I'll just 'it you on the bloody nowse."

Bill Wrenn stepped off the ladder and squared at him. He was sorry that the Cockney was smaller than Pete.

The Cockney came over, feinted in an absent-minded manner, made swift and confusing circles with his left hand, and hit Bill Wrenn on the aforesaid bloody nose, which immediately became a bleeding nose. Bill Wrenn felt dizzy and, sitting on a grain-sack, listened amazedly to the Cockney's apologetic:

"I'm sorry I ayn't got time to 'ave the law on you, but I could spare time to 'it you again."

Bill shook the blood from his nose and staggered at the Cockney, who seized his collar, set him down outside the stable with a jarring bump, and walked away, whistling:

"Come, oh come to our Sunday-school,
Ev-v-v-v-v-ry Sunday morn-ing."

"Gee!" mourned Mr. William Wrenn, "and I thought I was getting this hobo business down pat.... Gee! I wonder if Pete *was* so hard to lick?"

CHAPTER VI

HE IS AN ORPHAN

Sadly clinging to the plan of the walking-trip he was to have made with Morton, Mr. Wrenn crossed by ferry to Birkenhead, quite unhappily, for he wanted to be discussing with Morton the quaintness of the uniformed functionaries. He looked for the *Merian* half the way over. As he walked through Birkenhead, bound for Chester, he pricked himself on to note red-brick house-rows, almost shocking in their lack of high front stoops. Along the country road he reflected: "Wouldn't Morty enjoy this! Farm-yard all paved. Haystack with a little roof on it. Kitchen stove stuck in a kind of fireplace. Foreign as the deuce."

But Morton was off some place, in a darkness where there weren't things to enjoy. Mr. Wrenn had lost him forever. Once he heard himself wishing that even Tim, the hatter, or "good old McGarver" were along. A scene so British that it seemed proper to enjoy it alone he did find in a real garden-party, with what appeared to be a real curate, out of a story in *The Strand*, passing teacups; but he passed out of that hot glow into a cold plodding that led him to Chester and a dull hotel which might as well have been in Bridgeport or Hoboken.

He somewhat timidly enjoyed Chester the early part of the next day, docilely following a guide about the walls, gaping at the mill on the Dee and asking the guide two intelligent questions about Roman remains. He snooped through the galleried streets, peering up dark stairways set in heavy masonry that spoke of historic sieges, and imagined that he was historically besieging. For a time Mr. Wrenn's fancies contented him.

He smiled as he addressed glossy red and green postcards to Lee Theresa and Goaty, Cousin John and Mr. Guilfogle, writing on each a variation of "Having a splendid trip. This is a very interesting old town. Wish you were here." Pantingly, he found a panorama showing the hotel where he was staying—or at least two of its chimneys—and, marking it with a heavy cross and the announcement "This is my hotel where I am staying," he sent it to Charley Carpenter.

He was at his nearest to greatness at Chester Cathedral. He chuckled aloud as he passed the remains of a refectory of monastic days, in the close, where knights had tied their romantically pawing chargers, "just like he'd read about in a story about the olden times." He was really there. He glanced about and assured himself of it. He wasn't in the office. He was in an English cathedral close!

But shortly thereafter he was in an English temperance hotel, sitting still, almost weeping with the longing to see Morton. He walked abroad, feeling like an ntruder on the lively night crowd; in a tap-room he drank a glass of English porter and tried to make himself believe that he was acquainted with the others in the room, to which theory they gave but little support. All this while his loneliness shadowed him.

Of that loneliness one could make many books; how it sat down with him; how he crouched in his chair, be-spelled by it, till he violently rose and fled, with oneliness for companion in his flight. He was lonely. He sighed that he was "lonely as fits." Lonely—the word obsessed him. Doubtless he was a bit mad, as are all the isolated men who sit in distant lands longing for the voices of friendship.

Next morning he hastened to take the train for Oxford to get away from his oneliness, which lolled evilly beside him in the compartment. He tried to convey to a stodgy North Countryman his interest in the way the seats faced each other. The man said "Oh aye?" insultingly and returned to his Manchester newspaper.

Feeling that he was so offensive that it was a matter of honor for him to keep his eyes away, Mr. Wrenn dutifully stared out of the door till they reached Oxford.

There is a calm beauty to New College gardens. There is, Mr. Wrenn observed, "something simply *slick* about all these old quatrangleses," crossed by summering students in short flappy gowns. But he always returned to his exile's room, where he now began to hear the new voice of shapeless nameless Fear—fear of all this alien world that didn't care whether he loved it or not.

He sat thinking of the cattle-boat as a home which he had loved but which he would never see again. He had to use force on himself to keep from hurrying back to Liverpool while there still was time to return on the same boat.

No! He was going to "stick it out somehow, and get onto the hang of all this highbrow business."

Then he said: "Oh, darn it all. I feel rotten. I wish I was dead!"

"Those, sir, are the windows of the apartment once occupied by Walter Pater," said the cultured American after whom he was trailing. Mr. Wrenn viewed them attentively, and with shame remembered that he didn't know who Walter Pater was. But—oh yes, now he remembered; Walter was the guy that 'd murdered his whole family. So, aloud, "Well, I guess Oxford's sorry Walt ever come here, all right."

"My dear sir, Mr. Pater was the most immaculate genius of the nineteenth century," lectured Dr. Mittyford, the cultured American, severely.

Mr. Wrenn had met Mittyford, Ph.D., near the barges; had, upon polite request, still more politely lent him a match, and seized the chance to confide in somebody. Mittyford had a bald head, neat eye-glasses, a fair family income, a chatty good-fellowship at the Faculty Club, and a chilly contemptuousness in his rhetoric class-room at Leland Stanford, Jr., University. He wrote poetry, which he filed away under the letter "P" in his letter-file.

Dr. Mittyford grudgingly took Mr. Wrenn about, to teach him what not to enjoy. He pointed at Shelley's rooms as at a certificated angel's feather, but Mr.

Wrenn writhingly admitted that he had never heard of Shelley, whose name he confused with Max O'Rell's, which Dr. Mittyford deemed an error. Then, Pater's window. The doctor shrugged. Oh well, what could you expect of the proletariat! Swinging his stick aloofly, he stalked to the Bodleian and vouchsafed, "That, sir, is the *AEschylus* Shelley had in his pocket when he was drowned."

Though he heard with sincere regret the news that his new idol was drowned, Mr. Wrenn found that *AEschylus* left him cold. It seemed to be printed in a foreign language. But perhaps it was merely a very old book.

Standing before a case in which was an exquisite book in a queer wrigglesome language, bearing the legend that from this volume Fitzgerald had translated the *Rubaiyat*, Dr. Mittyford waved his hand and looked for thanks.

"Pretty book," said Mr. Wrenn.

"And did you note who used it?"

"Uh—yes." He hastily glanced at the placard. "Mr. Fitzgerald. Say, I think I read some of that Rubaiyat. It was something about a Persian kitten—I don't remember exactly."

Dr. Mittyford walked bitterly to the other end of the room.

About eight in the evening Mr. Wrenn's landlady knocked with, "There's a gentleman below to see you, sir."

"Me?" blurted Mr. Wrenn.

He galloped down-stairs, panting to himself that Morton had at last found him. He peered out and was overwhelmed by a motor-car, with Dr. Mittyford waiting in awesome fur coat, goggles, and gauntlets, centered in the car-lamplight that loomed in the shivery evening fog.

"Gee! just like a hero in a novel!" reflected Mr. Wrenn.

"Get on your things," said the pedagogue. "I'm going to give you the time of your life."

Mr. Wrenn obediently went up and put on his cap. He was excited, yet frightened and resentful at being "dragged into all this highbrow business" which he had resolutely been putting away the past two hours.

As he stole into the car Dr. Mittyford seemed comparatively human, remarking: "I feel bored this evening. I thought I would give you a *nuit blanche*. How would you like to go to the Red Unicorn at Brempton—one of the few untouched old inns?"

"That would be nice," said Mr. Wrenn, unenthusiastically.

His chilliness impressed Dr. Mittyford, who promptly told one of the best of his well-known whimsical yet scholarly stories.

"Ha! ha!" remarked Mr. Wrenn.

He had been saying to himself: "By golly! I ain't going to even try to be a society guy with him no more. I'm just going to be *me*, and if he don't like it he can go to the dickens."

So he was gentle and sympathetic and talked West Sixteenth Street slang, to the rhetorician's lofty amusement.

The tap-room of the Red Unicorn was lighted by candles and a fireplace. That is a simple thing to say, but it was not a simple thing for Mr. Wrenn to see. As he observed the trembling shadows on the sanded floor he wriggled and excitedly murmured, "Gee!... Gee whittakers!"

The shadows slipped in arabesques over the dust-gray floor and scampered as bravely among the rafters as though they were in such a tale as men told in believing days. Rustics in smocks drank ale from tankards; and in a corner was snoring an ear-ringed peddler with his beetle-black head propped on an oilcloth pack.

Stamping in, chilly from the ride, Mr. Wrenn laughed aloud. With a comfortable feeling on the side toward the fire he stuck his slight legs straight out before the old-time settle, looked devil-may-care, made delightful ridges on the sanded floor with his toe, and clapped a pewter pot on his knee with a small emphatic "Wop!" After about two and a quarter tankards he broke out, "Say, that peddler guy there, don't he look like he was a gipsy—you know—sneaking through the hedges around the manner-house to steal the earl's daughter, huh?"

"Yes.... You're a romanticist, then, I take it?"

"Yes, I guess I am. Kind of. Like to read romances and stuff." He stared at Mittyford beseechingly. "But, say—say, I wonder why—Somehow, I haven't enjoyed Oxford and the rest of the places like I ought to. See, I'd always thought I'd be simply nutty about the quatrangles and stuff, but I'm afraid they're too highbrow for me. I hate to own up, but sometimes I wonder if I can get away with this traveling stunt."

Mittyford, the magnificent, had mixed ale and whisky punch. He was mellowly instructive:

"Do you know, I've been wondering just what you *would* get out of all this. You really have a very fine imagination of a sort, you know, but of course you're lacking in certain factual bases. As I see it, your *metier* would be to travel with a pleasant wife, the two of you hand in hand, so to speak, looking at the more obvious public buildings and plesaunces—avenues and plesuances. There must be a certain portion of the tripper class which really has the ability `for to admire and for to see.'"

Dr. Mittyford finished his second toddy and with a wave of his hand presented to Mr. Wrenn the world and all the plesaunces thereof, for to see, though not, of course, to admire Mittyfordianly.

"But—what are you to do now about Oxford? Well, I'm afraid you're taken into captivity a bit late to be trained for that sort of thing. Do about Oxford? Why, go back, master the world you understand. By the way, have you seen my book on *Saxon Derivatives?* Not that I'm prejudiced in its favor, but it might give you a glimmering of what this difficile thing `culture' really is."

The rustics were droning a church anthem. The glow of the ale was in Mr. Wrenn. He leaned back, entirely happy, and it seemed confusedly to him that what little he had heard of his learned and affectionate friend's advice gratefully confirmed his own theory that what one wanted was friends—a "nice wife"— folks. "Yes, sir, by golly! It was awfully nice of the Doc." He pictured a tender girl in golden brown back in the New York he so much desired to see who would await him evenings with a smile that was kept for him. Homey—that was what *he* was going to be! He happily and thoughtfully ran his finger about the rim of his glass ten times.

"Time to go, I'm afraid," Dr. Mittyford was saying. Through the exquisite haze that now filled the room Mr. Wrenn saw him dimly, as a triangle of shirt-front and two gleaming ellipses for eyes.... His dear friend, the Doc!... As he walked through the room chairs got humorously in his way, but he good-naturedly picked a path among them, and fell asleep in the motor-car. All the ride back he made soft mouse-like sounds of snoring.

When he awoke in the morning with a headache and surveyed his unchangeably dingy room he realized slowly, after smothering his head in the pillow to shut off the light from his scorching eyeballs, that Dr. Mittyford had called him a fool for trying to wander. He protested, but not for long, for he hated to venture out there among the dreadfully learned colleges and try to understand stuff written in letters that look like crow-tracks.

He packed his suit-case slowly, feeling that he was very wicked in leaving Oxford's opportunities.

Mr. Wrenn rode down on a Tottenham Court Road bus, viewing the quaintness of London. Life was a rosy ringing valiant pursuit, for he was about to ship on a Mediterranean steamer laden chiefly with adventurous friends. The bus passed a victoria containing a man with a real monocle. A newsboy smiled up at him. The Strand roared with lively traffic.

But the gray stonework and curtained windows of the Anglo-Southern Steamship Company's office did not invite any Mr. Wrenns to come in and ship, nor did the hall porter, a beefy person with a huge collar and sparse painfully sleek hair, whose eyes were like cold boiled mackerel as Mr. Wrenn yearned:

"Please—uh—please will you be so kind and tell me where I can ship as a steward for the Med—"

"None needed."

"Or Spain? I just want to get any kind of a job at first. Peeling potatoes or—It don't make any difference—"

"None needed, I said, my man." The porter examined the hall clock extensively.

Bill Wrenn suddenly popped into being and demanded: "Look here, you; I want to see somebody in authority. I want to know what I *can* ship as."

The porter turned round and started. All his faith in mankind was destroyed by the shock of finding the fellow still there. "Nothing, I told you. No one needed."

"Look here; can I see somebody in authority or not?"

The porter was privately esteemed a wit at his motherin-law's. Waddling away, he answered, "Or not."

Mr. Wrenn drooped out of the corridor. He had planned to see the Tate Gallery, but now he hadn't the courage to face the difficulties of enjoying pictures. He zig-zagged home, mourning: "What's the use. And I'll be hung if I'll try any other offices, either. The icy mitt, that's what they hand you here. Some day I'll go down to the docks and try to ship there. Prob'ly. Gee! I feel rotten!"

Out of all this fog of unfriendliness appeared the waitress at the St. Brasten Cocoa House; first, as a human being to whom he could talk, second, as a woman. She was ignorant and vulgar; she misused English cruelly; she wore greasy cotton garments, planted her large feet on the floor with firm clumsiness, and always laughed at the wrong cue in his diffident jests. But she did laugh; she did listen while he stammered his ideas of meat-pies and St. Paul's and aeroplanes and Shelley and fog and tan shoes. In fact, she supposed him to be a gentleman and scholar, not an American.

He went to the cocoa-house daily.

She let him know that he was a man and she a woman, young and kindly, clear-skinned and joyous-eyed. She touched him with warm elbow and plump hip, leaning against his chair as he gave his order. To that he looked forward from meal to meal, though he never ceased harrowing over what he considered a shameful intrigue.

That opinion of his actions did not keep him from tingling one lunch-time when he suddenly understood that she was expecting to be tempted. He tempted her without the slightest delay, muttering, "Let's take a walk this evening?"

She accepted. He was shivery and short of breath while he was trying to smile at her during the rest of the meal, and so he remained all afternoon at the Tower of London, though he very well knew that all this history—"kings and gwillotines and stuff"—demanded real Wrenn thrills.

They were to meet on a street-corner at eight. At seven-thirty he was waiting for her. At eight-thirty he indignantly walked away, but he hastily returned, and stood there another half-hour. She did not come.

When he finally fled home he was glad to have escaped the great mystery of life, then distressingly angry at the waitress, and desolate in the desert stillness of his room.

He sat in his cold hygienic uncomfortable room on Tavistock Place trying to keep his attention on the "tick, tick, tick, tick" of his two-dollar watch, but really cowering before the vast shadowy presences that slunk in from the hostile city.

He didn't in the least know what he was afraid of. The actual Englishman whom he passed on the streets did not seem to threaten his life, yet his friendly watch and familiar suit-case seemed the only things he could trust in all the menacing world as he sat there, so vividly conscious of his fear and loneliness that he dared not move his cramped legs.

The tension could not last. For a time he was able to laugh at himself, and he made pleasant pictures—Charley Carpenter telling him a story at Drubel's; Morton companionably smoking on the top deck; Lee Theresa flattering him during an evening walk. Most of all he pictured the brown-eyed sweetheart he was going to meet somewhere, sometime. He thought with sophomoric shame of his futile affair with the waitress, then forgot her as he seemed almost to touch the comforting hand of the brown-eyed girl.

"Friends, that's what I want. You bet!" That was the work he was going to do—make acquaintances. A girl who would understand him, with whom he could trot about, seeing department-store windows and moving-picture shows.

It was then, probably, hunched up in the dowdy chair of faded upholstery, that he created the two phrases which became his formula for happiness. He desired "somebody to go home to evenings"; still more, "some one to work with and work for."

It seemed to him that he had mapped out his whole life. He sat back, satisfied, and caught the sound of emptiness in his room, emphasized by the stilly tick of his watch.

"Oh—Morton—" he cried.

He leaped up and raised the window. It was raining, but through the slow splash came the night rattle of hostile London. Staring down, he studied the desolate circle of light a street-lamp cast on the wet pavement. A cat gray as dish-water, its fur worn off in spots, lean and horrible, sneaked through the circle of light like the spirit of unhappiness, like London's sneer at solitary Americans in Russell Square rooms.

Mr. Wrenn gulped. Through the light skipped a man and a girl, so little aware of him that they stopped, laughingly, wrestling for an umbrella, then disappeared, and the street was like a forgotten tomb. A hansom swung by, the hoofbeats sharp and cheerless. The rain dripped. Nothing else. Mr. Wrenn slammed down the window.

He smoothed the sides of his suit-case and reckoned the number of miles it had traveled with him. He spun his watch about on the table, and listened to its rapid mocking speech, "Friends, friends; friends, friends."

Sobbing, he began to undress, laying down each garment as though he were going to the scaffold. When the room was dark the great shadowy forms of fear thronged unchecked about his narrow dingy bed.

Once during the night he woke. Some sound was threatening him. It was London, coming to get him and torture him. The light in his room was dusty, mottled, gray, lifeless. He saw his door, half ajar, and for some moments lay motionless, watching stark and bodiless heads thrust themselves through the opening and withdraw with sinister alertness till he sprang up and opened the door wide.

But he did not even stop to glance down the hall for the crowd of phantoms that had gathered there. Some hidden manful scorn of weakness made him sneer aloud, "Don't be a baby even if you *are* lonely."

His voice was deeper than usual, and he went to bed to sleep, throwing himself down with a coarse wholesome scorn of his nervousness.

He awoke after dawn, and for a moment curled in happy wriggles of satisfaction over a good sleep. Then he remembered that he was in the cold and friendless prison of England, and lay there panting with desire to get away, to get back to America, where he would be safe.

He wanted to leap out of bed, dash for the Liverpool train, and take passage for America on the first boat. But perhaps the officials in charge of the emigrants and the steerage (and of course a fellow would go steerage to save money) would want to know his religion and the color of his hair—as bad as trying to ship. They might hold him up for a couple of days. There were quarantines and customs and things, of which he had heard. Perhaps for two or even three days more he would have to stay in this nauseating prison-land.

This was the morning of August 3, 1910, two weeks after his arrival in London, and twenty-two days after victoriously reaching England, the land of romance.

CHAPTER VII

HE MEETS A TEMPERAMENT

Mr. Wrenn was sulkily breakfasting at Mrs. Cattermole's Tea House, which Mrs. Cattermole kept in a genteel fashion in a basement three doors from his rooming-house on Tavistock Place. After his night of fear and tragic portents he resented the general flowered-paper-napkin aspect of Mrs. Cattermole's establishment. "Hungh!" he grunted, as he jabbed at the fringed doily under the silly pink-and-white tea-cup on the green-and-white lacquered tray brought him by a fat waitress in a frilly apron which must have been made for a Christmas pantomime fairy who was not fat. "Hurump!" he snorted at the pictures of lambs and radishes and cathedrals and little duckies on Mrs. Cattermole's pink-and-white wall.

He wished it were possible—which, of course, it was not—to go back to the St. Brasten Cocoa House, where he could talk to the honest flat-footed galumping waitress, and cross his feet under his chair. For here he was daintily, yes, daintily, studied by the tea-room habitues—two bouncing and talkative daughters of an American tourist, a slender pale-haired English girl student of Assyriology with large top-barred eye-glasses over her protesting eyes, and a sprinkling of people living along Tavistock Place, who looked as though they wanted to know if your opinions on the National Gallery and abstinence were sound.

His disapproval of the lambiness of Mrs. Cattermole's was turned to a feeling of comradeship with the other patrons as he turned, with the rest, to stare hostilely at a girl just entering. The talk in the room halted, startled.

Mr. Wrenn gasped. With his head solemnly revolving, his eyes followed the young woman about his table to a table opposite. "A freak! Gee, what red hair!" was his private comment.

A slender girl of twenty-eight or twenty-nine, clad in a one-piece gown of sage-green, its lines unbroken by either belt or collar-brooch, fitting her as though it had been pasted on, and showing the long beautiful sweep of her fragile thighs and long-curving breast. Her collar, of the material of the dress, was so high that it touched her delicate jaw, and it was set off only by a fine silver chain, with a La Valliere of silver and carved Burmese jade. Her red hair, red as a poinsettia, parted and drawn severely back, made a sweep about the fair dead-white skin of her bored sensitive face. Bored blue-gray eyes, with pathetic crescents of faintly violet-hued wrinkles beneath them, and a scarce noticeable web of tinier wrinkles at the side. Thin long cheeks, a delicate nose, and a straight strong mouth of thin but startlingly red lips.

Such was the new patron of Mrs. Cattermole.

She stared about the tea-room like an officer inspecting raw recruits, sniffed at the stare of the thin girl student, ordered breakfast in a low voice, then languidly considered her toast and marmalade. Once she glanced about the room. Her heavy brows were drawn close for a second, making a deep-cleft wrinkle of ennui over her nose, and two little indentations, like the impressions of a box corner, in her forehead over her brows.

Mr. Wrenn's gaze ran down the line of her bosom again, and he wondered at her hands, which touched the heavy bread-and-butter knife as though it were a fine-point pen. Long hands, colored like ivory; the joint wrinkles etched into her skin; orange cigarette stains on the second finger; the nails—

He stared at them. To himself he commented, "Gee! I never did see such freak finger-nails in my life." Instead of such smoothly rounded nails as Theresa Zapp displayed, the new young lady had nails narrow and sharp-pointed, the ends like little triangles of stiff white writing-paper.

As she breakfasted she scanned Mr. Wrenn for a second. He was too obviously caught staring to be able to drop his eyes. She studied him all out, with almost as much interest as a policeman gives to a passing trolley-car, yawned delicately, and forgot him.

Though you should penetrate Greenland or talk anarchism to the daughter of a millionaire grocer, never shall you feel a more devouring chill than enveloped Mr. Wrenn as the new young lady glanced away from him, paid her check, rose slithily from her table, and departed. She rounded his table; not stalking out of its way, as Theresa would have done, but bending from the hips. Thus was it revealed to Mr. Wrenn that—

He was almost too horrified to put it into words.... He had noticed that there was something kind of funny in regard to her waist; he had had an impression of remarkably smooth waist curves and an unjagged sweep of back. Now he saw that—It was unheard of; not at all like Lee Theresa Zapp or ladies in the Subway. For—the freak girl wasn't wearing corsets!

When she had passed him he again studied her back, swiftly and covertly. No, sir. No question about it. It couldn't be denied by any one now that the girl was a freak, for, charitable though Our Mr. Wrenn was, he had to admit that there was no sign of the midback ridge and little rounded knobbinesses of corseted respectability. And he had a closer view of the texture of her sage-green crash gown.

"Golly!" he said to himself; "of all the doggone cloth for a dress! Reg'lar gunny-sacking. She's skinny, too. Bright-red hair. She sure is the prize freak. Kind of good-looking, but—get a brick!"

He hated to rule so clever-seeming a woman quite out of court. But he remembered her scissors glance at him, and his soft little heart became very hard.

How brittle are our steel resolves! When Mr. Wrenn walked out of Mrs. Cattermole's excellent establishment and heavily inspected the quiet Bloomsbury Street, with a cat's-meat-man stolidly clopping along the pavement, as loneliness rushed on him and he wondered what in the world he could do, he mused, "Gee! I bet that red-headed lady would be interestin' to know."

A day of furtive darts out from his room to do London, which glumly declined to be done. He went back to the Zoological Gardens and made friends with a tiger which, though it presumably came from an English colony, was the friendliest thing he had seen for a week. It did yawn, but it let him talk to it for a long while. He stood before the bars, peering in, and whenever no one else was about he murmured: "Poor fella, they won't let you go, heh? You got a worse boss 'n Goglefogle, heh? Poor old fella."

He didn't at all mind the disorder and rancid smell of the cage; he had no fear of the tiger's sleek murderous power. But he was somewhat afraid of the sound of his own tremorous voice. He had spoken aloud so little lately.

A man came, an Englishman in a high offensively well-fitting waistcoat, and stood before the cage. Mr. Wrenn slunk away, robbed of his new friend, the tiger, the forlornest person in all London, kicking at pebbles in the path.

As half-dusk made the quiet street even more detached, he sat on the steps of his rooming-house on Tavistock Place, keeping himself from the one definite thing he wanted to do—the thing he keenly imagined a happy Mr. Wrenn doing—dashing over to the Euston Station to find out how soon and where he could get a train for Liverpool and a boat for America.

A girl was approaching the house. He viewed her carelessly, then intently. It was the freak lady of Mrs. Cattermole's Tea House—the corsetless young woman of the tight-fitting crash gown and flame-colored hair. She was coming up the steps of his house.

He made room for her with feverish courtesy. She lived in the same house— He instantly, without a bit of encouragement from the uninterested way in which she snipped the door to, made up a whole novel about her. Gee! She was a French countess, who lived in a reg'lar chateau, and she was staying in Bloomsbury incognito, seeing the sights. She was a noble. She was—

Above him a window opened. He glanced up. The countess incog. was leaning out, scanning the street uncaringly. Why—her windows were next to his! He was living next room to an unusual person—as unusual as Dr. Mittyford.

He hurried up-stairs with a fervid but vague plan to meet her. Maybe she really was a French countess or somepun'. All evening, sitting by the window, he was comforted as he heard her move about her room. He had a friend. He had started that great work of making friends—well, not started, but started starting—then he got confused, but the idea was a flame to warm the fog-chilled spaces of the London street.

At his Cattermole breakfast he waited long. She did not come. Another day— but why paint another day that was but a smear of flat dull slate? Yet another breakfast, and the lady of mystery came. Before he knew he was doing it he had bowed to her, a slight uneasy bend of his neck. She peered at him, unseeing, and sat down with her back to him.

He got much good healthy human vindictive satisfaction in evicting her violently from the French chateau he had given her, and remembering that, of course, she was just a "fool freak Englishwoman—prob'ly a bloomin' stoodent" he scorned, and so settled *her!* Also he told her, by telepathy, that her new gown was freakier than ever—a pale-green thing, with large white buttons.

As he was coming in that evening he passed her in the hall. She was clad in what he called a bathrobe, and what she called an Arabian *burnoose*, of black embroidered with dull-gold crescents and stars, showing a V of exquisite flesh at her throat. A shred of tenuous lace straggled loose at the opening of the *burnoose*. Her radiant hair, tangled over her forehead, shone with a thousand various gleams from the gas-light over her head as she moved back against the wall and stood waiting for him to pass. She smiled very doubtfully, distantly—the smile, he felt, of a great lady from Mayfair. He bobbed his head, lowered his eyes abashedly, and noticed that along the shelf of her forearm, held against her waist, she bore many silver toilet articles, and such a huge heavy fringed Turkish bath-towel as he had never seen before.

He lay awake to picture her brilliant throat and shining hair. He rebuked himself for the lack of dignity in "thinking of that freak, when she wouldn't even return a fellow's bow." But her shimmering hair was the star of his dreams.

Napping in his room in the afternoon, Mr. Wrenn heard slight active sounds from her, next room. He hurried down to the stoop.

She stood behind him on the door-step, glaring up and down the street, as bored and as ready to spring as the Zoo tiger. Mr. Wrenn heard himself saying to the girl, "Please, miss, do you mind telling me—I'm an American; I'm a stranger in London—I want to go to a good play or something and what would I—what would be good—"

"I don't know, reahlly," she said, with much hauteur. "Everything's rather rotten this season, I fancy." Her voice ran fluting up and down the scale. Her a's were very broad.

"Oh—oh—y-you *are* English, then?"

"Yes!"

"Why—uh—"

"*Yes!*"

"Oh, I just had a fool idea maybe you might be French."

"Perhaps I am, y' know. I'm not reahlly English," she said, blandly.

"Why—uh—"

"What made you think I was French? Tell me; I'm interested."

"Oh, I guess I was just—well, it was almost make-b'lieve—how you had a castle in France—just a kind of a fool game."

"Oh, *don't* be ashamed of imagination," she demanded, stamping her foot, while her voice fluttered, low and beautifully controlled, through half a dozen notes. "Tell me the rest of your story about me."

She was sitting on the rail above him now. As he spoke she cupped her chin with the palm of her delicate hand and observed him curiously.

"Oh, nothing much more. You were a countess—"

"Please! Not just 'were.' Please, sir, mayn't I be a countess now?"

"Oh yes, of course you are!" he cried, delight submerging timidity. "And your father was sick with somepun' mysterious, and all the docs shook their heads and said 'Gee! we dunno what it is,' and so you sneaked down to the treasure-chamber—you see, your dad—your father, I should say—he was a cranky old Frenchman—just in the story, you know. He didn't think you could do anything yourself about him being mysteriously sick. So one night you—"

"Oh, was it dark? Very *very* dark? And silent? And my footsteps rang on the hollow flagstones? And I swiped the gold and went forth into the night?"

"Yes, *yes!* That's it."

"But why did I swipe it?"

"I'm just coming to that," he said, sternly.

"Oh, please, sir, I'm awful sorry I interrupted."

"It was like this: You wanted to come over here and study medicine so's you could cure your father."

"But please, sir," said the girl, with immense gravity, "mayn't I let him die, and not find out what's ailing him, so I can marry the *maire?*"

"Nope," firmly, "you got to—Say, gee! I didn't expect to tell you all this make-b'lieve…. I'm afraid you'll think it's awful fresh of me."

"Oh, I loved it—really I did—because you liked to make it up about poor Istra. (My name is Istra Nash.) I'm sorry to say I'm not reahlly"—her two "reallys" were quite different—"a countess, you know. Tell me—you live in this same house, don't you? Please tell me that you're not an interesting Person. Please!"

"I—gee! I guess I don't quite get you."

"Why, stupid, an Interesting Person is a writer or an artist or an editor or a girl who's been in Holloway Jail or Canongate for suffraging, or any one else who depends on an accident to be tolerable."

"No, I'm afraid not; I'm just a kind of clerk."

"Good! Good! My dear sir—whom I've never seen before—have I? By the way, please don't think I usually pick up stray gentlemen and talk to them about my pure white soul. But you, you know, made stories about me…. I was saying: If you could only know how I loathe and hate and despise Interesting People just now! I've seen so much of them. They talk and talk and talk—they're just like Kipling's bandar-log—What is it?

"See us rise in a flung festoon
Half-way up to the jealous moon.

Don't you wish you—

could know all about art and economics as we do?' That's what they say. Umph!"

Then she wriggled her fingers in the air like white butterflies, shrugged her shoulders elaborately, rose from the rail, and sat down beside him on the steps, quite matter-of-factly.

He gould feel his temple-pulses beat with excitement.

She turned her pale sensitive vivid face slowly toward him.

"When did you see me—to make up the story?"

"Breakfasts. At Mrs. Cattermole's."

"Oh yes.... How is it you aren't out sight-seeing? Or is it blessedly possible that you aren't a tripper—a tourist?"

"Why, I dunno." He hunted uneasily for the right answer. "Not exactly. I tried a stunt—coming over on a cattle-boat."

"That's good. Much better."

She sat silent while, with enormous and self-betraying pains to avoid detection, he studied her firm thin brilliantly red lips. At last he tried:

"Please tell me something about London. Some of you English— Oh, I dunno. I can't get acquainted easily."

"My dear child, I'm not English! I'm quite as American as yourself. I was born in California. I never saw England till two years ago, on my way to Paris. I'm an art student.... That's why my accent is so perishin' English—I can't afford to be just *ordinary* British, y' know."

Her laugh had an October tang of bitterness in it.

"Well, I'll—say, what do you know about that!" he said, weakly.

"Tell me about yourself—since apparently we're now acquainted.... Unless you want to go to that music-hall?"

"Oh no, no, no! Gee, I was just *crazy* to have somebody to talk to—somebody nice—I was just about nutty, I was so lonely," all in a burst. He finished, hesitatingly, "I guess the English are kinda hard to get acquainted with."

"Lonely, eh?" she mused, abrupt and bluffly kind as a man, for all her modulating woman's voice. "You don't know any of the people here in the house?"

"No'm. Say, I guess we got rooms next to each other."

"How romantic!" she mocked.

"Wrenn's my name; William Wrenn. I work for—I used to work for the Souvenir and Art Novelty Company. In New York."

"Oh. I see. Novelties? Nice little ash-trays with `Love from the Erie Station'? And woggly pin-cushions?"

"Yes! And fat pug-dogs with black eyes."

"Oh no-o-o! Please not black! Pale sympathetic blue eyes—nice honest blue eyes!"

"Nope. Black. Awful black.... Say, gee, I ain't talking too nutty, am I?"

"'Nutty'? You mean 'idiotically'? The slang's changed since—Oh yes, of course; you've succeeded in talking quite nice and 'idiotic.'"

"Oh, say, gee, I didn't mean to—When you been so nice and all to me—"

"Don't apologize!" Istra Nash demanded, savagely. "Haven't they taught you that?"

"Yes'm," he mumbled, apologetically.

She sat silent again, apparently not at all satisfied with the architecture of the opposite side of Tavistock Place. Diffidently he edged into speech:

"Honest, I did think you was English. You came from California? Oh, say, I wonder if you've ever heard of Dr. Mittyford. He's some kind of school-teacher. I think he teaches in Leland Stamford College."

"Leland Stanford? You know him?" She dropped into interested familiarity.

"I met him at Oxford."

"Really?... My brother was at Stanford. I think I've heard him speak of—Oh yes. He said that Mittyford was a cultural climber, if you know what I mean; rather—oh, how shall I express it?—oh, shall we put it, finicky about things people have just told him to be finicky about."

"Yes!" glowed Mr. Wrenn.

To the luxury of feeling that he knew the unusual Miss Istra Nash he sacrificed Dr. Mittyford, scholarship and eye-glasses and Shelley and all, without mercy.

"Yes, he was awfully funny. Gee! I didn't care much for him."

"Of course you know he's a great man, however?" Istra was as bland as though she had meant that all along, which left Mr. Wrenn nowhere at all when it came to deciding what she meant.

Without warning she rose from the steps, flung at him "G' night," and was off down the street.

Sitting alone, all excited happiness, Mr. Wrenn muttered: "Ain't she a wonder! Gee! she's striking-lookin'! Gee whittakers!"

Some hours later he said aloud, tossing about in bed: "I wonder if I was too fresh. I hope I wasn't. I ought to be careful."

He was so worried about it that he got up and smoked a cigarette, remembered that he was breaking still another rule by smoking too much, then got angry and snapped defiantly at his suit-case: "Well, what do I care if I *am* smoking too much? And I'll be as fresh as I want to." He threw a newspaper at the censorious suit-case and, much relieved, went to bed to dream that he was a rabbit making enormously amusing jests, at which he laughed rollickingly in half-dream, till he realized that he was being awakened by the sound of long sobs from the room of Istra Nash.

Afternoon; Mr. Wrenn in his room. Miss Nash was back from tea, but there was not a sound to be heard from her room, though he listened with mouth open, bent forward in his chair, his hands clutching the wooden seat, his finger-tips rubbing nervously back and forth over the rough under-surface of the wood. He wanted to help her—the wonderful lady who had been sobbing in the night. He had a plan, in which he really believed, to say to her, "Please let me help you, princess, jus' like I was a knight."

At last he heard her moving about. He rushed downstairs and waited on the stoop.

When she came out she glanced down and smiled contentedly. He was flutteringly sure that she expected to see him there. But all his plan of proffering assistance vanished as he saw her impatient eyes and her splendors of dress—another tight-fitting gown, of smoky gray, with faint silvery lights gliding along the fabric.

She sat on the rail above him, immediately, unhesitatingly, and answered his "Evenin'" cheerfully.

He wanted so much to sit beside her, to be friends with her. But, he felt, it took courage to sit beside her. She was likely to stare haughtily at him. However, he did go up to the rail and sit, shyly kicking his feet, beside her, and she did not stare haughtily. Instead she moved over an inch or two, glanced at him almost as though they were sharing a secret, and said, quietly:

"I thought quite a bit about you last evening. I believe you really have an imagination, even though you are a salesman—I mean so many don't; you know how it is."

"Oh yes."

You see, Mr. Wrenn didn't know he was commonplace.

"After I left here last night I went over to Olympia Johns', and she dragged me off to a play. I thought of you at it because there was an imaginative butler in it. You don't mind my comparing you to a butler, do you? He was really quite the nicest person in the play, y' know. Most of it was gorgeously rotten. It used to be a French farce, but they sent it to Sunday-school and gave it a nice fresh frock. It seemed that a gentleman-tabby had been trying to make a match between his nephew and his ward. The ward arted. Personally I think it was by tonsorial art. But, anyway, the uncle knew that nothing brings people together so well as hating the same person. You know, like hating the cousin, when you're a kiddy, hating the cousin that always keeps her nails clean?"

"Yes! That's *so!*"

"So he turned nasty, and of course the nephew and ward clinched till death did them part—which, I'm very sorry to have to tell you, death wasn't decent enough to do on the stage. If the play could only have ended with everybody's funeral I should have called it a real happy ending."

Mr. Wrenn laughed gratefully, though uncertainly. He knew that she had made jokes for him, but he didn't exactly know what they were.

"The imaginative butler, he was rather good. But the rest—Ugh!"

"That must have been a funny play," he said, politely.

She looked at him sidewise and confided, "Will you do me a favor?"

"Oh yes, I—"

"Ever been married?"

He was frightfully startled. His "No" sounded as though he couldn't quite remember.

She seemed much amused. You wouldn't have believed that this superior quizzical woman who tapped her fingers carelessly on her slim exquisite knee had ever sobbed in the night.

"Oh, that wasn't a personal question," she said. "I just wanted to know what you're like. Don't you ever collect people? I do—chloroform 'em quite cruelly and pin their poor little corpses out on nice clean corks…. You live alone in New York, do you?"

"Y-yes."

"Who do you play with—know?"

"Not—not much of anybody. Except maybe Charley Carpenter. He's assistant bookkeeper for the Souvenir Company. "He had wanted to, and immediately decided not to, invent *grandes mondes* whereof he was an intimate.

"What do—oh, you know—people in New York who don't go to parties or read much—what do they do for amusement? I'm so interested in types."

"Well—" said he.

That was all he could say till he had digested a pair of thoughts: Just what did she mean by "types"? Had it something to do with printing stories? And what could he say about the people, anyway? He observed:

"Oh, I don't know—just talk about—oh, cards and jobs and folks and things and—oh, you know; go to moving pictures and vaudeville and go to Coney Island and—oh, sleep."

"But you—?"

"Well, I read a good deal. Quite a little. Shakespeare and geography and a lot of stuff. I like reading."

"And how do you place Nietzsche?" she gravely desired to know.

"?"

"Nietzsche. You know—the German humorist."

"Oh yes—uh—let me see now; he's—uh—"

"Why, you remember, don't you? Haeckel and he wrote the great musical comedy of the century. And Matisse did the music—Matisse and Rodin."

"I haven't been to it," he said, vaguely. "...I don't know much German. Course I know a few words, like *Spricken Sie Dutch* and *Bitty, sir,* that Rabin at the Souvenir Company—he's a German Jew, I guess—learnt me.... But, say, isn't Kipling great! Gee! when I read *Kim* I can imagine I'm hiking along one of those roads in India just like I was there—you know, all those magicians and so on.... Readin's wonderful, ain't it!"

"Um. Yes."

"I bet you read an awful lot."

"Very little. Oh—D'Annunzio and some Turgenev and a little Tourgenieff.... That last was a joke, you know."

"Oh yes," disconcertedly.

"What sorts of plays do you go to, Mr. Wrenn?"

"Moving pictures mostly," he said, easily, then bitterly wished he hadn't confessed so low-life a habit.

"Well—tell me, my dear—Oh, I didn't mean that; artists use it a good deal; it just means 'old chap.' You *don't* mind my asking such beastly personal questions, do you? I'm interested in people.... And now I must go up and write a letter. I was going over to Olympia's—she's one of the Interesting People I spoke of—but you see you have been much more amusing. Good night. You're lonely in London, aren't you? We'll have to go sightseeing some day."

"Yes, I am lonely!" he exploded. Then, meekly: "Oh, thank you! I sh'd be awful pleased to.... Have you seen the Tower, Miss Nash?"

"No. Never. Have you?"

"No. You see, I thought it 'd be kind of a gloomy thing to see all alone. Is that why you haven't never been there, too?"

"My dear man, I see I shall have to educate you. Shall I? I've been taken in hand by so many people—it would be a pleasure to pass on the implied slur. Shall I?"

"Please do."

"One simply doesn't go and see the Tower, because that's what trippers do. Don't you understand, my dear? (Pardon the 'my dear' again.) The Tower is the sort of thing school superintendents see and then go back and lecture on in school assembly-room and the G. A. R. hall. I'll take you to the Tate Gallery." Then, very abruptly, "G' night," and she was gone.

He stared after her smooth back, thinking: "Gee! I wonder if she got sore at something I said. I don't think I was fresh this time. But she beat it so quick.... Them lips of hers—I never knew there was such red lips. And an artist—paints pictures!... Read a lot—Nitchy—German musical comedy. Wonder if that's that 'Merry Widow' thing?... That gray dress of hers makes me think of fog. Cur'ous."

In her room Istra Nash inspected her nose in a mirror, powdered, and sat down to write, on thick creamy paper:

Skilly dear, I'm in a fierce Bloomsbury boarding-house—bores —except for a Phe-nomenon—little man of 35 or 40 with embryonic imagination & a virgin soul. I'll try to keep from planting radical thoughts in the virgin soul, but I'm tempted.

Oh Skilly dear I'm lonely as the devil. Would it be too bromid. to say I wish you were here? I put out my hand in the darkness, & yours wasn't there. My dear, my dear, how desolate—Oh you understand it only too well with your supercilious grin & your superior eye-glasses & your beatific Oxonian ignorance of poor eager America.

I suppose I *am* just a barbarous Californian kiddy. It's just as Pere Dureon said at the atelier, "You haf a' onderstanding of the 'igher immorality, but I 'ope you can cook—paint you cannot."

He wins. I can't sell a single thing to the art editors here or get one single order. One horrid eye-glassed earnest youth who Sees People at a magazine, he vouchsafed that they "didn't use any Outsiders." Outsiders! And his hair was nearly as red as my wretched mop. So I came home & howled & burned Milan tapers before your picture. I did. Though you don't deserve it.

Oh damn it, am I getting sentimental? You'll read this at Petit Monsard over your drip & grin at your poor unnietzschean barbarian.

I. N.

CHAPTER VIII

HE TIFFINS

Mr. Wrenn, chewing and chewing and chewing the cud of thought in his room next evening, after an hour had proved two things; thus:

(a) The only thing he wanted to do was to go back to America at once, because England was a country where every one—native or American—was so unfriendly and so vastly wise that he could never understand them.

(b) The one thing in the world that he wanted to do was to be right here, for the most miraculous event of which he had ever heard was meeting Miss Nash. First one, then the other, these thoughts swashed back and forth like the swinging tides. He got away from them only long enough to rejoice that somehow—he didn't know how—he was going to be her most intimate friend, because they were both Americans in a strange land and because they both could make-believe.

Then he was proving that Istra would, and would not, be the perfect comrade among women when some one knocked at his door.

Electrified, his cramped body shot up from its crouch, and he darted to the door.

Istra Nash stood there, tapping her foot on the sill with apologetic haste in her manner. Abruptly she said:

"So sorry to bother you. I just wondered if you could let me have a match? I'm all out."

"Oh *yes!* Here's a whole box. Please take 'em. I got plenty more." [Which was absolutely untrue.]

"Thank you. S' good o' you," she said, hurriedly. "G' night."

She turned away, but he followed her into the hall, bashfully urging: "Have you been to another show? Gee! I hope you draw a better one next time 'n the one about the guy with the nephew."

"Thank you."

She glanced back in the half dark hall from her door—some fifteen feet from his. He was scratching at the wall-paper with a diffident finger, hopeful for a talk.

"Won't you come in?" she said, hesitatingly.

"Oh, thank you, but I guess I hadn't better."

Suddenly she flashed out the humanest of smiles, her blue-gray eyes crinkling with cheery friendship. "Come in, come in, child." As he hesitatingly entered she warbled: "Needn't both be so lonely all the time, after all, need we? Even if you *don't* like poor Istra. You don't—do you?" Seemingly she didn't expect an answer to her question, for she was busy lighting a Russian cigarette. It was the first time in his life that he had seen a woman smoke.

With embarrassed politeness he glanced away from her as she threw back her head and inhaled deeply. He blushingly scrutinized the room.

In the farther corner two trunks stood open. One had the tray removed, and out of the lower part hung a confusion of lacey things from which he turned away uncomfortable eyes. He recognized the black-and-gold burnoose, which was tumbled on the bed, with a nightgown of lace insertions and soft wrinkles in the lawn, a green book with a paper label bearing the title *Three Plays for Puritans*, a red slipper, and an open box of chocolates.

On the plain kitchen-ware table was spread a cloth of Reseda green, like a dull old leaf in color. On it lay a gold-mounted fountain-pen, huge and stub-pointed; a medley of papers and torn envelopes, a bottle of Creme Yvette, and a silver-framed portrait of a lean smiling man with a single eye-glass.

Mr. Wrenn did not really see all these details, but he had an impression of luxury and high artistic success. He considered the Yvette flask the largest bottle of perfume he'd ever seen; and remarked that there was "some guy's picture on the table." He had but a moment to reconnoiter, for she was astonishingly saying:

"So you were lonely when I knocked?"

"Why, how—"

"Oh, I could see it. We all get lonely, don't we? I do, of course. Just now I'm getting sorer and sorer on Interesting People. I think I'll go back to Paris. There even the Interesting People are—why, they're interesting. Savvy—you see I *am* an American—savvy?"

"Why—uh—uh—uh—I d-don't exactly get what you mean. How do you mean about 'Interesting People'?"

"My dear child, of course you don't get me." She went to the mirror and patted her hair, then curled on the bed, with an offhand "Won't you sit down?" and smoked elaborately, blowing the blue tendrils toward the ceiling as she continued: "Of course you don't get it. You're a nice sensible clerk who've had enough real work to do to keep you from being afraid that other people will think you're commonplace. You don't have to coddle yourself into working enough to earn a living by talking about temperament.

"Why, these Interesting People—You find 'em in London and New York and San Francisco just the same. They're convinced they're the wisest people on earth. There's a few artists and a bum novelist or two always, and some social workers.

The particular bunch that it amuses me to hate just now—and that I apparently can't do without—they gather around Olympia Johns, who makes a kind of salon out of her rooms on Great James Street, off Theobald's Road…. They might just as well be in New York; but they're even stodgier. They don't get sick of the game of being on intellectual heights as soon as New-Yorkers do.

"I'll have to take you there. It's a cheery sensation, you know, to find a man who has some imagination, but who has been unspoiled by Interesting People, and take him to hear them wamble. They sit around and growl and rush the growler—I hope you know growler-rushing—and rejoice that they're free spirits. Being Free, of course, they're not allowed to go and play with nice people, for when a person is Free, you know, he is never free to be anything but Free. That may seem confusing, but they understand it at Olympia's.

"Of course there's different sorts of intellectuals, and each cult despises all the others. Mostly, each cult consists of one person, but sometimes there's two—a talker and an audience—or even three. For instance, you may be a militant and a vegetarian, but if some one is a militant and has a good figure, why then—oof!… That's what I mean by `Interesting People.' I loathe them! So, of course, being one of them, I go from one bunch to another, and, upon my honor, every single time I think that the new bunch *is* interesting!"

Then she smoked in gloomy silence, while Mr. Wrenn remarked, after some mental labor, "I guess they're like cattlemen—the cattle-ier they are, the more romantic they look, and then when you get to know them the chief trouble with them is that they're cattlemen."

"Yes, that's it. They're—why, they're—Oh, poor dear, there, there, there! It *sha'n't* have so much intellekchool discussion, *shall* it!… I think you're a very nice person, and I'll tell you what we'll do. We'll have a small fire, shall we? In the fire-place."

"Yes!"

She pulled the old-fashioned bell-cord, and the old-fashioned North Country landlady came—tall, thin, parchment-faced, musty-looking as though she had been dressed up in Victorian garments in 1880 and left to stand in an unaired parlor ever since. She glowered silent disapproval at the presence of Mr. Wrenn in Istra's room, but sent a slavey to make the fire—"saxpence uxtry." Mr. Wrenn felt guilty till the coming of the slavey, a perfect Christmas-story-book slavey, a small and merry lump of soot, who sang out, "Chilly t'-night, ayn't it?" and made a fire that was soon singing "Chilly t'-night," like the slavey.

Istra sat on the floor before the fire, Turk-wise, her quick delicate fingers drumming excitedly on her knees.

"Come sit by me. You, with your sense of the romantic, ought to appreciate sitting by the fire. You know it's always done."

He slumped down by her, clasping his knees and trying to appear the dignified American business man in his country-house.

She smiled at him intimately, and quizzed:

"Tell me about the last time you sat with a girl by the fire. Tell poor Istra the dark secret. Was she the perfect among pink faces?"

"I've—never—sat—before—any—fireplace—with —any—one! Except when I was about nine—one Hallowe'en—at a party in Parthenon—little town up York State."

"Really? Poor kiddy!"

She reached out her hand and took his. He was terrifically conscious of the warm smoothness of her fingers playing a soft tattoo on the back of his hand, while she said:

"But you have been in love? Drefful in love?"

"I never have."

"Dear child, you've missed so much of the tea and cakes of life, haven't you? And you have an interest in life. Do you know, when I think of the jaded Interesting People I've met—Why do I leave you to be spoiled by some shop-girl in a flowered hat? She'd drag you to moving-picture shows.... Oh! You didn't tell me that you went to moving pictures, did you?"

"No!" he lied, fervently, then, feeling guilty, "I used to, but no more."

"It *shall* go to the nice moving pictures if it wants to! It shall take me, too. We'll forget there are any syndicalists or broken-colorists for a while, won't we? We'll let the robins cover us with leaves."

"You mean like the babes in the woods? But, say, I'm afraid you ain't just a babe in the woods! You're the first person with brains I ever met, 'cept, maybe, Dr. Mittyford; and the Doc never would play games, I don't believe. The very first one, really."

"Thank you!" Her warm pressure on his hand tightened. His heart was making the maddest gladdest leaps, and timidly, with a feeling of historic daring, he ventured to explore with his thumb-tip the fine lines of the side of her hand.... It actually was he, sitting here with a princess, and he actually did feel the softness of her hand, he pantingly assured himself.

Suddenly she gave his hand a parting pressure and sprang up.

"Come. We'll have tiffin, and then I'll send you away, and to-morrow we'll go see the Tate Gallery."

While Istra was sending the slavey for cakes and a pint of light wine Mr. Wrenn sat in a chair—just sat in it; he wanted to show that he could be dignified and not take advantage of Miss Nash's kindness by slouchin' round. Having read much Kipling, he had an idea that tiffin was some kind of lunch in the afternoon, but of course if Miss Nash used the word for evening supper, then he had been wrong.

Istra whisked the writing-table with the Reseda-green cover over before the fire, chucked its papers on the bed, and placed a bunch of roses on one end, moving the small blue vase two inches to the right, then two inches forward.

The wine she poured into a decanter. Wine was distinctly a problem to him.

He was excited over his sudden rise into a society where one took wine as a matter of course. Mrs. Zapp wouldn't take it as a matter of course. He rejoiced that he wasn't narrow-minded, like Mrs. Zapp. He worked so hard at not being narrow-minded like Mrs. Zapp that he started when he was called out of his daydream by a mocking voice:

"But you might look at the cakes. Just once, anyway. They are very nice cakes."

"Uh—"

"Yes, I know the wine is wine. Beastly of it."

"Say, Miss Nash, I did get you this time."

"Oh, don't tell me that my presiding goddessship is over already."

"Uh—sure! Now I'm going to be a cruel boss."

"Dee-lighted! Are you going to be a caveman?"

"I'm sorry. I don't quite get you on that."

"That's too bad, isn't it. I think I'd rather like to meet a caveman."

"Oh say, I know about that caveman—Jack London's guys. I'm afraid I ain't one. Still—on the cattle-boat—Say, I wish you could of seen it when the gang were tying up the bulls, before starting. Dark close place 'tween-decks, with the steers bellowin' and all parked tight together, and the stiffs gettin' seasick—so seasick we just kind of staggered around; and we'd get hold of a head rope and yank and then let go, and the bosses, d yell, 'Pull, or I'll brain you.' And then the fo'c'sle—men packed in like herrings."

She was leaning over the table, making a labyrinth with the currants from a cake and listening intently. He stopped politely, feeling that he was talking too much. But, "Go on, please do," she commanded, and he told simply, seeing it more and more, of Satan and the Grenadier, of the fairies who had beckoned to him from the Irish coast hills, and the comradeship of Morton.

She interrupted only once, murmuring, "My dear, it's a good thing you're articulate, anyway—" which didn't seem to have any bearing on hay-bales.

She sent him away with a light "It's been a good party, hasn't it, caveman? (If you *are* a caveman.) Call for me tomorrow at three. We'll go to the Tate Gallery."

She touched his hand in the fleetingest of grasps.

"Yes. Good night, Miss Nash," he quavered.

A morning of planning his conduct so that in accompanying Istra Nash to the Tate Gallery he might be the faithful shadow and beautiful transcript of Mittyford, Ph.D. As a result, when he stood before the large canvases of Mr. Watts at the Tate he was so heavy and correctly appreciative, so ready not to enjoy the stories in the pictures of Millais, that Istra suddenly demanded:

"Oh, my dear child, I have taken a great deal on my hands. You've got to learn to play. You don't know how to play. Come. I shall teach you. I don't know why I should, either. But—come."

She explained as they left the gallery: "First, the art of riding on the buses. Oh, it is an art, you know. You must appreciate the flower-girls and the gr-r-rand young bobbies. You must learn to watch for the blossoms on the restaurant terraces and roll on the grass in the parks. You're much too respectable to roll on the grass, aren't you? I'll try ever so hard to teach you not to be. And we'll go to tea. How many kinds of tea are there?"

"Oh, Ceylon and English Breakfast and—oh—Chinese."

"B—"

"And golf tees!" he added, excitedly, as they took a seat in front atop the bus.

"Puns are a beginning at least," she reflected.

"But how many kinds of tea *are* there, Istra?... Oh say, I hadn't ought to—"

"Course; call me Istra or anything else. Only, you mustn't call my bluff. What do I know about tea? All of us who play are bluffers, more or less, and we are ever so polite in pretending not to know the others are bluffing.... There's lots of kinds of tea. In the New York Chinatown I saw once—Do you know Chinatown? Being a New-Yorker, I don't suppose you do."

"Oh yes. And Italiantown. I used to wander round there."

"Well, down at the Seven Flowery Kingdoms Chop Suey and American Cooking there's tea at five dollars a cup that they advertise is grown on `cloud-covered mountain-tops.' I suppose when the tops aren't cloud-covered they only charge three dollars a cup.... But, serious-like, there's really only two kinds of teas—those you go to to meet the man you love and ought to hate, and those you give to spite the women you hate but ought to—hate! Isn't that lovely and complicated? That's playing. With words. My aged parent calls it `talking too much and not saying anything.' Note that last—not saying *anything!* It's one of the rules in playing that mustn't be broken."

He understood that better than most of the things she said. "Why," he exclaimed, "it's kind of talking sideways."

"Why, yes. Of course. Talking sideways. Don't you see now?"

Gallant gentleman as he was, he let her think she had invented the phrase.

She said many other things; things implying such vast learning that he made gigantic resolves to "read like thunder."

Her great lesson was the art of taking tea. He found, surprisedly, that they weren't really going to endanger their clothes by rolling on park grass. Instead, she led him to a tea-room behind a candy-shop on Tottenham Court Road, a low room with white wicker chairs, colored tiles set in the wall, and green Sedji-ware jugs with irregular bunches of white roses. A waitress with wild-rose cheeks and a busy step brought Orange Pekoe and lemon for her, Ceylon and Russian Caravan tea and a jug of clotted cream for him, with a pile of cinnamon buns.

"But—" said Istra. "Isn't this like Alice in Wonderland! But you must learn the buttering of English muffins most of all. If you get to be very good at it the flunkies will let you take tea at the Carleton. They are such hypercritical flunkies, and the one that brings the gold butter-measuring rod to test your skill, why, he always wears knee-breeches of silver gray. So you can see, Billy, how careful you have to be. And eat them without buttering your nose. For if you butter your nose they'll think you're a Greek professor. And you wouldn't like that, would you, honey?" He learned how to pat the butter into the comfortable brown insides of the muffins that looked so cold and floury without. But Istra seemed to have lost interest; and he didn't in the least follow her when she observed:

"Doubtless it *was* the best butter. But where, where, dear dormouse, are the hatter and hare? Especially the sweet bunny rabbit that wriggled his ears and loved Gralice, the *princesse d' outre-mer.*

> "Where, where are the hatter and hare,
> And where is the best butter gone?"

Presently: "Come on. Let's beat it down to Soho for dinner. Or—no! Now you shall lead me. Show me where you'd go for dinner. And you shall take me to a music-hall, and make me enjoy it. Now *you* teach *me* to play."

"Gee! I'm afraid I don't know a single thing to teach you."

"Yes, but—See here! We are two lonely Western barbarians in a strange land. We'll play together for a little while. We're not used to each other's sort of play, but that will break up the monotony of life all the more. I don't know how long we'll play or—Shall we?"

"Oh yes!"

"Now show me how you play."

"I don't believe I ever did much, really."

"Well, you shall take me to your kind of a restaurant."

"I don't believe you'd care much for penny meat-pies."

"Little meat-pies?"

"Um-huh."

"Little *crispy* ones? With flaky covers?"

"Um-huh."

"Why, course I would! And ha'p'ny tea? Lead me to it, O brave knight! And to a vaudeville."

He found that this devoted attendant of theaters had never seen the beautiful Italians who pounce upon protesting zylophones with small clubs, or the side-splitting juggler's assistant who breaks up piles and piles of plates. And as to the top hat that turns into an accordion and produces much melody, she was ecstatic.

At after-theater supper he talked of Theresa and South Beach, of Charley Carpenter and Morton—Morton—Morton.

They sat, at midnight, on the steps of the house in Tavistock Place.

"I do know you now, "she mused. "It's curious how any two babes in a strange-enough woods get acquainted. You *are* a lonely child, aren't you?" Her voice was mother-soft. "We will play just a little—"

"I wish I had some games to teach. But you know so much."

"And I'm a perfect beauty, too, aren't I?" she said, gravely.

"Yes, you are!" stoutly.

"You would be loyal…. And I need some one's admiration…. Mostly, Paris and London hold their sides laughing at poor Istra."

He caught her hand. "Oh, don't! They *must* 'preciate you. I'd like to kill anybody that didn't!"

"Thanks." She gave his hand a return pressure and hastily withdrew her own. "You'll be good to some sweet pink face…. And I'll go on being discontented. Oh, isn 't life the fiercest proposition!… We seem different, you and I, but maybe it's mostly surface—down deep we're alike in being desperately unhappy because we never know what we're unhappy about. Well—"

He wanted to put his head down on her knees and rest there. But he sat still, and presently their cold hands snuggled together.

After a silence, in which they were talking of themselves, he burst out: "But I don't see how Paris could help 'preciating you. I'll bet you're one of the best artists they ever saw…. The way you made up a picture in your mind about that juggler!"

"Nope. Sorry. Can't paint at all."

"Ah, stuff!" with a rudeness quite masterful. "I'll bet your pictures are corkers."

"Um."

"Please, would you let me see some of them some time. I suppose it would bother—"

"Come up-stairs. I feel inspired. You are about to hear some great though nasty criticisms on the works of the unfortunate Miss Nash."

She led the way, laughing to herself over something. She gave him no time to blush and hesitate over the impropriety of entering a lady's room at midnight, but stalked ahead with a brief "Come in."

She opened a large portfolio covered with green-veined black paper and yanked out a dozen unframed pastels and wash-drawings which she scornfully tossed on the bed, saying, as she pointed to a mass of Marseilles roofs:

"Do you see this sketch? The only good thing about it is the thing that last art editor, that red-headed youth, probably didn't like. Don't you hate red hair? You see these ridiculous glaring purple shadows under the *clocher?*"

She stared down at the picture interestedly, forgetting him, pinching her chin thoughtfully, while she murmured: "They're rather nice. Rather good. Rather good."

Then, quickly twisting her shoulders about, she poured out:

"But look at this. Consider this arch. It's miserably out of drawing. And see how I've faked this figure? It isn't a real person at all. Don't you notice how I've juggled with this stairway? Why, my dear man, every bit of the drawing in this thing would disgrace a seventh-grade drawing-class in Dos Puentes. And regard the bunch of lombardies in this other picture. They look like umbrellas upside down in a silly wash-basin. Uff! It's terrible. *Affreux!* Don't act as though you liked them. You really needn't, you know. Can't you see now that they're hideously out of drawing?"

Mr. Wrenn's fancy was walking down a green lane of old France toward a white cottage with orange-trees gleaming against its walls. In her pictures he had found the land of all his forsaken dreams.

"I—I—I—" was all he could say, but admiration pulsed in it.

"Thank you…. Yes, we *will* play. Good night. To-morrow!"

CHAPTER IX

HE ENCOUNTERS THE INTELLECTUALS

He wanted to find a cable office, stalk in, and nonchalantly send to his bank for more money. He could see himself doing it. Maybe the cable clerk would think he was a rich American. What did he care if he spent all he had? A guy, he admonished himself, just had to have coin when he was goin' with a girl like Miss Istra. At least seven times he darted up from the door-step, where he was on watch for her, and briskly trotted as far as the corner. Each time his courage melted, and he slumped back to the door-step. Sending for money—gee, he groaned, that was pretty dangerous.

Besides, he didn't wish to go away. Istra might come down and play with him.

For three hours he writhed on that door-step, till he came to hate it; it was as much a prison as his room at the Zapps' had been. He hated the areaway grill, and a big brown spot on the pavement, and, as a truck-driver hates a motorman, so did he hate a pudgy woman across the street who peeped out from a second-story window and watched him with cynical interest. He finally could endure no longer the world's criticism, as expressed by the woman opposite. He started as though he were going to go right now to some place he had been intending to go to all the time, and stalked away, ignoring the woman.

He caught a bus, then another, then walked a while. Now that he was moving, he was agonizedly considering his problem: What was Istra to him, really? What could he be to her? He *was* just a clerk. She could never love him. "And of course," he explained to himself, "you hadn't oughta love a person without you expected to marry them; you oughtn't never even touch her hand." Yet he did want to touch hers. He suddenly threw his chin back, high and firm, in defiance. He didn't care if he was wicked, he declared. He wanted to shout to Istra across all the city: Let us be great lovers! Let us be mad! Let us stride over the hilltops. Though that was not at all the way he phrased it.

Then he bumped into a knot of people standing on the walk, and came down from the hilltops in one swoop.

A crowd was collecting before Rothsey Hall, which bore the sign:

GLORY—GLORY—GLORY
SPECIAL SALVATION ARMY JUBILEE MEETING

EXPERIENCES OF ADJUTANT CRABBENTHWAITE IN AFRICA

He gaped at the sign. A Salvationist in the crowd, trim and well set up, his red-ribboned Salvation Army cap at a jaunty angle, said, "Won't you come in, brother?"

Mr. Wrenn meekly followed into the hall. Bill Wrenn was nowhere in sight.

Now it chanced that Adjutant Crabbenthwaite told much of Houssas and the N'Gombi, of saraweks and week-long treks, but Mr. Wrenn's imagination was not for a second drawn to Africa, nor did he even glance at the sun-bonneted Salvationist women packed in the hall. He was going over and over the Adjutant's denunciations of the Englishmen and Englishwomen who flirt on the mail-boats.

Suppose it had been himself and his madness over Istra—at the moment he quite called it madness—that the Adjutant had denounced!

A Salvationist near by was staring at him most accusingly....

He walked away from the jubilee reflectively. He ate his dinner with a grave courtesy toward the food and the waiter. He was positively courtly to his fork. For he was just reformed. He was going to "steer clear" of mad artist women—of all but nice good girls whom you could marry. He remembered the Adjutant's thundered words:

"Flirting you call it—flirting! Look into your hearts. God Himself hath looked into them and found flirtation the gateway to hell. And I tell you that these army officers and the bedizened women, with their wine and cigarettes, with their devil's calling-cards and their jewels, with their hell-lighted talk of the sacrilegious follies of socialism and art and horse-racing, O my brothers, it was all but a cloak for looking upon one another to lust after one another. Rotten is this empire, and shall fall when our soldiers seek flirtation instead of kneeling in prayer like the iron men of Cromwell."

Istra.... Card-playing.... Talk of socialism and art. Mr. Wrenn felt very guilty. Istra.... Smoking and drinking wine.... But his moral reflections brought the picture of Istra the more clearly before him—the persuasive warmth of her perfect fingers; the curve of her backward-bent throat as she talked in her melodious voice of all the beautiful things made by the wise hands of great men.

He dashed out of the restaurant. No matter what happened, good or bad, he had to see her. While he was climbing to the upper deck of a bus he was trying to invent an excuse for seeing her.... Of course one couldn't "go and call on ladies in their rooms without havin' some special excuse; they would think that was awful fresh."

He left the bus midway, at the sign of a periodical shop, and purchased a *Blackwood's* and a *Nineteenth Century*. Morton had told him these were the chief English "highbrow magazines."

He carried them to his room, rubbed his thumb in the lampblack on the gas-fixture, and smeared the magazine covers, then cut the leaves and ruffled the margins to make the magazines look dog-eared with much reading; not because he wanted to appear to have read them, but because he felt that Istra would not permit him to buy things just for her.

All this business with details so calmed him that he wondered if he really cared to see her at all. Besides, it was so late—after half-past eight.

"Rats! Hang it all! I wish I was dead. I don't know what I do want to do," he groaned, and cast himself upon his bed. He was sure of nothing but the fact that he was unhappy. He considered suicide in a dignified manner, but not for long enough to get much frightened about it.

He did not know that he was the toy of forces which, working on him through the strangeness of passionate womanhood, could have made him a great cad or a petty hero as easily as they did make him confusedly sorry for himself. That he wasn't very much of a cad or anything of a hero is a detail, an accident resulting from his thirty-five or thirty-six years of stodgy environment. Cad or hero, filling scandal columns or histories, he would have been the same William Wrenn.

He was thinking of Istra as he lay on his bed. In a few minutes he dashed to his bureau and brushed his thinning hair so nervously that he had to try three times for a straight parting. While brushing his eyebrows and mustache he solemnly contemplated himself in the mirror.

"I look like a damn rabbit," he scorned, and marched half-way to Istra's room. He went back to change his tie to a navy-blue bow which made him appear younger. He was feeling rather resentful at everything, including Istra, as he finally knocked and heard her "Yes? Come in."

There was in her room a wonderful being lolling in a wing-chair, one leg over the chair-arm; a young young man, with broken brown teeth, always seen in his perpetual grin, but a godlike Grecian nose, a high forehead, and bristly yellow hair. The being wore large round tortoise-shell spectacles, a soft shirt with a gold-plated collar-pin, and delicately gray garments.

Istra was curled on the bed in a leaf-green silk kimono with a great gold-mounted medallion pinned at her breast. Mr. Wrenn tried not to be shocked at the kimono.

She had been frowning as he came in and fingering a long thin green book of verses, but she glowed at Mr. Wrenn as though he were her most familiar friend, murmuring, "Mouse dear, I'm so glad you could come in."

Mr. Wrenn stood there awkwardly. He hadn't expected to find another visitor. He seemed to have heard her call him "Mouse." Yes, but what did Mouse mean? It wasn't his name at all. This was all very confusing. But how awful glad she was to see him!

"Mouse dear, this is one of our best little indecent poets, Mr. Carson Haggerty. From America—California—too. Mr. Hag'ty, Mr. Wrenn."

"Pleased meet you," said both men in the same tone of annoyance.

Mr. Wrenn implored: "I—uh—I thought you might like to look at these magazines. Just dropped in to give them to you." He was ready to go.

"Thank you—so good of you. *Please* sit down. Carson and I were only fighting—he's going pretty soon. We knew each other at art school in Berkeley. Now he knows all the toffs in London."

"Mr. Wrenn," said the best little poet, "I hope you'll back up my contention. Izzy says th—"

"Carson, I have told you just about enough times that I do not intend to stand for 'Izzy' any more! I should think that even *you* would be able to outgrow the standard of wit that obtains in first-year art class at Berkeley."

Mr. Haggerty showed quite all of his ragged teeth in a noisy joyous grin and went on, unperturbed: "Miss Nash says that the best European thought, personally gathered in the best salons, shows that the Rodin vogue is getting the pickle-eye from all the real yearners. What is your opinion?"

Mr. Wrenn turned to Istra for protection. She promptly announced: "Mr. Wrenn absolutely agrees with me. By the way, he's doing a big book on the recrudescence of Kipling, after his slump, and—"

"Oh, come off, now! Kipling! Blatant imperialist, anti-Stirner!" cried Carson Haggerty, kicking out each word with the assistance of his swinging left foot.

Much relieved that the storm-center had passed over him, Mr. Wrenn sat on the front edge of a cane-seated chair, with the magazines between his hands, and his hands pressed between his forward-cocked knees. Always, in the hundreds of times he went over the scene in that room afterward, he remembered how cool and smooth the magazine covers felt to the palms of his flattened hands. For he associated the papery surfaces with the apprehension he then had that Istra might give him up to the jag-toothed grin of Carson Haggerty, who would laugh him out of the room and out of Istra's world.

He hated the poetic youth, and would gladly have broken all of Carson's teeth short off. Yet the dread of having to try the feat himself made him admire the manner in which Carson tossed about long creepy-sounding words, like a bush-ape playing with scarlet spiders. He talked insultingly of Yeats and the commutation of sex-energy and Isadora Duncan and the poetry of Carson Haggerty.

Istra yawned openly on the bed, kicking a pillow, but she was surprised into energetic discussion now and then, till Haggerty intentionally called her Izzy again, when she sat up and remarked to Mr. Wrenn: "Oh, don't go yet. You can tell me about the article when Carson goes. Dear Carson said he was only going to stay till ten."

Mr. Wrenn hadn't had any intention of going, so he merely smiled and bobbed his head to the room in general, and stammered "Y-yes," while he tried to remember what he had told her about some article. Article. Perhaps it was a Souvenir Company novelty article. Great idea! Perhaps she wanted to design a motto for them. He decidedly hoped that he could fix it up for her—he'd sure do his best. He'd be glad to write over to Mr. Guilfogle about it. Anyway, she seemed willing to have him stick here.

Yet when dear Carson had jauntily departed, leaving the room still loud with the smack of his grin, Istra seemed to have forgotten that Mr. Wrenn was alive. She was scowling at a book on the bed as though it had said things to her. So he sat quiet and crushed the magazine covers more closely till the silence choked him, and he dared, "Mr. Carson is an awful well-educated man."

"He's a bounder," she snapped. She softened her voice as she continued: "He was in the art school in California when I was there, and he presumes on that.... It was good of you to stay and help me get rid of him.... I'm getting—I'm sorry I'm so dull to-night. I suppose I'll get sent off to bed right now, if I can't be more entertaining. It was sweet of you to come in, Mouse.... You don't mind my calling you `Mouse,' do you? I won't, if you do mind."

He awkwardly walked over and laid the magazines on the bed. "Why, it's all right.... What was it about some novelty—some article? If there's anything I could do—anything—"

"Article?"

"Why, yes. That you wanted to see me about."

"Oh! Oh, that was just to get rid of Carson.... His *insufferable* familiarity! The penalty for my having been a naive kiddy, hungry for friendship, once. And now, good n—. Oh, Mouse, he says my eyes—even with this green kimono on— Come here, dear. tell me what color my eyes are."

She moved with a quick swing to the side of her bed. Thrusting out her two arms, she laid ivory hands clutchingly on his shoulder. He stood quaking, forgetting every one of the Wrennish rules by which he had edged a shy polite way through life. He fearfully reached out his hands toward her shoulders in turn, but his arms were shorter than hers, and his hands rested on the sensitive warmth of her upper arms. He peered at those dear gray-blue eyes of hers, but he could not calm himself enough to tell whether they were china-blue or basalt-black.

"Tell me," she demanded; "*aren't* they green?"

"Yes," he quavered.

"You're sweet," she said.

Leaning out from the side of her bed, she kissed him. She sprang up, and hastened to the window, laughing nervously, and deploring: "I shouldn't have done that! I shouldn't! Forgive me!" Plaintively, like a child: "Istra was so bad, so bad. Now you must go." As she turned back to him her eyes had the peace of an old friend's.

Because he had wished to be kind to people, because he had been pitiful toward Goaty Zapp, Mr. Wrenn was able to understand that she was trying to be a kindly big sister to him, and he said "Good night, Istra," and smiled in a lively way and walked out. He got out the smile by wrenching his nerves, for which he paid in agony as he knelt by his bed, acknowledging that Istra would never love him and that therefore he was not to love, would be a fool to love, never would love her—and seeing again her white arms softly shadowed by her green kimono sleeves.

No sight of Istra, no scent of her hair, no sound of her always-changing voice for two days. Twice, seeing a sliver of light under her door as he came up the darkened stairs, he knocked, but there was no answer, and he marched into his room with the dignity of fury.

Numbers of times he quite gave her up, decided he wanted never to see her again. But after one of the savagest of these renunciations, while he was stamping defiantly down Tottenham Court Road, he saw in a window a walking-stick that he was sure she would like his carrying. And it cost only two-and-six. Hastily, before he changed his mind, he rushed in and slammed down his money. It was a very beautiful stick indeed, and of a modesty to commend itself to Istra, just a plain straight stick with a cap of metal curiously like silver. He was conscious that the whole world was leering at him, demanding "What're *you* carrying a cane for?" but he—the misunderstood—was willing to wait for the reward of this martyrdom in Istra's approval.

The third night, as he stood at the window watching two children playing in the dusk, there was a knock. It was Istra. She stood at his door, smart and inconspicuous in a black suit with a small toque that hid the flare of her red hair.

"Come," she said, abruptly. "I want you to take me to Olympia's—Olympia Johns' flat. I've been reading all the Balzac there is. I want to talk. Can you come?"

"Oh, of course—"

"Hurry, then!"

He seized his small foolishly round hat, and he tucked his new walking-stick under his arm without displaying it too proudly, waiting for her comment.

She led the way down-stairs and across the quiet streets and squares of Bloomsbury to Great James Street. She did not even see the stick.

She said scarce a word beyond:

"I'm sick of Olympia's bunch—I never want to dine in Soho with an inhibition and a varietistic sex instinct again—*jamais de la vie.* But one has to play with somebody."

Then he was so cheered that he tapped the pavements boldly with his stick and delicately touched her arm as they crossed the street. For she added:

"We'll just run in and see them for a little while, and then you can take me out and buy me a Rhine wine and seltzer.... Poor Mouse, it shall have its play!"

Olympia Johns' residence consisted of four small rooms. When Istra opened the door, after tapping, the living-room was occupied by seven people, all interrupting one another and drinking fourpenny ale; seven people and a fog of cigarette smoke and a tangle of papers and books and hats. A swamp of unwashed dishes appeared on a large table in the room just beyond, divided off from the living-room by a burlap curtain to which were pinned suffrage buttons and medallions. This last he remembered afterward, thinking over the room, for the medals' glittering points of light relieved his eyes from the intolerable glances of the people as he was hastily introduced to them. He was afraid that he would be dragged into a discussion, and sat looking away from them to the medals, and to the walls, on which were posters, showing mighty fists with hammers and flaming torches, or hog-like men lolling on the chests of workmen, which they seemed to enjoy more than the workmen. By and by he ventured to scan the group.

Carson Haggerty, the American poet, was there. But the center of them all was Olympia Johns herself—spinster, thirty-four, as small and active and excitedly energetic as an ant trying to get around a match. She had much of the ant's brownness and slimness, too. Her pale hair was always falling from under her fillet of worn black velvet (with the dingy under side of the velvet showing curled up at the edges). A lock would tangle in front of her eyes, and she would impatiently shove it back with a jab of her thin rough hands, never stopping in her machine-gun volley of words.

"Yes, yes, yes, yes," she would pour out. "Don't you *see?* We must do something. I tell you the conditions are intolerable, simply intolerable. We must *do* something."

The conditions were, it seemed, intolerable in the several branches of education of female infants, water rates in Bloomsbury, the cutlery industry, and ballad-singing.

And mostly she was right. Only her rightness was so demanding, so restless, that it left Mr. Wrenn gasping.

Olympia depended on Carson Haggerty for most of the "Yes, that's so's," though he seemed to be trying to steal glances at another woman, a young woman, a lazy smiling pretty girl of twenty, who, Istra told Mr. Wrenn, studied Greek archaeology at the Museum. No one knew why she studied it. She seemed peacefully ignorant of everything but her kissable lips, and she adorably poked at things with lazy graceful fingers, and talked the Little Language to Carson Haggerty, at which Olympia shrugged her shoulders and turned to the others.

There were a Mr. and Mrs. Stettinius—she a poet; he a bleached man, with goatish whiskers and a sanctimonious white neck-cloth, who was Puritanically, ethically, gloomily, religiously atheistic. Items in the room were a young man who taught in Mr. Jeney's Select School and an Established Church mission worker from Whitechapel, who loved to be shocked.

It was Mr. Wrenn who was really shocked, however, not by the noise and odor; not by the smoking of the women; not by the demand that "we" tear down the state; no, not by these was Our Mr. Wrenn of the Souvenir Company shocked, but by his own fascinated interest in the frank talk of sex. He had always had a quite undefined supposition that it was wicked to talk of sex unless one made a joke of it.

Then came the superradicals, to confuse the radicals who confused Mr. Wrenn.

For always there is a greater rebellion; and though you sell your prayer-book to buy Bakunine, and esteem yourself revolutionary to a point of madness, you shall find one who calls you reactionary. The scorners came in together—Moe Tchatzsky, the syndicalist and direct actionist, and Jane Schott, the writer of impressionistic prose—and they sat silently sneering on a couch.

Istra rose, nodded at Mr. Wrenn, and departed, despite Olympia's hospitable shrieks after them of "Oh stay! It's only a little after ten. Do stay and have something to eat."

Istra shut the door resolutely. The hall was dark. It was gratefully quiet. She snatched up Mr. Wrenn's hand and held it to her breast.

"Oh, Mouse dear, I'm so bored! I want some real things. They talk and talk in there, and every night they settle all the fate of all the nations, always the same way. I don't suppose there's ever been a bunch that knew more things incorrectly. You hated them, didn't you?"

"Why, I don't think you ought to talk about them so severe," he implored, as they started down-stairs. "I don't mean they're like you. They don't savvy like you do. I mean it! But I was awful int'rested in what that Miss Johns said about kids in school getting crushed into a mold. Gee! that's so; ain't it? Never thought of it before. And that Mrs. Stettinius talked about Yeats so beautiful."

"Oh, my dear, you make my task so much harder. I want you to be different. Can't you see your cattle-boat experience is realer than any of the things those half-baked thinkers have done? I *know*. I'm half-baked myself."

"Oh, I've never done nothing."

"But you're ready to. Oh, I don't know. I want—I wish Jock Seton—the filibuster I met in San Francisco—I wish he were here. Mouse, maybe I can make a filibuster of you. I've got to create something. Oh, those people! If you just knew them! That fool Mary Stettinius is mad about that Tchatzsky person, and her husband invites him to teas. Stettinius is mad about Olympia, who'll probably take Carson out and marry him, and he'll keep on hanging about the Greek girl. Ungh!"

"I don't know—I don't know—"

But as he didn't know what he didn't know she merely patted his arm and said, soothingly: "I won't criticize your first specimens of radicals any more. They are trying to do something, anyway." Then she added, in an irrelevant tone, "You're exactly as tall as I am. Mouse dear, you ought to be taller."

They were entering the drab stretch of Tavistock Place, after a silence as drab, when she exclaimed: "Mouse, I am *so* sick of everything. I want to get out, away, anywhere, and do something, anything, just so's it's different. Even the country. I'd like—Why couldn't we?"

"Let's go out on a picnic to-morrow, Istra."

"A picnic picnic? With pickles and a pillow cushion and several kinds of cake?... I'm afraid the Bois Boulogne has spoiled me for that.... Let me think."

She drooped down on the steps of their house. Her head back, her supple strong throat arched with the passion of hating boredom, she devoured the starlight dim over the stale old roofs across the way.

"Stars," she said. "Out on the moors they would come down by you.... What is *your* adventure—your formula for it?... Let's see; you take common roadside things seriously; you'd be dear and excited over a Red Lion Inn."

"Are there more than one Red Li—"

"My dear Mouse, England is a menagerie of Red Lions and White Lions and fuzzy Green Unicorns.... Why not, why not, *why not!* Let's walk to Aengusmere. It's a fool colony of artists and so on, up in Suffolk; but they *have* got some beautiful cottages, and they're more Celt than Dublin.... Start right now; take a train to Chelmsford, say, and tramp all night. Take a couple of days or so to get there. Think of it! Tramping through dawn, past English fields. Think of it, Yankee. And not caring what anybody in the world thinks. Gipsies. Shall we?"

"Wh-h-h-h-y—" He was sure she was mad. Tramping all night! He couldn't let her do this.

She sprang up. She stared down at him in revulsion, her hands clenched. Her voice was hostile as she demanded:

"What? Don't you want to? With *me?*"

He was up beside her, angry, dignified; a man.

"Look here. You know I want to. You're the elegantest—I mean you're—Oh, you ought to know! Can't you see how I feel about you? Why, I'd rather do this than anything I ever heard of in my life. I just don't want to do anything that would get people to talking about you."

"Who would know? Besides, my dear man, I don't regard it as exactly wicked to walk decently along a country road."

"Oh, it isn't that. Oh, please, Istra, don't look at me like that—like you hated me."

She calmed at once, drummed on his arm, sat down on the railing, and drew him to a seat beside her.

"Of course, Mouse. It's silly to be angry. Yes, I do believe you want to take care of me. But don't worry.... Come! Shall we go?"

"But wouldn't you rather wait till to-morrow?"

"No. The whole thing's so mad that if I wait till then I'll never want to do it. And you've got to come, so that I'll have some one to quarrel with.... I hate the smugness of London, especially the smugness of the anti-smug anti-bourgeois radicals, so that I have the finest mad mood! Come. We'll go."

Even this logical exposition had not convinced him, but he did not gainsay as they entered the hall and Istra rang for the landlady. His knees grew sick and old and quavery as he heard the landlady's voice loud below-stairs: "Now wot do they want? It's eleven o'clock. Aren't they ever done a-ringing and a-ringing?"

The landlady, the tired thin parchment-faced North Countrywoman, whose god was Respectability of Lodgings, listened in a frightened way to Istra's blandly superior statement: "Mr. Wrenn and I have been invited to join an excursion out of town that leaves to-night. We'll pay our rent and leave our things here."

"Going off together—"

"My good woman, we are going to Aengusmere. Here's two pound. Don't allow any one in my room. And I may send for my things from out of town. Be ready to pack them in my trunks and send them to me. Do you understand?"

"Yes, miss, but—"

"My good woman, do you realize that your `buts' are insulting?"

"Oh, I didn't go to be insulting—"

"Then that's all…. Hurry now, Mouse!"

On the stairs, ascending, she whispered, with the excitement not of a tired woman, but of a tennis-and-dancing-mad girl: "We're off! Just take a tooth-brush. Put on an outing suit—any old thing—and an old cap."

She darted into her room.

Now Mr. Wrenn had, for any old thing, as well as for afternoon and evening dress, only the sturdy undistinguished clothes he was wearing, so he put on a cap, and hoped she wouldn't notice. She didn't. She came knocking in fifteen minutes, trim in a khaki suit, with low thick boots and a jolly tousled blue tam-o'-shanter.

"Come on. There's a train for Chelmsford in half an hour, my time-table confided to me. I feel like singing."

CHAPTER X

HE GOES A-GIPSYING

They rode out of London in a third-class compartment, opposite a curate and two stodgy people who were just people and defied you (Istra cheerfully explained to Mr. Wrenn) to make anything of them but just people.

"Wouldn't they stare if they knew what idiocy we're up to!" she suggested.

Mr. Wrenn bobbed his head in entire agreement. He was trying, without any slightest success, to make himself believe that Mr. William Wrenn, Our Mr. Wrenn, late of the Souvenir Company, was starting out for a country tramp at midnight with an artist girl.

The night foreman of the station, a person of bedizenment and pride, stared at them as they alighted at Chelmsford and glanced around like strangers. Mr. Wrenn stared back defiantly and marched with Istra from the station, through the sleeping town, past its ragged edges, into the country.

They tramped on, a bit wearily. Mr. Wrenn was beginning to wonder if they'd better go back to Chelmsford. Mist was dripping and blind and silent about them, weaving its heavy gray with the night. Suddenly Istra caught his arm at the gate to a farm-yard, and cried, "Look!"

"Gee!... Gee! we're in England. We're abroad!"

"Yes—abroad."

A paved courtyard with farm outbuildings thatched and ancient was lit faintly by a lantern hung from a post that was thumbed to a soft smoothness by centuries.

"That couldn't be America," he exulted. "Gee! I'm just gettin' it! I'm so darn glad we came.... Here's real England. No tourists. It's what I've always wanted—a country that's old. And different.... Thatched houses!... And pretty soon it'll be dawn, summer dawn; with you, with Istra! *Gee!* It's the darndest adventure."

"Yes.... Come on. Let's walk fast or we'll get sleepy, and then your romantic heroine will be a grouchy Interesting People!... Listen! There's a sleepy dog barking, a million miles away.... I feel like telling you about myself. You don't know me. Or do you?"

"I dunno just how you mean."

"Oh, it shall have its romance! But some time I'll tell you—perhaps I will—how I'm not really a clever person at all, but just a savage from outer darkness, who pretends to understand London and Paris and Munich, and gets frightfully scared of them…. Wait! Listen! Hear the mist drip from that tree. Are you nice and drowned?"

"Uh—kind of. But I been worrying about you being soaked."

"Let me see. Why, your sleeve is wet clear through. This khaki of mine keeps out the water better…. But I don't mind getting wet. All I mind is being bored. I'd like to run up this hill without a thing on—just feeling the good healthy real mist on my skin. But I'm afraid it isn't done."

Mile after mile. Mostly she talked of the boulevards and Pere Dureon, of Debussy and artichokes, in little laughing sentences that sprang like fire out of the dimness of the mist.

Dawn came. From a hilltop they made out the roofs of a town and stopped to wonder at its silence, as though through long ages past no happy footstep had echoed there. The fog lifted. The morning was new-born and clean, and they fairly sang as they clattered up to an old coaching inn and demanded breakfast of an amazed rustic pottering about the inn yard in a smock. He did not know that to a "thrilling" Mr. Wrenn he—or perhaps it was his smock—was the hero in an English melodrama. Nor, doubtless, did the English crisp bacon and eggs which a sleepy housemaid prepared know that they were theater properties. Why, they were English eggs, served at dawn in an English inn—a stone-floored raftered room with a starling hanging in a little cage of withes outside the latticed window. And there were no trippers to bother them! (Mr. Wrenn really used the word "trippers" in his cogitations; he had it from Istra.)

When he informed her of this occult fact she laughed, "You know mighty well, Mouse, that you have a sneaking wish there were one Yankee stranger here to see our glory."

"I guess that's right."

"But maybe I'm just as bad."

For once their tones had not been those of teacher and pupil, but of comrades. They set out from the inn through the brightening morning like lively boys on a vacation tramp.

The sun crept out, with the warmth and the dust, and Istra's steps lagged. As they passed the outlying corner of a farm where a straw-stack was secluded in a clump of willows Istra smiled and sighed: "I'm pretty tired, dear. I'm going to sleep in that straw-stack. I've always wanted to sleep in a straw-stack. It's *comme il faut* for vagabonds in the best set, you know. And one can burrow. Exciting, eh?"

She made a pillow of her khaki jacket, while he dug down to a dry place for her. He found another den on the other side of the stack.

It was afternoon when he awoke. He sprang up and rushed around the stack. Istra was still asleep, curled in a pathetically small childish heap, her tired face in repose against the brown-yellow of her khaki jacket. Her red hair had come down and shone about her shoulders.

She looked so frail that he was frightened. Surely, too, she'd be very angry with him for letting her come on this jaunt.

He scribbled on a leaf from his address-book — religiously carried for six years, but containing only four addresses — this note:

Gone to get stuff for bxfst be right back. — W. W.

and, softly crawling up the straw, left the note by her head. He hastened to a farm-house. The farm-wife was inclined to be curious. O curious farm-wife, you of the cream-thick Essex speech and the shuffling feet, you were brave indeed to face Bill Wrenn the Great, with his curt self-possession, for he was on a mission for Istra, and he cared not for the goggling eyes of all England. What though he was a bunny-faced man with an innocuous mustache? Istra would be awakening hungry. That was why he bullied you into selling him a stew-pan and a bundle of faggots along with the tea and eggs and a bread loaf and a jar of the marmalade your husband's farm had been making these two hundred years. And you should have had coffee for him, not tea, woman of Essex.

When he returned to their outdoor inn the late afternoon glow lay along the rich fields that sloped down from their well-concealed nook. Istra was still asleep, but her cheek now lay wistfully on the crook of her thin arm. He looked at the auburn-framed paleness of her face, its lines of thought and ambition, unmasked, unprotected by the swift changes of expression which defended her while she was awake. He sobbed. If he could only make her happy! But he was afraid of her moods.

He built a fire by a brooklet beyond the willows, boiled the eggs and toasted the bread and made the tea, with cream ready in a jar. He remembered boyhood camping days in Parthenon and old camp lore. He returned to the stack and called, "Istra — oh, Is-tra!"

She shook her head, nestled closer into the straw, then sat up, her hair about her shoulders. She smiled and called down: "Good morning. Why, it's afternoon! Did you sleep well, dear?"

"Yes. Did you? Gee, I hope you did!"

"Never better in my life. I'm so sleepy yet. But comfy. I needed a quiet sleep outdoors, and it's so peaceful here. Breakfast! I roar for breakfast! Where's the nearest house?"

"Got breakfast all ready."

"You're a dear!"

She went to wash in the brook, and came back with eyes dancing and hair trim, and they laughed over breakfast, glancing down the slope of golden hazy fields. Only once did Istra pass out of the land of their intimacy into some hinterland of analysis — when she looked at him as he drank his tea aloud out of the stew-pan, and wondered: "Is this really you here with me? But you *aren't* a boulevardier. I must say I don't understand what you're doing here at all…. Nor a caveman, ei-ther. I don't understand it…. But you *sha'n't* be worried by bad Istra. Let's see; we went to grammar-school together."

"Yes, and we were in college. Don't you remember when I was baseball captain? You don't? Gee, you got a bad memory!"

At which she smiled properly, and they were away for Suffolk again.

"I suppose now it'll go and rain," said Istra, viciously, at dusk. It was the first time she had spoken for a mile. Then, after another quarter-mile: "Please don't mind my being silent. I'm sort of stiff, and my feet hurt most unromantically. You won't mind, will you?"

Of course he did mind, and of course he said he didn't. He artfully skirted the field of conversation by very West Sixteenth Street observations on a town through which they passed, while she merely smiled wearily, and at best remarked "Yes, that's so," whether it was so or not.

He was reflecting: "Istra's terrible tired. I ought to take care of her." He stopped at the wood-pillared entrance of a temperance inn and commanded: "Come! We'll have something to eat here." To the astonishment of both of them, she meekly obeyed with "If you wish."

It cannot be truthfully said that Mr. Wrenn proved himself a person of *savoir faire* in choosing a temperance hotel for their dinner. Istra didn't seem so much to mind the fact that the table-cloth was coarse and the water-glasses thick, and that everywhere the elbow ran into a superfluity of greasy pepper and salt castors. But when she raised her head wearily to peer around the room she started, glared at Mr. Wrenn, and accused: "Are you by any chance aware of the fact that this place is crowded with tourists? There are two family parties from Davenport or Omaha; I *know* they are!"

"Oh, they ain't such bad-looking people," protested Mr. Wrenn…. Just because he had induced her to stop for dinner the poor man thought his masculine superiority had been recognized.

"Oh, they're *terrible!* Can't you *see* it? Oh, you're *hopeless.*"

"Why, that big guy—that big man with the rimless spectacles looks like he might be a good civil engineer, and I think that lady opposite him—"

"They're Americans."

"So're we!"

"I'm not."

"I thought—why—"

"Of course I was born there, but—"

"Well, just the same, I think they're nice people."

"Now see here. Must I argue with you? Can I have no peace, tired as I am? Those trippers are speaking of `quaint English flavor.' Can you want anything more than that to damn them? And they've been touring by motor—seeing every inn on the road."

"Maybe it's fun for—"

"Now *don't* argue with me. I know what I'm talking about. Why do I have to explain everything? They're hopeless!"

Mr. Wrenn felt a good wholesome desire to spank her, but he said, most politely: "You're awful tired. Don't you want to stay here tonight? Or maybe some other hotel; and I'll stay here."

"No. Don't want to stay any place. Want to get away from myself," she said, exactly like a naughty child.

So they tramped on again.

Darkness was near. They had plunged into a country which in the night seemed to be a stretch of desolate moorlands. As they were silently plodding up a hill the rain came. It came with a roar, a pitiless drenching against which they fought uselessly, soaking them, slapping their faces, blinding their eyes. He caught her arm and dragged her ahead. She would be furious with him because it rained, of course, but this was no time to think of that; he had to get her to a dry place.

Istra laughed: "Oh, isn't this great! We're real vagabonds now."

"Why! Doesn't that khaki soak through? Aren't you wet?"

"To the skin!" she shouted, gleefully. "And I don't care! We're *doing* something. Poor dear, is it worried? I'll race you to the top of the hill."

The dark bulk of a building struck their sight at the top, and they ran to it. Just now Mr. Wrenn was ready to devour alive any irate householder who might try to turn them out. He found the building to be a ruined stable—the door off the hinges, the desolate thatch falling in. He struck a match and, holding it up, standing straight, the master, all unconscious for once in his deprecating life of the Wrennishness of Mr. Wrenn, he discovered that the thatch above the horse-manger was fairly waterproof.

"Come on! Up on the edge of the manger, Istra," he ordered.

"This is a perfectly good place for a murder," she grinned, as they sat swinging their legs.

He could fancy her grinning. He was sure about it, and well content.

"Have I been so very grouchy, Mouse? Don't you want to murder me? I'll try to find you a long pin."

"Nope; I don't think so, much. I guess we can get along without it this time."

"Oh dear, dear! This is very dreadful. You're so used to me now that you aren't even scared of me any more."

"Gee! I guess I'll be scared of you all right as soon as I get you into a dry place, but I ain't got time now. Sitting on a manger! Ain't this the funniest place!... Now I must beat it out and find a house. There ought to be one somewheres near here."

"And leave me here in the darknesses and wetnesses? Not a chance. The rain'll soon be over, anyway. Really, I don't mind a bit. I think it's rather fun."

Her voice was natural again, natural and companionable and brave. She laughed as she stroked her wet shoulder and held his hand, sitting quietly and bidding him listen to the soft forlorn sound of the rain on the thatch.

But the rain was not soon over, and their dangling position was very much like riding a rail.

"I'm so uncomfortable!" fretted Istra.

"See here, Istra, please, I think I'd better go see if I can't find a house for you to get dry in."

"I feel too wretched to go any place. Too wretched to move."

"Well, then, I'll make a fire here. There ain't much danger."

"The place will catch fire," she began, querulously.

But he interrupted her. "Oh, *let* the darn place catch fire! I'm going to make a fire, I tell you!"

"I don't want to move. It'll just be another kind of discomfort, that's all. Why couldn't you try and take a little bit of care of me, anyway?"

"Oh, hon-ey!" he wailed, in youthful bewilderment. "I did try to get you to stay at that hotel in town and get some rest."

"Well, you ought to have made me. Don't you realize that I took you along to take care of me?"

"Uh—"

"Now don't argue about it. I can't stand argument all the time."

He thought instantly of Lee Theresa Zapp quarreling with her mother, but he said nothing. He gathered the driest bits of thatch and wood he could find in the litter on the stable floor and kindled a fire, while she sat sullenly glaring at him, her face wrinkled and tired in the wan firelight. When the blaze was going steadily, a compact and safe little fire, he spread his coat as a seat for her, and called, cheerily, "Come on now, honey; here's a regular home and hearthstone for you."

She slipped down from the manger edge and stood in front of him, looking into his eyes—which were level with her own.

"You *are* good to me," she half whispered, and smoothed his cheek, then slipped down on the outspread coat, and murmured, "Come; sit here by me, and we'll both get warm."

All night the rain dribbled, but no one came to drive them away from the fire, and they dozed side by side, their hands close and their garments steaming. Istra fell asleep, and her head drooped on his shoulder. He straightened to bear its weight, though his back twinged with stiffness, and there he sat unmoving, through an hour of pain and happiness and confused meditation, studying the curious background—the dark roof of broken thatch, the age-corroded walls, the littered earthen floor. His hand pressed lightly the clammy smoothness of the wet khaki of her shoulder; his wet sleeve stuck to his arm, and he wanted to pull it free.

His eyes stung. But he sat tight, while his mind ran round in circles, considering that he loved Istra, and that he would not be entirely sorry when he was no longer the slave to her moods; that this adventure was the strangest and most romantic, also the most idiotic and useless, in history.

Toward dawn she stirred, and, slipping stiffly from his position, he moved her so that her back, which was still wet, faced the fire. He built up the fire again, and sat brooding beside her, dozing and starting awake, till morning. Then his head bobbed, and he was dimly awake again, to find her sitting up straight, looking at him in amazement.

"It simply can't be, that's all…. Did you curl me up? I'm nice and dry all over now. It was very good of you. You've been a most commendable person…. But I think we'll take a train for the rest of our pilgrimage. It hasn't been entirely successful, I'm afraid."

"Perhaps we'd better."

For a moment he hated her, with her smooth politeness, after a night when she had been unbearable and human by turns. He hated her bedraggled hair and tired face. Then he could have wept, so deeply did he desire to pull her head down on his shoulder and smooth the wrinkles of weariness out of her dear face, the dearer because they had endured the weariness together. But he said, "Well, let's try to get some breakfast first, Istra."

With their garments wrinkled from rain, half asleep and rather cross, they arrived at the esthetic but respectable colony of Aengusmere by the noon train.

CHAPTER XI

HE BUYS AN ORANGE TIE

The Aengusmere Caravanserai is so unyieldingly cheerful and artistic that it makes the ordinary person long for a dingy old-fashioned room in which he can play solitaire and chew gum without being rebuked with exasperating patience by the wall stencils and clever etchings and polished brasses. It is adjectiferous. The common room (which is uncommon for hotel parlor) is all in superlatives and chintzes.

Istra had gone up to her room to sleep, bidding Mr. Wrenn do likewise and avoid the wrong bunch at the Caravanserai; for besides the wrong bunch of Interesting People there were, she explained, a right bunch, of working artists. But he wanted to get some new clothes, to replace his rain-wrinkled ready-mades. He was tottering through the common room, wondering whether he could find a clothing-shop in Aengusmere, when a shrill gurgle from a wing-chair by the rough-brick fireplace halted him.

"Oh-h-h-h, *Mister* Wrenn; Mr. *Wrenn!*" There sat Mrs. Stettinius, the poet-lady of Olympia's rooms on Great James Street.

"Oh-h-h-h, Mr. Wrenn, you *bad* man, *do* come sit down and tell me all *about* your *wonderful* trek with Istra Nash. I *just* met *dear* Istra in the upper hall. Poor dear, she was *so* crumpled, but her hair was like a sunset over mountain peaks— you know, as Yeats says:

"A stormy sunset were her lips,
A stormy sunset on doomed ships,

only of course this was her *hair* and not her *lips*—and she told me that you had tramped all the *way* from London. I've never heard of anything so romantic—or no, I won't say 'romantic'—I *do* agree with dear Olympia—*isn't* she a mag_nifi-cent_ woman—*so* fearless and progressive—didn't you *adore* meeting her?—she is our modern Joan of Arc—such a *noble* figure—I *do* agree with her that *romantic* love is *passe*, that we have entered the era of glorious companionship that regards vari-etism as *exactly* as romantic as monogamy. But—but—where was I?—I think your gipsying down from London was *most* exciting. Now *do* tell us all about it, Mr. Wrenn. First, I want you to meet Miss Saxonby and Mr. Gutch and *dear* Yilyena Dourschetsky and Mr. Howard Bancock Binch—of course you know his poetry."

And then she drew a breath and flopped back into the wing-chair's muffling depths.

During all this Mr. Wrenn had stood, frightened and unprotected and rain-wrinkled, before the gathering by the fireless fireplace, wondering how Mrs. Stettinius could get her nose so blue and yet so powdery. Despite her encouragement he gave no fuller account of the "gipsying" than, "Why—uh—we just tramped down," till Russian-Jewish Yilyena rolled her ebony eyes at him and insisted, "Yez, you mus' tale us about it."

Now, Yilyena had a pretty neck, colored like a cigar of mild flavor, and a trick of smiling. She was accustomed to having men obey her. Mr. Wrenn stammered:

"Why—uh—we just walked, and we got caught in the rain. Say, Miss Nash was a wonder. She never peeped when she got soaked through—she just laughed and beat it like everything. And we saw a lot of quaint English places along the road—got away from all them tourists—trippers—you know."

A perfectly strange person, a heavy old man with horn spectacles and a soft shirt, who had joined the group unbidden, cleared his throat and interrupted:

"Is it not a strange paradox that in traveling, the most observant of all pursuits, one should have to encounter the eternal bourgeoisie!"

From the Cockney Greek chorus about the unlighted fire:

"Yes!"

"Everywhere."

"Uh—" began Mr. Gutch. He apparently had something to say. But the chorus went on:

"And just as swelteringly monogamic in Port Said as in Brum."

"Yes, that's so."

"Mr. Wr-r-renn," thrilled Mrs. Stettinius, the lady poet, "didn't you notice that they were perfectly oblivious of all economic movements; that their observations never post-dated ruins?"

"I guess they wanted to make sure they were admirin' the right things," ventured Mr. Wrenn, with secret terror.

"Yes, that's so," came so approvingly from the Greek chorus that the personal pupil of Mittyford, Ph.D., made his first epigram:

"It isn't so much what you like as what you don't like that shows if you're wise."

"Yes," they gurgled; and Mr. Wrenn, much pleased with himself, smiled *au prince* upon his new friends.

Mrs. Stettinius was getting into her stride for a few remarks upon the poetry of industrialism when Mr. Gutch, who had been "Uh—"ing for some moments, trying to get in his remark, winked with sly rudeness at Miss Saxonby and observed:

"I fancy romance isn't quite dead yet, y' know. Our friends here seem to have had quite a ro-mantic little journey." Then he winked again.

"Say, what do you mean?" demanded Bill Wrenn, hot-eyed, fists clenched, but very quiet.

"Oh, I'm not *blaming* you and Miss Nash—quite the reverse!" tittered the Gutch person, wagging his head sagely.

Then Bill Wrenn, with his fist at Mr. Gutch's nose, spoke his mind:

"Say, you white-faced unhealthy dirty-minded lump, I ain't much of a fighter, but I'm going to muss you up so's you can't find your ears if you don't apologize for those insinuations."

"Oh, Mr. Wrenn—"

"He didn't mean—"

"I didn't mean—"

"He was just spoofing—"

"I was just spoofing—"

Bill Wrenn, watching the dramatization of himself as hero, was enjoying the drama. "You apologize, then?"

"Why certainly, Mr. Wrenn. Let me explain—"

"Oh, don't explain," snortled Miss Saxonby.

"Yes!" from Mr. Bancock Binch, "explanations are *so* conventional, old chap."

Do you see them?—Mr. Wrenn, self-conscious and ready to turn into a blind belligerent Bill Wrenn at the first disrespect; the talkers sitting about and assassinating all the princes and proprieties and, poor things, taking Mr. Wrenn quite seriously because he had uncovered the great truth that the important thing in sight-seeing is not to see sights. He was most unhappy, Mr. Wrenn was, and wanted to be away from there. He darted as from a spring when he heard Istra's voice, from the edge of the group, calling, "Come here a sec', Billy."

She was standing with a chair-back for support, tired but smiling.

"I can't get to sleep yet. Don't you want me to show you some of the buildings here?"

"Oh *yes!*"

"If Mrs. Stettinius can spare you!"

This by way of remarking on the fact that the female poet was staring volubly.

"G-g-g-g-g—" said Mrs. Stettinius, which seemed to imply perfect consent.

Istra took him to the belvedere on a little slope overlooking the lawns of Aengusmere, scattered with low bungalows and rose-gardens.

"It is beautiful, isn't it? Perhaps one could be happy here—if one could kill all the people except the architect," she mused.

"Oh, it is," he glowed.

Standing there beside her, happiness enveloping them, looking across the marvelous sward, Bill Wrenn was at the climax of his comedy of triumph. Admitted to a world of lawns and bungalows and big studio windows, standing in a belvedere beside Istra Nash as her friend—

"Mouse dear," she said, hesitatingly, "the reason why I wanted to have you come out here, why I couldn't sleep, I wanted to tell you how ashamed I am for having been peevish, being petulant, last night. I'm so sorry, because you were very patient with me, you were very good to me. I don't want you to think of me just as a crochety woman who didn't appreciate you. You are very kind, and when I hear that you're married to some nice girl I'll be as happy as can be."

"Oh, Istra," he cried, grasping her arm, "I don't want any girl in the world—I mean—oh, I just want to be let go 'round with you when you'll let me—"

"No, no, dear. You must have seen last night; that's impossible. Please don't argue about it now; I'm too tired. I just wanted to tell you I appreciated—And when you get back to America you won't be any the worse for playing around with poor Istra because she told you about different things from what you've played with, about rearing children as individuals and painting in *tempera* and all those things? And—and I don't want you to get too fond of me, because we're—different.... But we have had an adventure, even if it was a little moist." She paused; then, cheerily: "Well, I'm going to beat it back and try to sleep again. Good-by, Mouse dear. No, don't come back to the Cara-advanced-serai. Play around and see the animiles. G'-by."

He watched her straight swaying figure swing across the lawn and up the steps of the half-timbered inn. He watched her enter the door before he hastened to the shops which clustered about the railway- station, outside of the poetic preserves of the colony proper.

He noticed, as he went, that the men crossing the green were mostly clad in Norfolk jackets and knickers, so he purchased the first pair of unrespectable un-ankle-concealing trousers he had owned since small boyhood, and a jacket of rough serge, with a gaudy buckle on the belt. Also, he actually dared an orange tie!

He wanted something for Istra at dinner—"a s'prise," he whispered under his breath, with fond babying. For the first time in his life he entered a florist's shop.... Normally, you know, the poor of the city cannot afford flowers till they are dead, and then for but one day.... He came out with a bunch of orchids, and remembered the days when he had envied the people he had seen in florists' shops actually buying flowers. When he was almost at the Caravanserai he wanted to go back and change the orchids for simpler flowers, roses or carnations, but he got himself not to.

The linen and glassware and silver of the Caravanserai were almost as coarse as those of a temperance hotel, for all the raftered ceiling and the etchings in the dining-room. Hunting up the stewardess of the inn, a bustling young woman who was reading Keats energetically at an office-like desk, Mr. Wrenn begged: "I wonder could I get some special cups and plates and stuff for high tea tonight. I got a kind of party—"

"How many?" The stewardess issued the words as though he had put a penny in the slot.

"Just two. Kind of a birthday party." Mendacious Mr. Wrenn!

"Certainly. Of course there's a small extra charge. I have a Royal Satsuma tea-service—practically Royal Satsuma, at least—and some special Limoges."

"I think Royal Sats'ma would be nice. And some silverware?"

"Surely."

"And could we get some special stuff to eat?"

"What would you like?"

"Why—"

Mendacious Mr. Wrenn! as we have commented. He put his head on one side, rubbed his chin with nice consideration, and condescended, "What would you suggest?"

"For a party high tea? Why, perhaps consomme and omelet Bergerac and a salad and a sweet and *cafe diable*. We have a chef who does French eggs rather remarkably. That would be simple, but—"

"Yes, that would be very good," gravely granted the patron of cuisine. "At six; for two."

As he walked away he grinned within. "Gee! I talked to that omelet Berg' rac like I'd known it all my life!"

Other s'prises for Istra's party he sought. Let's see; suppose it really were her birthday, wouldn't she like to have a letter from some important guy? he queried of himself. He'd write her a make-b'lieve letter from a duke. Which he did. Purchasing a stamp, he humped over a desk in the common room and with infinite pains he inked the stamp in imitation of a postmark and addressed the letter to "Lady Istra Nash, Mouse Castle, Suffolk."

Some one sat down at the desk opposite him, and he jealously carried the task upstairs to his room. He rang for pen and ink as regally as though he had never sat at the wrong end of a buzzer. After half an hour of trying to visualize a duke writing a letter he produced this:

LADY ISTRA NASH,
Mouse Castle.

DEAR MADAM,—We hear from our friend Sir William Wrenn that some folks are saying that to-day is not your birthday & want to stop your celebration, so if you should need somebody to make them believe to-day is your birthday we have sent our secretary, Sir Percival Montague. Sir William Wrenn will hide him behind his chair, and if they bother you just call for Sir Percival and he will tell them. Permit us, dear Lady Nash, to wish you all the greetings of the season, and in close we beg to remain, as ever,

Yours sincerely,

DUKE VERE DE VERE.

He was very tired. When he lay down for a minute, with a pillow tucked over his head, he was almost asleep in ten seconds. But he sprang up, washed his prickly eyes with cold water, and began to dress. He was shy of the knickers and golf-stockings, but it was the orange tie that gave him real alarm. He dared it, though, and went downstairs to make sure they were setting the table with glory befitting the party.

As he went through the common room he watched the three or four groups scattered through it. They seemed to take his clothes as a matter of course. He was glad. He wanted so much to be a credit to Istra.

Returning from the dining-room to the common room, he passed a group standing in a window recess and looking away from him. He overheard:

"Who is the remarkable new person with the orange tie and the rococo buckle on his jacket belt—the one that just went through? Did you ever *see* anything so funny! His collar didn't come within an inch and a half of fitting his neck. He must be a poet. I wonder if his verses are as jerry-built as his garments!"

Mr. Wrenn stopped.

Another voice:

"And the beautiful lack of development of his legs! It's like the good old cycling days, when every draper's assistant went bank-holidaying.... I don't know him, but I suppose he's some tuppeny-ha'p'ny illustrator."

"Or perhaps he has convictions about fried bananas, and dines on a bean saute. O Aengusmere! Shades of Aengus!"

"Not at all. When they look as gentle as he they always hate the capitalists as a militant hates a cabinet minister. He probably dines on the left ear of a South-African millionaire every evening before exercise at the barricades.... I say, look over there; there's a real artist going across the green. You can tell he's a real artist because he's dressed like a navvy and—"

Mr. Wrenn was walking away, across the common room, quite sure that every one was eying him with amusement. And it was too late to change his clothes. It was six already.

He stuck out his jaw, and remembered that he had planned to hide the "letter from the duke" in Istra's napkin that it might be the greater surprise. He sat down at their table. He tucked the letter into the napkin folds. He moved the vase of orchids nearer the center of the table, and the table nearer the open window giving on the green. He rebuked himself for not being able to think of something else to change. He forgot his clothes, and was happy.

At six-fifteen he summoned a boy and sent him up with a message that Mr. Wrenn was waiting and high tea ready.

The boy came back muttering, "Miss Nash left this note for you, sir, the stewardess says."

Mr. Wrenn opened the green-and-white Caravanserai letter excitedly. Perhaps Istra, too, was dressing for the party! He loved all s'prises just then. He read:

> Mouse dear, I'm sorrier than I can tell you, but you know I warrned you that bad Istra was a creature of moods, and just now my mood orders me to beat it for Paris, which I'm doing, on the 5.17 train. I won't say good-by—I hate good-bys, they're so stupid, don't you think? Write me some time, better make it care Amer. Express Co., Paris, because I don't know yet just where I'll be. And please don't look me up in Paris, because it's always better to end up an affair without explanations, don't you think? You have been wonderfully kind to me, and I'll send you some good thought-forms, shall I?
>
> I. N.

He walked to the office of the Caravanserai, blindly, quietly. He paid his bill, and found that he had only fifty dollars left. He could not get himself to eat the waiting high tea. There was a seven-fourteen train for London. He took it. Meantime he wrote out a cable to his New York bank for a hundred and fifty dollars. To keep from thinking in the train he talked gravely and gently to an old man about the brave days of England, when men threw quoits. He kept thinking over and over, to the tune set by the rattling of the train trucks: "Friends... I got to make friends, now I know what they are.... Funny some guys don't make friends. Mustn't forget. Got to make lots of 'em in New York. Learn how to make 'em."

He arrived at his room on Tavistock Place about eleven, and tried to think for the rest of the night of how deeply he was missing Morton of the cattle-boat now that—now that he had no friend in all the hostile world.

In a London A. B. C. restaurant Mr. Wrenn was talking to an American who had a clipped mustache, brisk manners, a Knight-of-Pythias pin, and a mind for duck-shooting, hardware-selling, and cigars.

"No more England for mine," the American snapped, good-humoredly. "I'm going to get out of this foggy hole and get back to God's country just as soon as I can. I want to find out what's doing at the store, and I want to sit down to a plate of flapjacks. I'm good and plenty sick of tea and marmalade. Why, I wouldn't take this fool country for a gift. No, sir! Me for God's country—Sleepy Eye, Brown County, Minnesota. You bet!"

"You don't like England much, then?" Mr. Wrenn carefully reasoned.

"Like it? Like this damp crowded hole, where they can't talk English, and have a fool coinage—Say, that's a great system, that metric system they've got over in France, but here—why, they don't know whether Kansas City is in Kansas or Missouri or both.... 'Right as rain'—that's what a fellow said to me for 'all right'! Ever hear such nonsense?.... And tea for breakfast! Not for me! No, sir! I'm going to take the first steamer!"

With a gigantic smoke-puff of disgust the man from Sleepy Eye stalked out, jingling the keys in his trousers pocket, cocking up his cigar, and looking as though he owned the restaurant.

Mr. Wrenn, picturing him greeting the Singer Tower from an incoming steamer, longed to see the tower.

"Gee! I'll do it!"

He rose and, from that table in the basement of an A. B. C. restaurant, he fled to America.

He dashed up-stairs, fidgeted while the cashier made his change, rang for a bus, whisked into his room, slammed his things into his suit-case, announced to it wildly that they were going home, and scampered to the Northwestern Station. He walked nervously up and down till the Liverpool train departed. "Suppose Istra wanted to make up, and came back to London?" was a terrifying thought that hounded him. He dashed into the waiting-room and wrote to her, on a souvenir post-card showing the Abbey: "Called back to America—will write. Address care of Souvenir Company, Twenty-eighth Street." But he didn't mail the card.

Once settled in a second-class compartment, with the train in motion, he seemed already much nearer America, and, humming, to the great annoyance of a lady with bangs, he planned his new great work—the making of friends; the discovery, some day, if Istra should not relent, of "somebody to go home to." There was no end to the "societies and lodges and stuff" he was going to join directly he landed.

At Liverpool he suddenly stopped at a post-box and mailed his card to Istra. That ended his debate. Of course after that he had to go back to America.

He sailed exultantly, one month and seventeen days after leaving Portland.

CHAPTER XII
HE DISCOVERS AMERICA

In his white-painted steerage berth Mr. Wrenn lay, with a scratch-pad on his raised knees and a small mean pillow doubled under his head, writing sample follow-up letters to present to the Souvenir and Art Novelty Company, interrupting his work at intervals to add to a list of the books which, beginning about five minutes after he landed in New York, he was going to master. He puzzled over Marie Corelli. Morton liked Miss Corelli so much; but would her works appeal to Istra Nash?

He had worked for many hours on a letter to Istra in which he avoided mention of such indecent matters as steerages and immigrants. He was grateful, he told her, for "all you learned me," and he had thought that Aengusmere was a beautiful place, though he now saw "what you meant about them interesting people," and his New York address would be the Souvenir Company.

He tore up the several pages that repeated that oldest most melancholy cry of the lover, which rang among the deodars, from viking ships, from the moonlit courtyards of Provence, the cry which always sounded about Mr. Wrenn as he walked the deck: "I want you so much; I miss you so unendingly; I am so lonely for you, dear." For no more clearly, no more nobly did the golden Aucassin or lean Dante word that cry in their thoughts than did Mr. William Wrenn, Our Mr. Wrenn.

A third-class steward with a mangy mustache and setter-like tan eyes came teetering down-stairs, each step like a nervous pencil tap on a table, and peered over the side of Mr. Wrenn's berth. He loved Mr. Wrenn, who was proven a scholar by the reading of real bound books—an English history and a second-hand copy of *Haunts of Historic English Writers*, purchased in Liverpool—and who was willing to listen to the steward's serial story of how his woman, Mrs. Wargle, faithlessly consorted with Foddle, the cat's-meat man, when the steward was away, and, when he was home, cooked for him lights and liver that unquestionably were purchased from the same cat's-meat man. He now leered with a fond and watery gaze upon Mr. Wrenn's scholarly pursuits, and announced in a whisper:

"They've sighted land."

"Land?"

"Oh aye."

Mr. Wrenn sat up so vigorously that he bumped his head. He chucked his papers beneath the pillow with his right hand, while the left was feeling for the side of the berth. "Land!" he bellowed to drowsing cabin-mates as he vaulted out.

The steerage promenade-deck, iron-sided, black-floored, ending in the iron approaches to the galley at one end and the iron superstructures about a hatch at the other, was like a grim swart oilily clean machine-shop aisle, so inclosed, so over-roofed, that the side toward the sea seemed merely a long factory window. But he loved it and, except when he had guiltily remembered the books he had to read, he had stayed on deck, worshiping the naive bright attire of immigrants and the dark roll and glory of the sea.

Now, out there was a blue shading, made by a magic pencil; land, his land, where he was going to become the beloved comrade of all the friends whose likenesses he saw in the white-caps flashing before him.

Humming, he paraded down to the buffet, where small beer and smaller tobacco were sold, to buy another pound of striped candy for the offspring of the Russian Jews.

The children knew he was coming. "Fat rascals," he chuckled, touching their dark cheeks, pretending to be frightened as they pounded soft fists against the iron side of the ship or rolled unregarded in the scuppers. Their shawled mothers knew him, too, and as he shyly handed about the candy the chattering stately line of Jewish elders nodded their beards like the forest primeval in a breeze, saying words of blessing in a strange tongue.

He smiled back and made gestures, and shouted "Land! Land!" with several variations in key, to make it sound foreign.

But he withdrew for the sacred moment of seeing the Land of Promise he was newly discovering—the Long Island shore; the grass-clad redouts at Fort Wadsworth; the vast pile of New York sky-scrapers, standing in a mist like an enormous burned forest.

"Singer Tower.... Butterick Building," he murmured, as they proceeded toward their dock. "That's something like.... Let's see; yes, sir, by golly, right up there between the Met. Tower and the *Times*—good old Souvenir Company office. Jiminy! `One Dollar to Albany'—something *like* a sign, that is—good old dollar! To thunder with their darn shillings. Home!... Gee! there's where I used to moon on a wharf!... Gosh! the old town looks good."

And all this was his to conquer, for friendship's sake.

He went to a hotel. While he had to go back to the Zapps', of course, he did not wish, by meeting those old friends, to spoil his first day. No, it was cheerfuler to stand at a window of his cheap hotel on Seventh Avenue, watching the "good old American crowd"—Germans, Irishmen, Italians, and Jews. He went to the Nickelorion and grasped the hand of the ticket-taker, the Brass-button Man, ejaculating: "How are you? Well, how's things going with the old show?... I been away couple of months."

"Fine and dandy! Been away, uh? Well, it's good to get back to the old town, heh? Summer hotel?"

"Unk?"

"Why, you're the waiter at Pat Maloney's, ain't you?"

Next morning Mr. Wrenn made himself go to the Souvenir and Art Novelty Company. He wanted to get the teasing, due him for staying away so short a time, over as soon as possible. The office girl, addressing circulars, seemed surprised when he stepped from the elevator, and blushed her usual shy gratitude to the men of the office for allowing her to exist and take away six dollars weekly.

Then into the entry-room ran Rabin, one of the traveling salesmen.

"Why, hul-lo, Wrenn! Wondered if that could be you. Back so soon? Thought you were going to Europe."

"Just got back. Couldn't stand it away from you, old scout!"

"You must have been learning to sass back real smart, in the Old Country, heh? Going to be with us again? Well, see you again soon. Glad see you back."

He was not madly excited at seeing Rabin; still, the drummer was part of the good old Souvenir Company, the one place in the world on which he could absolutely depend, the one place where they always wanted him.

He had been absently staring at the sample-tables, noting new novelties. The office girl, speaking sweetly, but as to an outsider, inquired, "Who did you wish to see, Mr. Wrenn?"

"Why! Mr. Guilfogle."

"He's busy, but if you'll sit down I think you can see him in a few minutes."

Mr. Wrenn felt like the prodigal son, with no calf in sight, at having to wait on the callers' bench, but he shook with faint excited gurgles of mirth at the thought of the delightful surprise Mr. Mortimer R. Guilfogle, the office manager, was going to have. He kept an eye out for Charley Carpenter. If Charley didn't come through the entry-room he'd go into the bookkeeping-room, and—"talk about your surprises—"

"Mr. Guilfogle will see you now," said the office girl.

As he entered the manager's office Mr. Guilfogle made much of glancing up with busy amazement.

"Well, well, Wrenn! Back so soon? Thought you were going to be gone quite a while."

"Couldn't keep away from the office, Mr. Guilfogle," with an uneasy smile.

"Have a good trip?"

"Yes, a dandy."

"How'd you happen to get back so soon?"

"Oh, I wanted to—Say, Mr. Guilfogle, I really wanted to get back to the office again. I'm awfully glad to see it again."

"Glad see *you*. Well, where did you go? I got the card you sent me from Chesterton with the picture of the old church on it."

"Why, I went to Liverpool and Oxford and London and—well—Kew and Ealing and places and—And I tramped through Essex and Suffolk—all through—on foot. Aengusmere and them places."

"Just a moment. (Well, Rabin, what is it? Why certainly. I've told you that already about five times. *Yes*, I said—that's what I had the samples made up for. I wish you'd be a little more careful, d' ye hear?) You went to London, did you, Wrenn? Say, did you notice any novelties we could copy?"

"No, I'm afraid I didn't, Mr. Guilfogle. I'm awfully sorry. I hunted around, but I couldn't find a thing we could use. I mean I couldn't find anything that began to come up to our line. Them English are pretty slow."

"Didn't, eh? Well, what's your plans now?"

"Why—uh—I kind of thought—Honestly, Mr. Guilfogle, I'd like to get back on my old job. You remember—it was to be fixed so—"

"Afraid there's nothing doing just now, Wrenn. Not a thing. Course I can't tell what may happen, and you want to keep in touch with us, but we're pretty well filled up just now. Jake is getting along better than we thought. He's learning—" Not one word regarding Jake's excellence did Mr. Wrenn hear.

Not get the job back? He sat down and stammered:

"Gee! I hadn't thought of that. I'd kind of banked on the Souvenir Company, Mr. Guilfogle."

"Well, you know I told you I thought you were an idiot to go. I warned you."

He timidly agreed, mourning: "Yes, that so; I know you did. But uh—well—"

"Sorry, Wrenn. That's the way it goes in business, though. If you will go beating it around—A rolling stone don't gather any moss. Well, cheer up! Possibly there may be something doing in—"

"Tr-r-r-r-r-r," said the telephone.

Mr. Guilfogle remarked into it: "Hello. Yes, it's me. Well, who did you think it was? The cat? Yuh. Sure. No. Well, to-morrow, probably. All right. Good-by."

Then he glanced at his watch and up at Mr. Wrenn impatiently.

"Say, Mr. Guilfogle, you say there'll be—when will there be likely to be an opening?"

"Now, how can I tell, my boy? We'll work you in if we can—you ain't a bad clerk; or at least you wouldn't be if you'd be a little more careful. By the way, of course you understand that if we try to work you in it'll take lots of trouble, and we'll expect you to not go flirting round with other firms, looking for a job. Understand that?"

"Oh yes, sir."

"All right. We appreciate your work all right, but of course you can 't expect us to fire any of our present force just because you take the notion to come back whenever you want to…. Hiking off to Europe, leaving a good job!… You didn't get on the Continent, did you?"

"No, I—"

"Well…. Oh, say, how's the grub in London? Cheaper than it is here? The wife was saying this morning we'd have to stop eating if the high cost of living goes on going up."

"Yes, it's quite a little cheaper. You can get fine tea for two and three cents a cup. Clothes is cheaper, too. But I don't care much for the English, though there is all sorts of quaint places with a real flavor…. Say, Mr. Guilfogle, you know I inherited a little money, and I can wait awhile, and you'll kind of keep me in mind for a place if one—"

"Didn't I *say* I would?"

"Yes, but—"

"You come around and see me a week from now. And leave your address with Rosey. I don't know, though, as we can afford to pay you quite the same salary at first, even if we can work you in—the season's been very slack. But I'll do what I can for you. Come in and see me in about a week. Goo' day."

Rabin, the salesman, waylaid Mr. Wrenn in the corridor.

"You look kind of peeked, Wrenn. Old Goglefogle been lighting into you? Say, I ought to have told you first. I forgot it. The old rat, he's been planning to stick the knife into you all the while. 'Bout two weeks ago me and him had a couple of cocktails at Mouquin's. You know how chummy he always gets after a couple of smiles. Well, he was talking about—I was saying you're a good man and hoping you were having a good time—and he said, 'Yes,' he says, 'he's a good man, but he sure did lay himself wide open by taking this trip. I've got him dead to rights,' he says to me. 'I've got a hunch he'll be back here in three or four months,' he says to me. 'And do you think he'll walk in and get what he wants? Not him. I'll keep him waiting a month before I give him back his job, and then you watch, Rabin,' he says to me, 'you'll see he'll be tickled to death to go back to work at less salary than he was getting, and he'll have sense enough to not try this stunt of getting off the job again after that. And the trip'll be good for him, anyway—he'll do better work—vacation at his own expense—save us money all round. I tell you, Rabin,' he says to me, 'if any of you boys think you can get the best of the company or me you just want to try it, that's all.' Yessir, that's what the old rat told me. You want to watch out for him."

"Oh, I will; indeed I will—"

"Did he spring any of this fairy tale just now?"

"Well, kind of. Say, thanks, I'm awful obliged to—"

"Say, for the love of Mike, don't let him know I told you."

"No, no, I sure won't."

They parted. Eager though he was for the great moment of again seeing his comrade, Charley Carpenter, Mr. Wrenn dribbled toward the bookkeeping-room mournfully, planning to tell Charley of Guilfogle's wickedness.

The head bookkeeper shook his head at Mr. Wrenn's inquiry:

"Charley ain't here any longer."

"Ain't *here?*"

"No. He got through. He got to boozing pretty bad, and one morning about three weeks ago, when he had a pretty bad hang-over, he told Guilfogle what he thought of him, so of course Guilfogle fired him."

"Oh, that's too *bad*. Say, you don't know his address, do you?"

"—East a Hundred and Eighteenth.... Well, I'm glad to see you back, Wrenn. Didn't expect to see you back so soon, but always glad to see you. Going to be with us?"

"I ain't sure," said Mr. Wrenn, crabbedly, then shook hands warmly with the bookkeeper, to show there was nothing personal in his snippishness.

For nearly a hundred blocks Mr. Wrenn scowled at an advertisement of Corn Flakes in the Third Avenue Elevated without really seeing it.... Should he go back to the Souvenir Company at all?

Yes. He would. That was the best way to start making friends. But he would "get our friend Guilfogle at recess," he assured himself, with an out-thrust of the jaw like that of the great Bill Wrenn. He knew Guilfogle's lead now, and he would show that gentleman that he could play the game. He'd take that lower salary and pretend to be frightened, but when he got the chance—

He did not proclaim even to himself what dreadful thing he was going to do, but as he left the Elevated he said over and over, shaking his closed fist inside his coat pocket:

"When I get the chance—when I *get* it—"

The flat-building where Charley Carpenter lived was one of hundreds of pressed-brick structures, apparently all turned out of the same mold. It was filled with the smells of steamy washing and fried fish. Languid with the heat, Mr. Wrenn crawled up an infinity of iron steps and knocked three times at Charley's door. No answer. He crawled down again and sought out the janitress, who stopped watching an ice-wagon in the street to say:

"I guess you'll be finding him asleep up there, sir. He do be lying there drunk most of the day. His wife's left him. The landlord's give him notice to quit, end of August. Warm day, sir. Be you a bill-collector? Mostly, it's bill-collectors that—"

"Yes, it is hot."

Superior in manner, but deeply dejected, Mr. Wrenn rang the down-stairs bell long enough to wake Charley, pantingly got himself up the interminable stairs, and kicked the door till Charley's voice quavered inside:

"Who zhat?"

"It's me, Charley. Wrenn."

"You're in Yurp. Can't fool me. G' 'way from there."

Three other doors on the same landing were now partly open and blocked with the heads of frowsy inquisitive women. The steamy smell was thicker in the darkness. Mr. Wrenn felt prickly, then angry at this curiosity, and again demanded:

"Lemme in, I say."

"Tell you it ain't you. I know you!"

Charley Carpenter's pale face leered out. His tousled hair was stuck to his forehead by perspiration; his eyes were red and vaguely staring. His clothes were badly wrinkled. He wore a collarless shirt with a frilled bosom of virulent pink, its cuffs grimy and limp.

"It's ol' Wrenn. C'm in. C'm in quick. Collectors always hanging around. They can't catch me. You bet."

He closed the door and wabbled swiftly down the long drab hall of the "railroad flat," evidently trying to walk straight. The reeking stifling main room at the end of the hall was terrible as Charley's eyes. Flies boomed everywhere. The oak table, which Charley and his bride had once spent four happy hours in selecting, was littered with half a dozen empty whisky-flasks, collars, torn sensational newspapers, dirty plates and coffee-cups. The cheap brocade cover, which a bride had once joyed to embroider with red and green roses, was half pulled off and dragged on the floor amid the cigarette butts, Durham tobacco, and bacon rinds which covered the green-and-yellow carpet-rug.

This much Mr. Wrenn saw. Then he set himself to the hard task of listening to Charley, who was muttering:

"Back quick, ain't you, ol' Wrenn? You come up to see me, didn't you? You're m' friend, ain't you, eh? I got an awful hang-over, ain't I? You don't care, do you, ol' Wrenn?"

Mr. Wrenn stared at him weakly, but only for a minute. Perhaps it was his cattle-boat experience which now made him deal directly with such drunkenness as would have nauseated him three months before; perhaps his attendance on a weary Istra.

"Come now, Charley, you got to buck up," he crooned.

"*All* ri'."

"What's the trouble? How did you get going like this?"

"Wife left me. I was drinking. You think I'm drunk, don't you? But I ain't. She went off with her sister—always hated me. She took my money out of savings-bank—three hundred; all money I had 'cept fifty dollars. I'll fix her. I'll kill her. Took to hitting the booze. Goglefogle fired me. Don't care. Drink all I want. Keep young fellows from getting it! Say, go down and get me pint. Just finished up pint. Got to have one-die of thirst. Bourbon. Get—"

"I'll go and get you a drink, Charley—just one drink, savvy?—if you'll promise to get cleaned up, like I tell you, afterward."

"*All* ri'."

Mr. Wrenn hastened out with a whisky-flask, muttering, feverishly, "Gee! I got to save him." Returning, he poured out one drink, as though it were medicine for a refractory patient, and said, soothingly:

"Now we'll take a cold bath, heh? and get cleaned up and sobered up. Then we'll talk about a job, heh?"

"Aw, don't want a bath. Say, I feel better now. Let's go out and have a drink. Gimme that flask. Where j' yuh put it?"

Mr. Wrenn went to the bathroom, turned on the cold-water tap, returned, and undressed Charley, who struggled and laughed and let his whole inert weight rest against Mr. Wrenn's shoulder. Though normally Charley could have beaten three Mr. Wrenns, he was run into the bath-room and poked into the tub.

Instantly he began to splash, throwing up water in handfuls, singing. The water poured over the side of the tub. Mr. Wrenn tried to hold him still, but the wet sleek shoulders slipped through his hand like a wet platter. Wholesomely vexed, he turned off the water and slammed the bathroom door.

In the bedroom he found an unwrinkled winter-weight suit and one clean shirt. In the living-room he hung up his coat, covering it with a newspaper, pulled the broom from under the table, and prepared to sweep.

The disorder was so great that he made one of the inevitable discoveries of every housekeeper, and admitted to himself that he "didn't know where to begin." He stumblingly lugged a heavy pile of dishes from the center-table to the kitchen, shook and beat and folded the table-cover, stuck the chairs atop the table, and began to sweep.

At the door a shining wet naked figure stood, bellowing:

"Hey! What d' yuh think you're doing? Cut it out."

"Just sweeping, Charley," from Mr. Wrenn, and an uninterrupted "Tuff, tuff, tuff" from the broom.

"Cut it out, I said. Whose house *is* this?"

"Gwan back in the bath-tub, Charley."

"Say, d' yuh think you can run me? Get out of this, or I'll throw you out. Got house way I want it."

Bill Wrenn, the cattleman, rushed at him, smacked him with the broom, drove him back into the tub, and waited. He laughed. It was all a good joke; his friend Charley and he were playing a little game. Charley also laughed and splashed some more. Then he wept and said that the water was cold, and that he was now deserted by his only friend.

"Oh, shut up," remarked Bill Wrenn, and swept the bathroom floor.

Charley stopped swashing about to sneer:

"Li'l ministering angel, ain't you? You think you're awful good, don't you? Come up here and bother me. When I ain't well. Salvation Army. You——. Aw, lemme 'lone, will you?" Bill Wrenn kept on sweeping. "Get out, you——."

There was enough energy in Charley's voice to indicate that he was getting sober. Bill Wrenn soused him under once more, so thoroughly that his own cuffs were reduced to a state of flabbiness. He dragged Charley out, helped him dry himself, and drove him to bed.

He went out and bought dish-towels, soap, washing-powder, and collars of Charley's size, which was an inch larger than his own. He finished sweeping and dusting and washing the dishes—all of them. He—who had learned to comfort Istra—he really enjoyed it. His sense of order made it a pleasure to see a plate yellow with dried egg glisten iridescently and flash into shining whiteness; or a room corner filled with dust and tobacco flakes become again a "nice square clean corner with the baseboard shining, gee! just like it was new."

An irate grocer called with a bill for fifteen dollars. Mr. Wrenn blandly heard his threats all through, pretending to himself that this was his home, whose honor was his honor. He paid the man eight dollars on account and loftily dismissed him. He sat down to wait for Charley, reading a newspaper most of the time, but rising to pursue stray flies furiously, stumbling over chairs, and making murderous flappings with a folded newspaper.

When Charley awoke, after three hours, clear of mind but not at all clear as regards the roof of his mouth, Mr. Wrenn gave him a very little whisky, with considerable coffee, toast, and bacon. The toast was not bad.

"Now, Charley," he said, cheerfully, "your bat's over, ain't it, old man?"

"Say, you been darn' decent to me, old man. Lord! how you've been sweeping up! How was I—was I pretty soused?"

"Honest, you were fierce. You will sober up, now, won't you?"

"Well, it's no wonder I had a classy hang-over, Wrenn. I was at the Amusieren Rathskeller till four this morning, and then I had a couple of nips before breakfast, and then I didn't have any breakfast. But sa-a-a-ay, man, I sure did have some fiesta last night. There was a little peroxide blonde that—"

"Now you look here, Carpenter; you listen to me. You're sober now. Have you tried to find another job?"

"Yes, I did. But I got down in the mouth. Didn't feel like I had a friend left."

"Well, you h—"

"But I guess I have now, old Wrennski."

"Look here, Charley, you know I don't want to pull off no Charity Society stunt or talk like I was a preacher. But I like you so darn much I want to see you sober up and get another job. Honestly I do, Charley. Are you broke?"

"Prett' nearly. Only got about ten dollars to my name…. I *will* take a brace, old man. I know you ain't no preacher. Course if you came around with any 'holier-than-thou' stunt I'd have to go right out and get soused on general principles.... Yuh—I'll try to get a job."

"Here's ten dollars. Please take it—aw—please, Charley."

"*All* right; anything to oblige."

"What 've you got in sight in the job line?"

"Well, there's a chance at night clerking in a little hotel where I was a bell-hop long time ago. The night clerk's going to get through, but I don't know just when—prob'ly in a week or two."

"Well, keep after it. And *please* come down to see me—the old place—West Sixteenth Street."

"What about the old girl with the ingrowing grouch? What's her name? She ain't stuck on me."

"Mrs. Zapp? Oh—hope she chokes. She can just kick all she wants to. I'm just going to have all the visitors I want to."

"All right. Say, tell us something about your trip."

"Oh, I had a great time. Lots of nice fellows on the cattle-boat. I went over on one, you know. Fellow named Morton—awfully nice fellow. Say, Charley, you ought to seen me being butler to the steers. Handing 'em hay. But say, the sea was fine; all kinds of colors. Awful dirty on the cattle-boat, though."

"Hard work?"

"Yuh—kind of hard. Oh, not so very."

"What did you see in England?"

"Oh, a lot of different places. Say, I seen some great vaudeville in Liverpool, Charley, with Morton—he's a slick fellow; works for the Pennsylvania, here in town. I got to look him up. Say, I wish we had an agency for college sofa-pillows and banners and souvenir stuff in Oxford. There's a whole bunch of colleges there, all right in the same town. I met a prof. there from some American college—he hired an automobubble and took me down to a reg'lar old inn—"

"Well, well!"

"—like you read about; sanded floor!"

"Get to London?"

"Yuh. Gee! it's a big place. Say, that Westminster Abbey's a great place. I was in there a couple of times. More darn tombs of kings and stuff. And I see a bishop, with leggins on! But I got kind of lonely. I thought of you a lot of times. Wished we could go out and get an ale together. Maybe pick up a couple of pretty girls."

"Oh, you sport!... Say, didn't get over to gay Paree, did you?"

"Nope.... Well, I guess I'd better beat it now. Got to move in—I'm at a hotel. You will come down and see me to-night, won't you?"

"So you thought of me, eh?... Yuh—sure, old socks. I'll be down to-night. And I'll get right after that job."

It is doubtful whether Mr. Wrenn would ever have returned to the Zapps' had he not promised to see Charley there. Even while he was carrying his suit-case down West Sixteenth, broiling by degrees in the sunshine, he felt like rushing up to Charley's and telling him to come to the hotel instead.

Lee Theresa, taking the day off with a headache, answered the bell, and ejaculated:

"Well! So it's you, is it?"

"I guess it is."

"What, are you back so soon? Why, you ain't been gone more than a month and a half, have you?"

Beware, daughter of Southern pride! The little Yankee is regarding your full-blown curves and empty eyes with rebellion, though he says, ever so meekly:

"Yes, I guess it is about that, Miss Theresa."

"Well, I just knew you couldn't stand it away from us. I suppose you'll want your room back. Ma, here's Mr. Wrenn back again—Mr. Wrenn! *Ma!*"

"Oh-h-h-h!" sounded Goaty Zapp's voice, in impish disdain, below. "Mr. Wrenn's back. Hee, hee! Couldn't stand it. Ain't that like a Yankee!"

A slap, a wail, then Mrs. Zapp's elephantine slowness on the stairs from the basement. She appeared, buttoning her collar, smiling almost pleasantly, for she disliked Mr. Wrenn less than she did any other of her lodgers.

"Back already, Mist' Wrenn? Ah declare, Ah was saying to Lee Theresa just yest'day, Ah just knew you'd be wishing you was back with us. Won't you come in?"

He edged into the parlor with, "How is the sciatica, Mrs. Zapp?"

"Ah ain't feeling right smart."

"My room occupied yet?"

He was surveying the airless parlor rather heavily, and his curt manner was not pleasing to the head of the house of Zapp, who remarked, funereally:

"It ain't taken just now, Mist' Wrenn, but Ah dunno. There was a gennulman a-looking at it just yesterday, and he said he'd be permanent if he came. Ah declare, Mist' Wrenn, Ah dunno's Ah like to have my gennulmen just get up and go without giving me notice."

Lee Theresa scowled at her.

Mr. Wrenn retorted, "I *did* give you notice."

"Ah know, but—well, Ah reckon Ah can let you have it, but Ah'll have to have four and a half a week instead of four. Prices is all going up so, Ah declare, Ah was just saying to Lee T'resa Ah dunno what we're all going to do if the dear Lord don't look out for us. And, Mist' Wrenn, Ah dunno's Ah like to have you coming in so late nights. But Ah reckon Ah can accommodate you."

"It's a good deal of a favor, isn't it, Mrs. Zapp?"

Mr. Wrenn was dangerously polite. Let gentility look out for the sharp practices of the Yankee.

"Yes, but—"

It was our hero, our madman of the seven and seventy seas, our revolutionist friend of Istra, who leaped straight from the salt-incrusted decks of his laboring steamer to the musty parlor and declared, quietly but unmovably-practically unmovably—"Well, then, I guess I'd better not take it at all."

"So that's the way you're going to treat us!" bellowed Mrs. Zapp. "You go off and leave us with an unoccupied room and— Oh! You poor white trash—you—"

"*Ma!* You shut up and go down-stairs-s-s-s!" Theresa hissed. "Go on."

Mrs. Zapp wabbled regally out. Lee Theresa spoke to Mr. Wrenn:

"Ma ain't feeling a bit well this afternoon. I'm sorry she talked like that. You will come back, won't you?" She showed all her teeth in a genuine smile, and in her anxiety reached his heart. "Remember, you promised you would."

"Well, I will, but—"

Bill Wrenn was fading, an affrighted specter. The "but" was the last glimpse of him, and that Theresa overlooked, as she bustlingly chirruped: "I *knew* you would understand. I'll skip right up and look at the room and put on fresh sheets."

One month, one hot New York month, passed before the imperial Mr. Guilfogle gave him back The Job, and then at seventeen dollars and fifty cents a week instead of his former nineteen dollars. Mr. Wrenn refused, upon pretexts, to go out with the manager for a drink, and presented him with twenty suggestions for new novelties and circular letters. He rearranged the unsystematic methods of Jake, the cub, and two days later he was at work as though he had never in his life been farther from the Souvenir Company than Newark.

CHAPTER XIII

HE IS "OUR MR. WRENN"

DEAR ISTRA,—I am back in New York feeling very well & hope this finds you the same. I have been wanting to write to you for quite a while now but there has not been much news of any kind & so I have not written to you. But now I am back working for the Souvenir Company. I hope you are having a good time in Paris it must be a very pretty city & I have often wished to be there perhaps some day I shall go. I [several erasures here] have been reading quite a few books since I got back & think now I shall get on better with my reading. You told me so many things about books & so on & I do appreciate it. In closing, I am yours very sincerely,

WILLIAM WRENN.

There was nothing else he could say. But there were a terrifying number of things he could think as he crouched by the window overlooking West Sixteenth Street, whose dull hue had not changed during the centuries while he had been tramping England. Her smile he remembered—and he cried, "Oh, I want to see her so much." Her gallant dash through the rain—and again the cry.

At last he cursed himself, "Why don't you *do* something that 'd count for her, and not sit around yammering for her like a fool?"

He worked on his plan to "bring the South into line"—the Souvenir Company's line. Again and again he sprang up from the writing-table in his hot room when the presence of Istra came and stood compellingly by his chair. But he worked.

The Souvenir Company salesmen had not been able to get from the South the business which the company deserved if right and justice were to prevail. On the steamer from England Mr. Wrenn had conceived the idea that a Dixieland Ink-well, with the Confederate and Union flags draped in graceful cast iron, would make an admirable present with which to draw the attention of the Southern trade. The ink-well was to be followed by a series of letters, sent on the slightest provo-cation, on order or re-order, tactfully hoping the various healths of the Southland were good and the baseball season important; all to insure a welcome to the sales-men on the Southern route.

He drew up his letters; he sketched his ink-well; he got up the courage to talk with the office manager.... To forget love and the beloved, men have ascended in aeroplanes and conquered African tribes. To forget love, a new, busy, much absorbed Mr. Wrenn, very much Ours, bustled into Mr. Guilfogle's office, slapped down his papers on the desk, and demanded: "Here's that plan about gettin' the South interested that I was telling you about. Say, honest, I'd like awful much to try it on. I'd just have to have part time of one stenographer."

"Well, you know our stenographers are pretty well crowded. But you can leave the outline with me. I'll look it over," said Mr. Guilfogle.

That same afternoon the manager enthusiastically O. K.'d the plan. To enthusiastically — O. K. is an office technology for saying, gloomily, "Well, I don't suppose it 'd hurt to try it, anyway, but for the love of Mike be careful, and let me see any letters you send out."

So Mr. Wrenn dictated a letter to each of their Southern merchants, sending him a Dixieland Ink-well and inquiring about the crops. He had a stenographer, an efficient intolerant young woman who wrote down his halting words as though they were examples of bad English she wanted to show her friends, and waited for the next word with cynical amusement.

"By gosh!" growled Bill Wrenn, the cattleman, "I'll show her I'm running this. I'll show her she's got another think coming." But he dictated so busily and was so hot to get results that he forgot the girl's air of high-class martyrdom.

He watched the Southern baseball results in the papers. He seized on every salesman on the Southern route as he came in, and inquired about the religion and politics of the merchants in his district. He even forgot to worry about his next rise in salary, and found it much more exciting to rush back for an important letter after a quick lunch than to watch the time and make sure that he secured every minute of his lunch-hour.

When October came — October of the vagabond, with the leaves brilliant out on the Palisades, and Sixth Avenue moving-picture palaces cool again and gay — Mr. Wrenn stayed late, under the mercury-vapor lights, making card cross-files of the Southern merchants, their hobbies and prejudices, and whistling as he worked, stopping now and then to slap the desk and mutter, "By gosh! I'm gettin' 'em — gettin' 'em."

He rarely thought of Istra till he was out on the street again, proud of having worked so late that his eyes ached. In fact, his chief troubles these days came when Mr. Guilfogle wouldn't "let him put through an idea."

Their first battle was over Mr. Wrenn's signing the letters personally; for the letters, the office manager felt, were as much Ours as was Mr. Wrenn, and should be signed by the firm. After some difficulty Mr. Wrenn persuaded him that one of the best ways to handle a personal letter was to make it personal. They nearly cursed each other before Mr. Wrenn was allowed to use his own judgment.

It's not at all certain that Mr. Guilfogle should have yielded. What's the use of a manager if his underlings use judgment?

The next battle Mr. Wrenn lost. He had demanded a monthly holiday for his stenographer. Mr. Guilfogle pointed out that she'd merely be the worse off for a holiday, that it 'd make her discontented, that it was a kindness to her to keep her mind occupied. Mr. Wrenn was, however, granted a new typewriter, in a manner which revealed the fact that the Souvenir Company was filled with almost too much mercy in permitting an employee to follow his own selfish and stubborn desires.

You cannot trust these employees. Mr. Wrenn was getting so absorbed in his work that he didn't even act as though it was a favor when Mr. Guilfogle allowed him to have his letters to the trade copied by carbon paper instead of having them blurred by the wet tissue-paper of a copy-book. The manager did grant the request, but he was justly indignant at the curt manner of the rascal, whereupon our bumptious revolutionist, our friend to anarchists and red-headed artists, demanded a "raise" and said that he didn't care a hang if the [qualified] letters never went out. The kindness of chiefs! For Mr. Guilfogle apologized and raised the madman's wage from seventeen dollars and fifty cents a week to his former nineteen dollars. [He had expected eighteen dollars; he had demanded twenty-two dollars and fifty cents; he was worth on the labor market from twenty-five to thirty dollars; while the profit to the Souvenir Company from his work was about sixty dollars minus whatever salary he got.]

Not only that. Mr. Guilfogle slapped him on the back and said: "You're doing good work, old man. It's fine. I just don't want you to be too reckless."

That night Wrenn worked till eight.

After his raise he could afford to go to the theater, since he was not saving money for travel. He wrote small letters to Istra and read the books he believed she would approve—a Paris Baedeker and the second volume of Tolstoi's *War and Peace*, which he bought at a second-hand book-stall for five cents. He became interested in popular and inaccurate French and English histories, and secreted any amount of footnote anecdotes about Guy Fawkes and rush-lights and the divine right of kings. He thought almost every night about making friends, which he intended—just as much as ever—to do as soon as Sometime arrived.

On the day on which one of the Southern merchants wrote him about his son—"fine young fellow, sir—has every chance of rising to a lieutenancy on the Atlanta police force"—Mr. Wrenn's eyes were moist. Here was a friend already. Sure. He would make friends. Then there was the cripple with the Capitol Corner News and Souvenir Stand in Austin, Texas. Mr. Wrenn secreted two extra Dixieland Ink-wells and a Yale football banner and sent them to the cripple for his brothers, who were in the Agricultural College.

The orders—yes, they were growing larger. The Southern salesmen took him out to dinner sometimes. But he was shy of them. They were so knowing and had so many smoking-room stories. He still had not found the friends he desired.

Miggleton's restaurant, on Forty-second Street, was a romantic discovery. Though it had "popular prices"—plain omelet, fifteen cents—it had red and green bracket lights, mission-style tables, and music played by a sparrowlike pianist and a violinist. Mr. Wrenn never really heard the music, but while it was quavering he had a happier appreciation of the Silk-Hat-Harry humorous pictures in the *Journal*, which he always propped up against an oil-cruet. [That never caused him inconvenience; he had no convictions in regard to salads.] He would drop the paper to look out of the window at the Lazydays Improvement Company's electric sign, showing gardens of paradise on the instalment plan, and dream of—well, he hadn't the slightest idea what—something distant and deliciously likely to become intimate. Once or twice he knew that he was visioning the girl in soft brown whom he would "go home to," and who, in a Lazydays suburban residence, would play just such music for him and the friends who lived near by. She would be as clever as Istra, but "oh, more so's you can go regular places with her."… Often he got good ideas about letters South, to be jotted down on envelope backs, from that music.

At last comes the historic match-box incident.

On that October evening in 1910 he dined early at Miggleton's. The thirty-cent table d'hote was perfect. The cream-of-corn soup was, he went so far as to remark to the waitress, "simply slick"; the Waldorf salad had two whole walnuts in his portion alone.

The fat man with the white waistcoat, whom he had often noted as dining in this same corner of the restaurant, smiled at him and said "Pleasant evening" as he sat down opposite Mr. Wrenn and smoothed the two sleek bangs which decorated the front of his nearly bald head.

The music included a "potpourri of airs from 'The Merry Widow,'" which set his foot tapping. All the while he was conscious that he'd made the Seattle Novelty and Stationery Corner Store come through with a five-hundred-dollar order on one of his letters.

The *Journal* contained an editorial essay on "Friendship" which would have been, and was, a credit to Cicero.

He laid down the paper, stirred his large cup of coffee, and stared at the mother-of-pearl buttons on the waistcoat of the fat man, who was now gulping down soup, opposite him. "My land!" he was thinking, "friendship! I ain't even begun to make all those friends I was going to. Haven't done a thing. Oh, I will; I must!"

"Nice night," said the fat man.

"Yuh—it sure is," brightly agreed Mr. Wrenn.

"Reg'lar Indian-Summer weather."

"Yes, isn't it! I feel like taking a walk on Riverside Drive—b'lieve I will."

"Wish I had time. But I gotta get down to the store—cigar-store. I'm on nights, three times a week."

"Yuh. I've seen you here most every time I eat early," Mr. Wrenn purred.

"Yuh. The rest of the time I eat at the boarding-house."

Silence. But Mr. Wrenn was fighting for things to say, means of approach, for the chance to become acquainted with a new person, for all the friendly human ways he had desired in nights of loneliness.

"Wonder when they'll get the Grand Central done?" asked the fat man.

"I s'pose it'll take quite a few years," said Mr. Wrenn, conversationally.

"Yuh. I s'pose it will."

Silence.

Mr. Wrenn sat trying to think of something else to say. Lonely people in city restaurants simply do not get acquainted. Yet he did manage to observe, "Great building that'll be," in the friendliest manner.

Silence.

Then the fat man went on:

"Wonder what Wolgast will do in his mill? Don't believe he can stand up."

Wolgast was, Mr. Wrenn seemed to remember, a pugilist. He agreed vaguely:

"Pretty hard, all right."

"Go out to the areoplane meet?" asked the fat man.

"No. But I'd like to see it. Gee! there must be kind of—kind of adventure in them things, heh?"

"Yuh—sure is. First machine I saw, though—I was just getting off the train at Belmont Park, and there was an areoplane up in the air, and it looked like one of them big mechanical beetles these fellows sell on the street buzzing around up there. I was kind of disappointed. But what do you think? It was that J. A. D. McCurdy, in a Curtiss biplane—I think it was—and by golly! he got to circling around and racing and tipping so's I thought I'd loose my hat off, I was so excited. And, say, what do you think? I see McCurdy himself, afterward, standing near one of the—the handgars—handsome young chap, not over twenty-eight or thirty, built like a half-miler. And then I see Ralph Johnstone and Arch Hoxey—"

"Gee!" Mr. Wrenn was breathing.

"—dipping and doing the—what do you call it?—Dutch sausage-roll or something like that. Yelled my head off."

"Oh, it must have been great to see 'em, and so close, too."

"Yuh—it sure was."

There seemed to be no other questions to settle. Mr. Wrenn slowly folded up his paper, pursued his check under three plates and the menu-card to its hiding-place beyond the catsup-bottle, and left the table with a regretful "Good night."

At the desk of the cashier, a decorative blonde, he put a cent in the machine which good-naturedly drops out boxes of matches. No box dropped this time, though he worked the lever noisily.

"Out of order?" asked the cashier lady. "Here's two boxes of matches. Guess you've earned them."

"Well, well, well, well!" sounded the voice of his friend, the fat man, who stood at the desk paying his bill. "Pretty easy, heh? Two boxes for one cent! Sting the restaurant." Cocking his head, he carefully inserted a cent in the slot and clattered the lever, turning to grin at Mr. Wrenn, who grinned back as the machine failed to work.

"Let me try it," caroled Mr. Wrenn, and pounded the lever with the enthusiasm of comradeship.

"Nothing doing, lady," crowed the fat man to the cashier.

"I guess *I* draw two boxes, too, eh? And I'm in a cigar-store. How's that for stinging your competitors, heh? Ho, ho, ho!"

The cashier handed him two boxes, with an embarrassed simper, and the fat man clapped Mr. Wrenn's shoulder joyously.

"My turn!" shouted a young man in a fuzzy green hat and a bright-brown suit, who had been watching with the sudden friendship which unites a crowd brought together by an accident.

Mr. Wrenn was glowing. "No, it ain't—it's mine," he achieved. "I invented this game." Never had he so stood forth in a crowd. He was a Bill Wrenn with the cosmopolitan polish of a floor-walker. He stood beside the fat man as a friend of sorts, a person to be taken perfectly seriously.

It is true that he didn't add to this spiritual triumph the triumph of getting two more boxes of matches, for the cashier-girl exclaimed, "No indeedy; it's my turn!" and lifted the match machine to a high shelf behind her. But Mr. Wrenn went out of the restaurant with his old friend, the fat man, saying to him quite as would a wit, "I guess we get stung, eh?"

"Yuh!" gurgled the fat man.

Walking down to your store?"

"Yuh—sure—won't you walk down a piece?"

"Yes, I would like to. Which way is it?"

"Fourth Avenue and Twenty-eighth."

"Walk down with you."

"Fine!"

And the fat man seemed to mean it. He confided to Mr. Wrenn that the fishing was something elegant at Trulen, New Jersey; that he was some punkins at the casting of flies in fishing; that he wished exceedingly to be at Trulen fishing with flies, but was prevented by the manager of the cigar-store; that the manager was an old devil; that his (the fat man's own) name was Tom Poppins; that the store had a slick new brand of Manila cigars, kept in a swell new humidor bought upon the advice of himself (Mr. Poppins); that one of the young clerks in the store had done fine in the Modified Marathon; that the Cubs had had a great team this year; that he'd be glad to give Mr.—Mr. Wrenn, eh?—one of those Manila cigars—great cigars they were, too; and that he hadn't "laughed so much for a month of Sundays as he had over the way they stung Miggleton's on them matches."

All this in the easy, affectionate, slightly wistful manner of fat men. Mr. Poppins's large round friendly childish eyes were never sarcastic. He was the man who makes of a crowd in the Pullman smoking-room old friends in half an hour. In turn, Mr. Wrenn did not shy off; he hinted at most of his lifelong ambitions and a fair number of his sorrows and, when they reached the store, not only calmly accepted, but even sneezingly ignited one of the "slick new Manila cigars."

As he left the store he knew that the golden age had begun. He had a friend!

He was to see Tom Poppins the coming Thursday at Miggleton's. And now he was going to find Morton! He laughed so loudly that the policeman at Thirty-fourth Street looked self-conscious and felt secretively to find out what was the matter with his uniform. Now, this evening, he'd try to get on the track of Morton. Well, perhaps not this evening—the Pennsylvania offices wouldn't be open, but some time this week, anyway.

Two nights later, as he waited for Tom Poppins at Miggleton's, he lashed himself with the thought that he had not started to find Morton; good old Morton of the cattle-boat. But that was forgotten in the wonder of Tom Poppins's account of Mrs. Arty's, a boarding-house "where all the folks likes each other."

"You've never fed at a boarding-house, eh?" said Tom. "Well, I guess most of 'em are pretty poor feed. And pretty sad bunch. But Mrs. Arty's is about as near like home as most of us poor bachelors ever gets. Nice crowd there. If Mrs. Arty— Mrs. R. T. Ferrard is her name, but we always call her Mrs. Arty—if she don't take to you she don't mind letting you know she won't take you in at all; but if she does she'll worry over the holes in your socks as if they was her husband's. All the bunch there drop into the parlor when they come in, pretty near any time clear up till twelve-thirty, and talk and laugh and rush the growler and play Five Hundred. Just like home!

"Mrs. Arty's nearly as fat as I am, but she can be pretty spry if there's something she can do for you. Nice crowd there, too except that Teddem—he's one of these here Willy-boy actors, always out of work; I guess Mrs. Arty is kind of sorry for him. Say, Wrenn—you seem to me like a good fellow—why don't you get acquainted with the bunch? Maybe you'd like to move up there some time. You was telling me about what a cranky old party your landlady is. Anyway, come on up there to dinner. On me. Got anything on for next Monday evening?"

"N-no."

"Come on up then——East Thirtieth."

"Gee, I'd like to!"

"Well, why don't you, then? Get there about six. Ask for me. Monday. Monday, Wednesday, and Friday I don't have to get to the store evenings. Come on; you'll find out if you like the place."

"By jiminy, I will!" Mr. Wrenn slapped the table, socially.

At last he was "through, just *through* with loafing around and not getting acquainted," he told himself. He was tired of Zapps. There was nothing to Zapps. He would go up to Mrs. Arty's and now—he was going to find Morton. Next morning, marveling at himself for not having done this easy task before, he telephoned to the Pennsylvania Railroad offices, asked for Morton, and in one-half minute heard:

"Yes? This is Harry Morton."

"Hullo, Mr. Morton! I'll just bet you can't guess who this is."

"I guess you've got me."

"Well, who do you think it—"

"Jack?"

"Hunka."

"Uncle Henry?"

"Nope." Mr. Wrenn felt lonely at finding himself so completely outside Morton's own world that he was not thought of. He hastened to claim a part in that world:

"Say, Mr. Morton, I wonder if you've ever heard of a cattle-boat called the *Merian?*"

"I—Say! Is this Bill Wrenn?"

"Yes."

"Well, well, well! Where areyou? When'd you get back?"

"Oh, I been back quite a little while, Morty. Tried to get hold of you—almost called up couple of times. I'm in my office—Souvenir Company—now. Back on the old job. Say, I'd like to see you."

"Well, I'd like to see *you*, old Bill!"

"Got a date for dinner this evening, Morty?"

"N-no. No, I don't *think* I've got anything on." Morton's voice seemed to sound a doubt. Mr. Wrenn reflected that Morton must be a society person; and he made his invitation highly polite:

"Well, say, old man, I'd be awful happy if you could come over and feed on me. Can't you come over and meet me, Morty?"

"Y-yes, I guess I can. Yes, I'll do it. Where'll I meet you?"

"How about Twenty-eighth and Sixth Avenue?"

"That'll be all right, Bill. 'Bout six o'clock?"

"Fine! Be awful nice to see you again, old Morty."

"Same here. Goo'-by."

Gazing across the table at Miggleton's, Mr. Wrenn saw, in the squat familiar body and sturdy face of Morton of the cattle-boat, a stranger, slightly uneasy and very quiet, wearing garments that had nothing whatever to do with the cattle-boats—a crimson scarf with a horseshoe-pin of "Brazilian diamonds," and sleek brown ready-made clothes with ornately curved cuffs and pocket flaps.

Morton would say nothing of his wanderings after their parting in Liverpool beyond: "Oh, I just bummed around. Places.... Warm to-night. For this time of year." Thrice he explained, "I was kind of afraid you'd be sore at me for the way I left you; that's why I've never looked you up." Thrice Mr. Wrenn declared that he had not been "sore," then ceased trying to make himself understood.

Their talk wilted. Both of them played with their knives a good deal. Morton built a set of triangles out of toothpicks while pretending to give hushed attention to the pianist's rendition of "Mammy's Little Cootsie Bootsie Coon," while Mr. Wrenn stared out of the window as though he expected to see the building across get afire immediately. When either of them invented something to say they started chattering with guilty haste, and each agreed hectically with any opinion the other advanced.

Mr. Wrenn surprised himself in the thought that Morton hadn't anything very new to say, which made him feel so disloyal that he burst out, effusively:

"Say, come on now, old man; I just got to hear about what you did after you left Liverpool."

"I—"

"Well—"

"I never got out of Liverpool! Worked in a restaurant.... But next time—! I'll go clean to Constantinople!" Morton exploded. "And I did see a lot of English life in Liverpool."

Mr. Wrenn talked long and rapidly of the world's baseball series, and Regal *vs.* Walkover shoes.

He tried to think of something they could do. Suddenly:

"Say, Morty, I know an awful nice guy down here in a cigar-store. Let's go down and see him."

"All right."

Tom Poppins was very cordial to them. He dragged brown canvas stools out of the tobacco-scented room where cigars were made, and the three of them squatted in the back of the store, while Tom gossiped of the Juarez races, Taft, cigar-wrappers, and Jews. Morton was aroused to tell the time-mellowed story of the judge and the darky. He was cheerful and laughed much and frequently said "Ah there, cull!" in general commendation. But he kept looking at the clock on the jog in the wall over the watercooler. Just at ten he rose abashedly, hesitated, and murmured, "Well, I guess I'll have to be beating it home."

From Mr. Wrenn: "Oh, Morty! So early?"

Tom: "What's the big hurry?"

"I've got to run clear over to Jersey City." Morton was cordial, but not convincing.

"Say—uh—Morton," said Tom, kindly of face, his bald head shining behind his twin bangs, as he rose, "I'm going to have Wrenn up to dinner at my boarding-house next Monday. Like to have you come along. It's a fine place—Mrs.

Arty—she's the landlady—she's a wonder. There's going to be a vacant room there—maybe you two fellows could frame it up to take it, heh? Understand, I don't get no rake-off on this, but we all like to do what we can for M—"

"No, no!" said Morton. "Sorry. Couldn't do it. Staying with my brother-in-law—costs me only 'bout half as much as it would I don't do much chasing around when I'm in town.... I'm going to save up enough money for a good long hike. I'm going clean to St. Petersburg!... But I've had a good time to-night."

"Glad. Great stuff about you fellows on the cattle-ship," said Tom.

Morton hastened on, protectively, a bit critically: "You fellows sport around a good deal, don't you?... I can't afford to.... Well, good night. Glad to met you, Mr. Poppins. G' night, old Wr—"

"Going to the ferry? For Jersey? I'll walk over with you," said Mr. Wrenn.

Their walk was quiet and, for Mr. Wrenn, tragically sad. He saw Morton (presumably) doing the wandering he had once planned. He felt that, while making his vast new circle of friends, he was losing all the wild adventurousness of Bill Wrenn. And he was parting with his first friend.

At the ferry-house Morton pronounced his "Well, so long, old fellow" with an affection that meant finality.

Mr. Wrenn fled back to Tom Poppins's store. On the way he was shocked to find himself relieved at having parted with Morton. The cigar-store was closed.

At home Mrs. Zapp waylaid him for his rent (a day overdue), and he was very curt. That was to keep back the "O God, how rotten I feel!" with which, in his room, he voiced the desolation of loneliness.

The ghost of Morton, dead and forgotten, was with him all next day, till he got home and unbelievably found on the staid black-walnut Zapp hat-rack a letter from Paris, in a gray foreign-appearing envelope with Istra's intensely black scrawl on it.

He put off the luxury of opening the letter till after the rites of brushing his teeth, putting on his slippers, pounding his rocking-chair cushion into softness. Panting with the joy to come, he stared out of the window at a giant and glorious figure of Istra—the laughing Istra of breakfast camp-fire—which towered from the street below. He sighed joyously and read:

> Mouse dear, just a word to let you know I haven't forgotten you and am very glad indeed to get your letters. Not much to write about. Frightfully busy with work and fool parties. You *are* a dear good soul and I hope you'll keep on writing me. In haste,
>
> I. N.

Longer letter next time.

He came to the end so soon. Istra was gone again.

CHAPTER XIV

HE ENTERS SOCIETY

England, in all its Istra-ness, scarce gave Mr. Wrenn a better thrill for his collection than the thrill he received on the November evening when he saw the white doorway of Mrs. R. T. Ferrard, in a decorous row of houses on Thirtieth Street near Lexington Avenue.

It is a block where the citizens have civic pride. A newspaper has not the least chance of lying about on the asphalt—some householder with a frequently barbered mustache will indignantly pounce upon it inside of an hour. No awe. is caused by the sight of vestibules floored with marble in alternate black and white tiles, scrubbed not by landladies, but by maids. There are dotted Swiss curtains at the basement windows and Irish point curtains on the first floors. There are two polished brass doorplates in a stretch of less than eight houses. Distinctly, it is not a quarter where children fill the street with shouting and little sticks.

Occasionally a taxicab drives up to some door without a crowd of small boys gathering; and young men in evening clothes are not infrequently seen to take out young ladies wearing tight-fitting gowns of black, and light scarfs over their heads. A Middle Western college fraternity has a club-house in the block, and four of the houses are private—one of them belonging to a police inspector and one to a school principal who wears spats.

It is a block that is satisfied with itself; as different from the Zapp district, where landladies in gingham run out to squabble with berry-venders, as the Zapp district is from the Ghetto.

Mrs. Arty Ferrard's house is a poor relation to most of the residences there. The black areaway rail is broken, and the basement-door grill is rusty. But at the windows are red-and-white-figured chintz curtains, with a $2.98 bisque figurine of an unclothed lady between them; the door is of spotless white, with a bell-pull of polished brass.

Mr. Wrenn yanked this bell-pull with an urbane briskness which, he hoped, would conceal his nervousness and delight in dining out. For he was one of the lonely men in New York. He had dined out four times in eight years.

The woman of thirty-five or thirty-eight who opened the door to him was very fat, two-thirds as fat as Mrs. Zapp, but she had young eyes. Her mouth was small, arched, and quivering in a grin.

"This is Mr. Wrenn, isn't it?" she gurgled, and leaned against the doorpost, merry, apparently indolent. "I'm Mrs. Ferrard. Mr. Poppins told me you were coming, and he said you were a terribly nice man, and I was to be sure and welcome you. Come right in."

Her indolence turned to energy as she charged down the hall to the large double door on the right and threw it open, revealing to him a scene of splendor and revelry by night.

Several persons [they seemed dozens, in their liveliness] were singing and shouting to piano music, in the midst of a general redness and brightness of furnishings—red paper and worn red carpet and a high ceiling with circular moldings tinted in pink. Hand-painted pictures of old mills and ladies brooding over salmon sunsets, and an especially hand-painted Christmas scene with snow of inlaid mother-of-pearl, animated the walls. On a golden-oak center-table was a large lamp with a mosaic shade, and through its mingled bits of green and red and pearl glass stormed the brilliance of a mantle-light.

The room was crowded with tufted plush and imitation-leather chairs, side-tables and corner brackets, a couch and a "lady's desk." Green and red and yellow vases adorned with figures of youthful lovers crammed the top of the piano at the farther end of the room and the polished black-marble mantel of the fireplace. The glaring gas raced the hearth-fire for snap and glare and excitement. The profusion of furniture was like a tumult; the redness and oakness and polishedness of furniture was a dizzying activity; and it was all overwhelmingly magnified by the laughter and singing about the piano.

Tom Poppins lumbered up from a couch of terrifically new and red leather, and Mr. Wrenn was introduced to the five new people in the room with dismaying swiftness. There seemed to be fifty times five unapproachable and magnificent strangers from whom he wanted to flee. Of them all he was sure of only two—a Miss Nelly somebody and what sounded like Horatio Hood Tem (Teddem it was).

He wished that he had caught Miss Nelly's last name (which, at dinner, proved to be Croubel), for he was instantly taken by her sweetness as she smiled, held out a well-shaped hand, and said, "So pleased meet you, Mr. Wrenn."

She returned to the front of the room and went on talking to a lank spinster about ruchings, but Mr. Wrenn felt that he had known her long and as intimately as it was possible to know so clever a young woman.

Nelly Croubel gave him the impression of a delicate prettiness, a superior sort of prettiness, like that of the daughter of the Big White House on the Hill, the Squire's house, at Parthenon; though Nelly was not unusually pretty. Indeed, her mouth was too large, her hair of somewhat ordinary brown. But her face was always changing with emotions of kindliness and life. Her skin was perfect; her features fine, rather Greek; her smile, quick yet sensitive. She was several inches shorter than Mr. Wrenn, and all curves. Her blouse of white silk lay tenderly along the adorably smooth softness of her young shoulders. A smart patent-leather belt encircled her sleek waist. Thin black lisle stockings showed a modestly arched and rather small foot in a black pump.

She looked as though she were trained for business; awake, self-reliant, self-respecting, expecting to have to get things done, all done, yet she seemed indestructibly gentle, indestructibly good and believing, and just a bit shy.

Nelly Croubel was twenty-four or twenty-five in years, older in business, and far younger in love. She was born in Upton's Grove, Pennsylvania. There, for eighteen years, she had played Skip to Malue at parties, hid away the notes with which the boys invited her to picnics at Baptist Beach, read much Walter Scott, and occasionally taught Sunday-school. Her parents died when she was beginning her fourth year in high school, and she came to New York to work in Wanamacy's toy department at six dollars a week during the holiday rush. Her patience with fussy old shoppers and her large sales-totals had gained her a permanent place in the store.

She had loftily climbed to the position of second assistant buyer in the lingerie department, at fourteen dollars and eighty cents a week That was quite all of her history except that she attended a Presbyterian church nearly every Sunday. The only person she hated was Horatio Hood Teddem, the cheap actor who was playing the piano at Mr. Wrenn's entrance.

Just now Horatio was playing ragtime with amazing rapidity, stamping his foot and turning his head to smirk at the others.

Mrs. Arty led her chattering flock to the basement dining-room, which had pink wall-paper and a mountainous sideboard. Mr. Wrenn was placed between Mrs. Arty and Nelly Croubel. Out of the mist of strangeness presently emerged the personality of Miss Mary Proudfoot, a lively but religious spinster of forty who made doilies for the Dorcas Women's Exchange and had two hundred dollars a year family income. To the right of the red-glass pickle-dish were the elderly Ebbitts—Samuel Ebbitt, Esq., also Mrs. Ebbitt. Mr. Ebbitt had come from Hartford five years before, but he always seemed just to have come from there. He was in a real-estate office; he was gray, ill-tempered, impatiently honest, and addicted to rheumatism and the newspapers. Mrs. Ebbitt was addicted only to Mr. Ebbitt.

Across the table was felt the presence of James T. Duncan, who looked like a dignified red-mustached Sunday-school superintendent, but who traveled for a cloak and suit house, gambled heavily on poker and auction pinochle, and was esteemed for his straight back and knowledge of trains.

Which is all of them.

As soon as Mrs. Arty had guided Annie, the bashful maid, in serving the vegetable soup, and had coaxed her into bringing Mr. Wrenn a napkin, she took charge of the conversation, a luxury which she would never have intrusted to her flock's amateurish efforts. Mr. Poppins, said she, had spoken of meeting a friend of Mr. Wrenn's; Mr. Morton, was it not? A very nice man, she understood. Was it true that Mr. Wrenn and Mr. Morton had gone clear across the Atlantic on a cattle-boat? It really was?

"Oh, how interesting!" contributed pretty Nelly Croubel, beside Mr. Wrenn, her young eyes filled with an admiration which caused him palpitation and difficulty in swallowing his soup. He was confused by hearing old Samuel Ebbitt state:

"Uh-h-h-h—back in 18—uh—1872 the vessel *Prissie*—no, it was 1873; no, it must have been '72—"

"It was 1872, father," said Mrs. Ebbitt.

"1873. I was on a coasting-vessel, young man. But we didn't carry cattle." Mr. Ebbitt inspected Horatio Hood Teddem darkly, clicked his spectacle case sharply shut, and fell to eating, as though he had settled all this nonsense.

With occasional witty interruptions from the actor, Mr. Wrenn told of pitching hay, of the wit of Morton, and the wickedness of Satan, the boss.

"But you haven't told us about the brave things *you* did," cooed Mrs. Arty. She appealed to Nelly Croubel: "I'll bet he was a cool one. Don't you think he was, Nelly?"

"I'm sure he was." Nelly's voice was like a flute.

Mr. Wrenn knew that there was just one thing in the world that he wanted to do; to persuade Miss Nelly Croubel that (though he was a solid business man, indeed yes, and honorable) he was a cool one, who had chosen, in wandering o'er this world so wide, the most perilous and cattle-boaty places. He tried to think of something modest yet striking to say, while Tom was arguing with Miss Mary Proudfoot, the respectable spinster, about the ethics of giving away street-car transfers.

As they finished their floating custard Mr. Wrenn achieved, "Do you come from New York, Miss Croubel?" and listened to the tale of sleighing-parties in Upton's Grove, Pennsylvania. He was absolutely happy.

"This is like getting home," he thought. "And they're classy folks to get home to—now that I can tell 'em apart. Gee! Miss Croubel is a peach. And brains—golly!"

He had a frightened hope that after dinner he would be able to get into a corner and talk with Nelly, but Tom Poppins conferred with Horatio Hood Teddenm and called Mr. Wrenn aside. Teddem had been acting with a moving-picture company for a week, and had three passes to the celebrated Waldorf Photoplay Theater.

Mr. Wrenn had bloodthirstily disapproved Horatio Hood's effeminate remarks, such as "Tee *hee!*" and "Oh, you naughty man," but when he heard that this molly-coddle had shared in the glory of making moving pictures he went proudly forth with him and Tom. He had no chance to speak to Mrs. Arty about taking the room to be vacated.

He wished that Charley Carpenter or the Zapps could see him sitting right beside an actor who was shown in the pictures miraculously there before them, asking him how they made movies, just as friendly as though they had known each other always.

He wanted to do something to entertain his friends beyond taking them out for a drink. He invited them down to his room, and they came.

Teddem was in wonderful form; he mimicked every one they saw so amiably that Tom Poppins knew the actor wanted to borrow money. The party were lovingly humming the popular song of the time—"Any Little Girl That's a Nice Little Girl is the Right Little Girl for Me"—as they frisked up the gloomy steps of the Zapps. Entering, Poppins and Teddem struck attitudes on the inside stairs and sang aloud.

Mr. Wrenn felt enormously conscious of Mrs. Zapp down below. He kept listening, as he led them up-stairs and lighted the gas. But Teddem so imitated Colonel Roosevelt, with two water-glasses for eye-glasses and a small hat-brush for mustache, that Mr. Wrenn was moved wrigglingly to exclaim: "Say, I'm going out and get some beer. Or 'd you rather have something else? Some cheese sandwiches? How about 'em?"

"Fine," said Tom and Teddem together.

Not only did Mr. Wrenn buy a large newspaper-covered bundle of bottles of beer and Swiss-cheese sandwiches, but also a small can of caviar and salty crackers. In his room he spread a clean towel, then two clean towels, on the bureau, and arrayed the feast, with two water-glasses and a shaving-mug for cups.

Horatio Hood Teddem, spreading caviar on a sandwich, and loudly singing his masterpiece, "Waal I swan," stopped short and fixed amazed eyes on the door of the room.

Mr. Wrenn hastily turned. The light fell—as on a cliff of crumbly gray rock—on Mrs. Zapp, in the open door, vast in her ungirdled gray wrapper, her arms folded, glowering speechlessly.

"Mist' Wrenn," she began, in a high voice that promised to burst into passion.

But she was addressing the formidable adventurer, Bill Wrenn. He had to protect his friends. He sprang up and walked across to her.

He said, quietly, "I didn't hear you knock, Mrs. Zapp."

"Ah *didn't* knock, and Ah want you should—"

"Then please do knock, unless you want me to give notice."

He was quivering. His voice was shrill.

From the hall below Theresa called up, "Ma, come down here. *Ma!*"

But Mrs. Zapp was too well started. "If you think Ah'm going to stand for a lazy sneaking little drunkard keeping the whole street awake, and here it is prett' nearly midnight—"

Just then Mr. William Wrenn saw and heard the most astounding thing of his life, and became an eternal slave to Tom Poppins.

Tom's broad face became hard, his voice businesslike. He shouted at Mrs. Zapp:

"Beat it or I'll run you in. Trouble with you is, you old hag, you don't appreciate a nice quiet little chap like Wrenn, and you try to bully him—and him here for years. Get out or I'll put you out. I'm no lamb, and I won't stand for any of your monkey-shines. Get out. This ain't your room; he's rented it—he's paid the rent—it's his room. Get out!"

Kindly Tom Poppins worked in a cigar-store and was accustomed to talk back to drunken men six feet tall. His voice was tremendous, and he was fatly immovable; he didn't a bit mind the fact that Mrs. Zapp was still "glaring speechless."

But behold an ally to the forlorn lady. When Theresa, in the hall below, heard Tom, she knew that Mr. Wrenn would room here no more. She galloped up-stairs and screeched over her mother's shoulder:

"You will pick on a lady, will you, you drunken scum—you—you cads—I'll have you arrested so quick you—"

"Look here, lady," said Tom, gently. "I'm a plain-clothes man, a detective." His large voice purred like a tiger-tabby's. "I don't want to run you in, but I will if you don't get out of here and shut that door. Or you might go down and call the cop on this block. He'll run you in—for breaking Code 2762 of the Penal Law! Trespass and flotsam—that's what it is!"

Uneasy, frightened, then horrified, Mrs. Zapp swung bulkily about and slammed the door.

Sick, guilty, banished from home though he felt, Mr. Wrenn's voice quavered, with an attempt at dignity:

"I'm awful sorry she butted in while you fellows was here. I don't know how to apologize"

"Forget it, old man," rolled out Tom's bass. "Come on, let's go up to Mrs. Arty's."

"But, gee! it's nearly a quarter to eleven."

"That's all right. We can get up there by a little after, and Mrs. Arty stays up playing cards till after twelve."

"Golly!" Mr. Wrenn agitatedly ejaculated under his breath, as they noisily entered Mrs. Arty's—though not noisily on his part.

The parlor door was open. Mrs. Arty's broad back was toward them, and she was announcing to James T. Duncan and Miss Proudfoot, with whom she was playing three-handed Five Hundred, "Well, I'll just bid seven on hearts if you're going to get so set up." She glanced back, nodded, said, "Come in, children," picked up the "widow," and discarded with quick twitches of the cards. The frightened Mr. Wrenn, feeling like a shipwrecked land-lubber, compared this gaming smoking woman unfavorably with the intense respectability of his dear lost patron, Mrs. Zapp. He sat uneasy till the hand of cards was finished, feeling as though they were only tolerating him. And Nelly Croubel was nowhere in sight.

Suddenly said Mrs. Arty, "And now you would like to look at that room, Mr. Wrenn, unless I'm wrong."

"Why—uh—yes, I guess I would like to."

"Come with me, child," she said, in pretended severity. "Tom, you take my hand in the game, and don't let me hear you've been bidding ten on no suit without the joker." She led Mr. Wrenn to the settee hat-rack in the hall. "The third-floor-back will be vacant in two weeks, Mr. Wrenn. We can go up and look at it now if you'd like to. The man who has it now works nights—he's some kind of a head waiter at Rector's, or something like that, and he's out till three or four. Come."

When he saw that third-floor-back, the room that the smart people at Mrs. Arty's were really willing to let him have, he felt like a man just engaged. It was all in soft green—grass-green matting, pale-green walls, chairs of white wicker with green cushions; the bed, a couch with a denim cover and four sofa pillows. It gave him the impression of being a guest on Fifth Avenue.

"It's kind of a plain room," Mrs. Arty said, doubtfully. "The furniture is kind of plain. But my head-waiter man—it was furnished for a friend of his—he says he likes it better than any other room in the house. It *is* comfortable, and you get lots of sunlight and—"

"I'll take—How much is it, please, with board?"

She spoke with a take-it-or-leave-it defiance. "Eleven-fifty a week."

It was a terrible extravagance; much like marrying a sick woman on a salary of ten a week, he reflected; nine-teen minus eleven-fifty left him only seven-fifty for clothes and savings and things and—but—" I'll take it," he said, hastily. He was frightened at himself, but glad, very glad. He was to live in this heaven; he was going to be away from that Zapp woman; and Nelly Croubel—Was she engaged to some man? he wondered.

Mrs. Arty was saying: "First, I want to ask you some questions, though. Please sit down." As she creaked into one of the wicker chairs she suddenly changed from the cigarette-rolling chaffing card-player to a woman dignified, reserved, commanding. "Mr. Wrenn, you see, Miss Proudfoot and Miss Croubel are on this floor. Miss Proudfoot can take care of herself, all right, but Nelly is such a trusting little thing—She's like my daughter. She's the only one I've ever given a reduced rate to—and I swore I never would to anybody!… Do you—uh—drink—drink much, I mean?"

Nelly on this floor! Near him! Now! He had to have this room. He forced himself to speak directly.

"I know how you mean, Mrs. Ferrard. No, I don't drink much of any—hardly at all; just a glass of beer now and then; sometimes I don't even touch that a week at a time. And I don't gamble and—and I do try to keep—er—straight—and all that sort of thing."

"That's good."

"I work for the Souvenir and Art Novelty Company on Twenty-eighth Street. If you want to call them up I guess the manager'll give me a pretty good recommend."

"I don't believe I'll need it, Mr. Wrenn. It's my business to find out what sort of animiles men are by just talking to them." She rose, smiled, plumped out her hand. "You *will* be nice to Nelly, *won't* you! I'm going to fire that Teddem out—don't tell him, but I am—because he gets too fresh with her."

"Yes!"

She suddenly broke into laughter, and ejaculated: "*Say*, that was hard work! Don't you *hate* to have to be serious? Let's trot down, and I'll make Tom or Duncan rush us a growler of beer to welcome you to our midst…. I'll bet your socks aren't darned properly. I'm going to sneak in and take a look at them, once I get you caged up here…. But I won't read your love-letters! Now let's go down by the fire, where it's comfy."

CHAPTER XV

HE STUDIES FIVE HUNDRED, SAVOUIR FAIRE, AND LOTSA-SNAP OFFICE MOTTOES

On a couch of glossy red leather with glossy black buttons and stiff fringes also of glossy red leather, Mr. William Wrenn sat upright and was very confiding to Miss Nelly Croubel, who was curled among the satin pillows with her skirts drawn carefully about her ankles. He had been at Mrs. Arty's for two weeks now. He wore a new light-blue tie, and his trousers were pressed like sheet steel.

"Yes, I suppose you're engaged to some one, Miss Nelly, and you'll go off and leave us—go off to that blamed Upton's Grove or some place."

"I am *not* engaged. I've told you so. Who would want to marry me? You stop teasing me—you're mean as can be; I'll just have to get Tom to protect me!"

"Course you're engaged."

"Ain't."

"Are."

"Ain't. Who would want to marry poor little me?"

"Why, anybody, of course."

"You *stop* teasing me…. Besides, probably you're in love with twenty girls."

"I am *not*. Why, I've never hardly known but just two girls in my life. One was just a girl I went to theaters with once or twice—she was the daughter of the landlady I used to have before I came here."

> "If you don't make love to the landlady's daughter
> You won't get a second piece of pie!"

quoted Nelly, out of the treasure-house of literature.

"Sure. That's it. But I bet you—"

"Who was the other girl?"

"Oh! She…. She was a—an artist. I liked her—a lot. But she was—oh, awful highbrow. Gee! if—But—"

A sympathetic silence, which Nelly broke with:

"Yes, they're funny people. Artists…. Do you have your lesson in Five Hundred tonight? Your very first one?"

"I think so. Say, is it much like this here bridge-whist? Oh say, Miss Nelly, why do they call it Five Hundred?"

"That's what you have to make to go out. No, I guess it isn't very much like bridge; though, to tell the truth, I haven't ever played bridge. . My! it must be a nice game, though."

"Oh, I thought prob'ly you could play it. You can do 'most everything. Honest, I've never seen nothing like it."

"Now you stop, Mr. Wrenn. I know I'm a—what was it Mr. Teddem used to call me? A minx. But—"

"Miss *Nelly!* You *aren't* a minx!"

"Well—"

"Or a mink, either. You're a—let's see—an antelope."

"I am not! Even if I can wriggle my nose like a rabbit. Besides, it sounds like a muskmelon. But, anyway, the head buyer said I was crazy to-day."

"If I heard him say you were crazy—"

"Would you beat him for me?" She cuddled a cushion and smiled gratefully. Her big eyes seemed to fill with light.

He caught himself wanting to kiss the softness of her shoulder, but he said only, "Well, I ain't much of a scrapper, but I'd try to make it interesting for him."

"Tell me, did you ever have a fight? When you were a boy? Were you *such* a bad boy?"

"I never did when I was a boy, but—well—I did have a couple of fights when I was on the cattle-boat and in England. Neither of them amounted to very much, though, I guess. I was scared stiff!"

"Don't believe it!"

"Sure I was."

"I don't believe you'd be scared. You're too earnest."

"Me, Miss Nelly? Why, I'm a regular cut-up."

"You stop making fun of yourself! I *like* it when you're earnest—like when you saw that beautiful snowfall last night…. Oh dear, isn't it hard to have to miss so many beautiful things here in the city—there's just the parks, and even there there aren't any birds, real wild birds, like we used to have in Pennsylvania."

"Yes, isn't it! Isn't it hard!" Mr. Wrenn drew nearer and looked sympathy.

"I'm afraid I'm getting gushy. Miss Hartenstein—she's in my department—she'd laugh at me…. But I do love birds and squirrels and pussy-willows and all those things. In summer I love to go on picnics on Staten Island or tramp in Van Cortlandt Park."

"Would you go on a picnic with me some day next spring?" Hastily, "I mean with Miss Proudfoot and Mrs. Arty and me?"

"I should be pleased to." She was prim but trusting about it. "Oh, listen, Mr. Wrenn; did you ever tramp along the Palisades as far as Englewood? It's lovely there—the woods and the river and all those funny little tugs puffing along, way *way* down below you—why, I could lie on the rocks up there and just dream and dream for hours. After I've spent Sunday up there"—she was dreaming now, he saw, and his heart was passionately tender toward her—"I don't hardly mind a bit having to go back to the store Monday morning.... You've been up along there, haven't you?"

"Me? Why, I guess I'm the guy that discovered the Palisades!... Yes, it is *won*-derful up there!"

"Oh, you are, are you? I read about that in American history!... But honestly, Mr. Wrenn, I do believe you care for tramps and things—not like that Teddem or Mr. Duncan—they always want to just stay in town—or even Tom, though he's an old dear."

Mr. Wrenn looked jealous, with a small hot jealousy. She hastened on with: "Of course, I mean he's just like a big brother. To all of us."

It was sweet to both of them, to her to declare and to him to hear, that neither Tom nor any other possessed her heart. Their shy glances were like an outreach of tenderly touching hands as she confided, "Mrs. Arty and he get up picnics, and when we're out on the Palisades he says to me—you know, sometimes he almost makes me think he *is* sleepy, though I do believe he just sneaks off under a tree and talks to Mrs. Arty or reads a magazine—but I was saying: he always says to me, 'Well, sister, I suppose you want to mousey round and dream by yourself—you won't talk to a growly old bear like me. Well, I'm glad of it. I want to sleep. I don't want to be bothered by you and your everlasting chatter. Get out!' I b'lieve he just says that 'cause he knows I wouldn't want to run off by myself if they didn't think it was proper."

As he heard her lively effort to imitate Tom's bass Mr. Wrenn laughed and pounded his knee and agreed: "Yes, Tom's an awfully fine fellow, isn't he!... I love to get out some place by myself, too. I like to wander round places and make up the doggondest fool little stories to myself about them; just as bad as a kiddy, that way."

"And you read such an awful lot, Mr. Wrenn! My! Oh, tell me, have you ever read anything by Harold Bell Wright or Myrtle Reed, Mr. Wrenn? They write such sweet stories."

He had not, but he expressed an unconquerable resolve so to do, and with immediateness. She went on:

"Mrs. Arty told me you had a real big library—nearly a hundred books and— Do you mind? I went in your room and peeked at them."

"No, course I don't mind! If there's any of them you'd like to borrow any time, Miss Nelly, I would be awful glad to lend them to you.... But, rats! Why, I haven't got hardly any books."

"That's why you haven't wasted any time learning Five Hundred and things, isn't it? Because you've been so busy reading and so on?"

"Yes, kind of." Mr. Wrenn looked modest.

"Haven't you always been lots of—oh, haven't you always 'magined lots?"

She really seemed to care.

Mr. Wrenn felt excitedly sure of that, and imparted: "Yes, I guess I have…. And I've always wanted to travel a lot."

"So have I! Isn't it wonderful to go around and see new places!"

"Yes, *isn't* it!" he breathed. "It was great to be in England—though the people there are kind of chilly some ways. Even when I'm on a wharf here in New York I feel just like I was off in China or somewheres. I'd like to see China. And India…. Gee! when I hear the waves down at Coney Island or some place—you know how the waves sound when they come in. Well, sometimes I almost feel like they was talking to a guy—you know—telling about ships. And, oh say, you know the whitecaps—aren't they just like the waves was motioning at you—they want you to come and beat it with you—over to China and places."

"Why, Mr. Wrenn, you're a regular poet!"

He looked doubtful.

"Honest; I'm not teasing you; you are a poet. And I think it's fine that Mr. Teddem was saying that nobody could be a poet or like that unless they drank an awful lot and—uh—oh, not be honest and be on a job. But you aren't like that. *Are* you?"

He looked self-conscious and mumbled, earnestly, "Well, I try not to be."

"But I am going to make you go to church. You'll be a socialist or something like that if you get to be too much of a poet and don't—"

"Miss Nelly, please *may* I go to church with you?"

"Why—"

"Next Sunday?"

"Why, yes, I should be pleased. Are you a Presbyterian, though?"

"Why—uh—I guess I'm kind of a Congregationalist; but still, they're all so much alike."

"Yes, they really are. And besides, what does it matter if we all believe the same and try to do right; and sometimes that's hard, when you're poor, and it seems like—like—"

"Seems like what?" Mr. Wrenn insisted.

"Oh—nothing…. My, you'll have to get up awful early Sunday morning if you'd like to go with me. My church starts at ten-thirty."

"Oh, I'd get up at five to go with you."

"Stupid! Now you're just trying to jolly me; you *are*; because you men aren't as fond of church as all that, I know you aren't. You're real lazy Sunday mornings, and just want to sit around and read the papers and leave the poor women—But please tell me some more about your reading and all that."

"Well, I'll be all ready to go at nine-thirty.... I don't know; why, I haven't done much reading. But I would like to travel and—Say, wouldn't it be great to—I suppose I'm sort of a kid about it; of course, a guy has to tend right to business, but it would be great—Say a man was in Europe with—with—a friend, and they both knew a lot of history—say, they both knew a lot about Guy Fawkes (he was the guy that tried to blow up the English Parliament), and then when they were there in London they could almost think they saw him, and they could go round together and look at Shelley's window—he was a poet at Oxford—Oh, it would be great with a—with a friend."

"Yes, wouldn't it?... I wanted to work in the book department one time. It's so nice your being—"

"Ready for Five Hundred?" bellowed Tom Poppins in the hall below. "Ready partner—you, Wrenn?"

Tom was to initiate Mr. Wrenn into the game, playing with him against Mrs. Arty and Miss Mary Proudfoot.

Mrs. Arty sounded the occasion's pitch of high merriment by delivering from the doorway the sacred old saying, "Well, the ladies against the men, eh?"

A general grunt that might be spelled "Hmmmmhm" assented.

"I'm a good suffragette," she added. "Watch us squat the men, Mary."

"Like to smash windows? Let's see—it's red fours, black fives up?" remarked Tom, as he prepared the pack of cards for playing.

"Yes, I would! It makes me so tired," asseverated Mrs. Arty, "to think of the old goats that men put up for candidates when they *know* they're solemn old fools! I'd just like to get out and vote my head off."

"Well, I think the woman's place is in the home," sniffed Miss Proudfoot, de-cisively, tucking away a doily she was finishing for the Women's Exchange and jabbing at her bangs.

They settled themselves about the glowing, glancing, glittering, golden-oak center-table. Miss Proudfoot shuffled sternly. Mr. Wrenn sat still and frightened, like a shipwrecked professor on a raft with two gamblers and a press-agent, though Nelly was smiling encouragingly at him from the couch where she had started her embroidery—a large Christmas lamp mat for the wife of the Presbyterian pastor at Upton's Grove.

"Don't you wish your little friend Horatio Hood Teddem was here to play with you?" remarked Tom.

"I *do* not," declared Mrs. Arty. "Still, there was one thing about Horatio. I never had to look up his account to find out how much he owed me. He stopped calling me, Little Buttercup, when he owed me ten dollars, and he even stopped slamming the front door when he got up to twenty. O Mr. Wrenn, did I ever tell you about the time I asked him if he wanted to have Annie sweep—"

"Gerty!" protested Miss Proudfoot, while Nelly, on the couch, ejaculated mechanically, "That story!" but Mrs. Arty chuckled fatly, and continued:

"I asked him if he wanted me to have Annie sweep his nightshirt when she swept his room. He changed it next day."

"Your bid, Mr. Poppins, "said Miss Proudfoot, severely.

"First, I want to tell Wrenn how to play. You see, Wrenn, here's the schedule. We play Avondale Schedule, you know."

"Oh yes," said Mr. Wrenn, timorously…. He had once heard of Carbondale—in New Jersey or Pennsylvania or somewhere—but that didn't seem to help much.

"Well, you see, you either make or go back," continued Tom. "Plus and minus, you know. Joker is high, then right bower, left, and ace. Then—uh—let's see; high bid takes the cat—widdie, you know—and discards. Ten tricks. Follow suit like whist, of course. I guess that's all—that ought to give you the hang of it, anyway. I bid six on no trump."

As Tom Poppins finished these instructions, given in the card-player's rapid don't-ask-me-any-more-fool-questions manner, Mr. Wrenn felt that he was choking. He craned up his neck, trying to ease his stiff collar. So, then, he was a failure, a social outcast already.

So, then, he couldn't learn Five Hundred! And he had been very proud of knowing one card from another perfectly, having played a number of games of two-handed poker with Tim on the cattle-boat. But what the dickens did "left—cat—follow suit" mean?

And to fail with Nelly watching him! He pulled at his collar again.

Thus he reflected while Mrs. Arty and Tom were carrying on the following brilliant but cryptic society-dialogue:

> *Mrs. Arty:* Well, I don't know.
>
> *Tom:* Not failure, but low bid is crime, little one.
>
> *Mrs. Arty:* Mary, shall I make—
>
> *Tom:* Hey! No talking 'cross table!
>
> *Mrs. Arty:* Um—let—me—see.
>
> *Tom:* Bid up, bid up! Bid a little seven on hearts?
>
> *Mrs. Arty:* Just for that I *will* bid seven on hearts, smarty!
>
> *Tom:* Oh, how we will squat you!… What you bidding, Wrenn?

Behind Mr. Wrenn, Nelly Croubel whispered to him: "Bid seven on no suit. You've got the joker." Her delicate forefinger, its nail shining, was pointing at a curious card in his hand.

"Seven nosut," he mumbled.

"Eight hearts," snapped Miss Proudfoot.

Nelly drew up a chair behind Mr. Wrenn's. He listened to her soft explanations with the desperate respect and affection which a green subaltern would give to a general in battle.

Tom and he won the hand. He glanced back at Nelly with awe, then clutched his new hand, fearfully, dizzily, staring at it as though it might conceal one of those malevolent deceivers of which Nelly had just warned him — a left bower.

"Good! Spades — see," said Nelly.

Fifteen minutes later Mr. Wrenn felt that Tom was hoping he would lead a club. He played one, and the whole table said: "That's right. Fine!"

On his shoulder he felt a light tap, and he blushed like a sunset as he peeped back at Nelly.

Mr. Wrenn, the society light, was Our Mr. Wrenn of the Souvenir Company all this time. Indeed, at present he intended to keep on taking The Job seriously until that most mistily distant time, which we all await, "when something turns up." His fondling of the Southern merchants was showing such results that he had grown from an interest in whatever papers were on his desk to a belief in the divine necessity of The Job as a whole. Not now, as of old, did he keep the personal letters in his desk tied up, ready for a sudden departure for Vienna or Kamchatka. Also, he wished to earn much more money for his new career of luxury. Mr. Guilfogle had assured him that there might be chances ahead — business had been prospering, two new road salesmen and a city-trade man had been added to the staff, and whereas the firm had formerly been jobbers only, buying their novelties from manufacturers, now they were having printed for them their own Lotsa-Snap Cardboard Office Mottoes, which were making a big hit with the trade.

Through his friend Rabin, the salesman, Mr. Wrenn got better acquainted with two great men — Mr. L. J. Glover, the purchasing agent of the Souvenir Company, and John Hensen, the newly engaged head of motto manufacturing. He "wanted to get onto all the different lines of the business so's he could step right in anywhere"; and from these men he learned the valuable secrets of business wherewith the marts of trade build up prosperity for all of us: how to seat a selling agent facing the light, so you can see his face better than he can see yours. How much ahead of time to telephone the motto-printer that "we've simply got to have proof this afternoon; what's the matter with you, down there? Don't you want our business any more?" He also learned something of the various kinds of cardboard and ink-well glass, though these, of course, were merely matters of knowledge, not of brilliant business tactics, and far less important than what Tom Poppins and Rabin called "handing out a snappy line of talk."

"Say, you're getting quite chummy lately — reg'lar society leader," Rabin informed him.

Mr. Wrenn's answer was in itself a proof of the soundness of Rabin's observation:

"Sure — I'm going to borrow some money from you fellows. Got to make an impression, see?"

A few hours after this commendation came Istra's second letter:

> Mouse dear, I'm so glad to hear about the simpatico board-
> ing- house. Yes indeed I would like to hear about the people in it.
> And you are reading history? That's good. I'm getting sick of Par-
> is and some day I'm going to stop an absinthe on the boulevard
> and slap its face to show I'm a sturdy moving-picture Western
> Amurrican and then leap to saddle and pursue the bandit. I'm
> working like the devil but what's the use. That is I mean unless
> one is doing the job well, as I'm glad you are. My Dear, keep it up.
> You know I want you to be *real* whatever you are. I didn't mean to
> preach but you know I hate people who aren't real—that's why I
> haven't much of a flair for myself.
>
> *Au recrire,*   I. N.

After he had read her letter for the third time he was horribly shocked and regarded himself as a traitor, because he found that he was only pretending to be enjoyably excited over it…. It seemed so detached from himself. "Flair"—"*au recri-re.*" Now, what did those mean? And Istra was always so discontented. "What 'd she do if she had to be on the job like Nelly?… Oh, Istra *is* wonderful. But—gee!—I dunno—"

And when he who has valorously loved says "But—gee!—I dunno—" love flees in panic.

He walked home thoughtfully.

After dinner he said abruptly to Nelly, "I had a letter from Paris to-day."

"Honestly? Who is she?"

"G-g-g-g—"

"Oh, it's always a she."

"Why—uh—it *is* from a girl. I started to tell you about her one day. She's an artist, and once we took a long tramp in the country. I met her—she was staying at the same place as I was in London. But—oh, gee! I dunno; she's so blame literary. She *is* a *fine* person—Do you think you'd like a girl like that?"

"Maybe I would."

"If she was a man?"

"Oh, yes-s! Artists are so romantic."

"But they ain't on the job more 'n half the time," he said, jealously.

"Yes, that's *so*."

His hand stole secretly, craftily skirting a cushion, to touch hers—which she withdrew, laughing:

"Hump-a! You go hold your artist's hand!"

"Oh, Miss Nelly! When I *told* you about her *myself!*"

"Oh yes, of course."

She was contrite, and they played Five Hundred animatedly all evening.

CHAPTER XVI

HE BECOMES MILDLY RELIGIOUS AND HIGHLY LITERARY

The hero of the one-act play at Hammerstein's Victoria vaudeville theater on that December evening was, it appeared, a wealthy young mine-owner in disguise. He was working for the "fake mine promoter" because he loved the promoter's daughter with a love that passed all understanding except that of the girls in the gallery. When the postal authorities were about to arrest the promoter our young hero saved him by giving him a real mine, and the ensuing kiss of the daughter ended the suspense in which Mr. Wrenn and Nelly, Mrs. Arty and Tom had watched the play from the sixth row of the balcony.

Sighing happily, Nelly cried to the group: "Wasn't that grand? I got so excited! Wasn't that young miner a dear?"

"Awfully nice," said Mr. Wrenn. "And, gee! wasn't that great, that office scene—with that safe and the rest of the stuff—just like you was in a real office. But, say, they wouldn't have a copying-press in an office like that; those fake mine promoters send out such swell letters; they'd use carbon copies and not muss the letters all up."

"By gosh, that's right!" and Tom nodded his chin toward his right shoulder in approval. Nelly cried, "That's so; they would"; while Mrs. Arty, not knowing what a copying-press was, appeared highly commendatory, and said nothing at all.

During the moving pictures that followed, Mr. Wrenn felt proudly that he was taken seriously, though he had known them but little over a month. He followed up his conversational advantage by leading the chorus in wondering, "which one of them two actors the heroine was married to?" and "how much a week they get for acting in that thing?" It was Tom who invited them to Miggleton's for coffee and fried oysters. Mr. Wrenn was silent for a while. But as they were stamping through the rivulets of wheel-tracks that crisscrossed on a slushy street-crossing Mr. Wrenn regained his advantage by crying, "Say, don't you think that play 'd have been better if the promoter 'd had an awful grouch on the young miner and 'd had to crawfish when the miner saved him?"

"Why, yes; it would!" Nelly glowed at him.

"Wouldn't wonder if it would," agreed Tom, kicking the December slush off his feet and patting Mr. Wrenn's back.

"Well, look here," said Mr. Wrenn, as they left Broadway, with its crowds betokening the approach of Christmas, and stamped to the quieter side of Forty-second, "why wouldn't this make a slick play: say there's an awfully rich old guy; say he's a railway president or something, d' you see? Well, he's got a secretary there in the office—on the stage, see? The scene is his office. Well, this guy's—the rich old guy's—daughter comes in and says she's married to a poor man and she won't tell his name, but she wants some money from her dad. You see, her dad's been planning for her to marry a marquise or some kind of a lord, and he's sore as can be, and he won't listen to her, and he just cusses her out something fierce, see? Course he doesn't really cuss, but he's awful sore; and she tells him didn't he marry her mother when he was a poor young man; but he won't listen. Then the secretary butts in—my idea is he's been kind of keeping in the background, see—and *he's* the daughter's husband all the while, see? and he tells the old codger how he's got some of his—some of the old fellow's—papers that give it away how he done something that was crooked—some kind of deal—rebates and stuff, see how I mean?—and the secretary's going to spring this stuff on the newspapers if the old man don't come through and forgive them; so of course the president has to forgive them, see?"

"You mean the secretary was the daughter's husband all along, and he heard what the president said right there?" Nelly panted, stopping outside Miggleton's, in the light from the oyster-filled window.

"Yes; and he heard it all."

"Why, I think that's just a *fine* idea," declared Nelly, as they entered the restaurant. Though her little manner of dignity and even restraint was evident as ever, she seemed keenly joyous over his genius.

"Say, that's a corking idea for a play, Wrenn," exclaimed Tom, at their table, gallantly removing the ladies' wraps.

"It surely is," agreed Mrs. Arty.

"Why don't you write it?" asked Nelly.

"Aw—I couldn't write it!"

"Why, sure you could, Bill," insisted Tom. "Straight; you ought to write it. (Hey, waiter! Four fries and coffee!) You ought to write it. Why, it's a wonder; it 'd make a dev— 'Scuse me, ladies. It'd make a howling hit. You might make a lot of money out of it."

The renewed warmth of their wet feet on the red-tile floor, the scent of fried oysters, the din of "Any Little Girl" on the piano, these added color to this moment of Mr. Wrenn's great resolve. The four stared at one another excitedly. Mr. Wrenn's eyelids fluttered. Tom brought his hand down on the table with a soft flat "plob" and declared: "Say, there might be a lot of money in it. Why, I've heard that Harry Smith—writes the words for these musical comedies—makes a *mint* of money."

"Mr. Poppins ought to help you in it—he's seen such a lot of plays," Mrs. Arty anxiously advised.

"That's a good idea," said Mr. Wrenn. It had, apparently, been ordained that he was to write it. They were now settling important details. So when Nelly cried, "I think it's just a fine idea; I knew you had lots of imagination," Tom interrupted her with:

"No; you write it, Bill. I'll help you all I can, of course…. Tell you what you ought to do: get hold of Teddem—he's had a lot of stage experience; he'd help you about seeing the managers. That 'd be the hard part—you can write it, all right, but you'd have to get next to the guys on the inside, and Teddem—Say, you cer_tain_ly ought to write this thing, Bill. Might make a lot of money."

"Oh, a lot!" breathed Nelly.

"Heard about a fellow," continued Tom—" fellow named Gene Wolf, I think it was—that was so broke he was sleeping in Bryant Park, and he made a *hundred thousand dollars* on his first play—or, no; tell you how it was: he sold it outright for ten thousand—something like that, anyway. I got that right from a fellow that's met him."

"Still, an author's got to go to college and stuff like that." Mr. Wrenn spoke as though he would be pleased to have the objection overruled at once, which it was with a universal:

"Oh, rats!"

Crunching oysters in a brown jacket of flour, whose every lump was a crisp delight, hearing his genius lauded and himself called Bill thrice in a quarter-hour, Mr. Wrenn was beatified. He asked the waiter for some paper, and while the four hotly discussed things which "it would be slick to have the president's daughter do" he drew up a list of characters on a sheet of paper he still keeps. It is headed, "Miggleton's Forty-second Street Branch." At the bottom appear numerous scribblings of the name Nelly.

"I think I'll call the heroine 'Nelly,'" he mused.

Nelly Croubel blushed. Mrs. Arty and Tom glanced at each other. Mr. Wrenn realized that he had, even at this moment of social triumph, "made a break."

He said, hastily; "I always liked that name. I—I had an aunt named that!"

"Oh—" started Nelly.

"She was fine to me when I was a kid, "Mr. Wrenn added, trying to remember whether it was right to lie when in such need.

"Oh, it's a horrid name," declared Nelly. "Why don't you call her something nice, like Hazel—or—oh—Dolores."

"Nope; Nelly's an elegant name—an *elegant* name."

MIGGLETON'S
Forty-second Street Branch
POPULAR PRICES ◆ MUSIC ◆ BEST SERVICE

New York———19

Vaudeville Play
Dramitis Persone

Nelly Warrington
Mr. Warrington
    her Father - a R/R Prest.
Reginald Thorne - Secy.

IN AN OFFICE

Typewriter table ... Footlights
Her. Nelly

Nelly Nelly
N Nelly
Nelly Croubel
Nelly Croubel
William
William Wren

He walked with Nelly behind the others, along Forty-second Street. To the outsider's eye he was a small respectable clerk, slightly stooped, with a polite mustache and the dignity that comes from knowing well a narrow world; wearing an overcoat too light for winter; too busily edging out of the way of people and guiding the nice girl beside him into clear spaces by diffidently touching her elbow, too pettily busy to cast a glance out of the crowd and spy the passing poet or king, or the iron night sky. He was as undistinguishable a bit of the evening street life as any of the file of street-cars slashing through the wet snow. Yet, he was the chivalrous squire to the greatest lady of all his realm; he was a society author, and a man of great prospective wealth and power over mankind!

"Say, we'll have the grandest dinner you ever saw if I get away with the play," he was saying. "Will you come, Miss Nelly?"

"Indeed I will! Oh, you sha'n't leave me out! Wasn't I there when—"

"Indeed you were! Oh, we'll have a reg'lar feast at the Astor—artichokes and truffles and all sorts of stuff.... Would—would you like it if I sold the play?"

"*Course* I would, silly!"

"I'd buy the business and make Rabin manager—the Souvenir Company.

So he came to relate all those intimacies of The Job; and he was overwhelmed at the ease with which she "got onto old Goglefogle."

His preparations for writing the play were elaborate.

He paced Tom's room till twelve-thirty, consulting as to whether he had to plan the stage-setting; smoking cigarettes in attitudes on chair arms. Next morning in the office he made numerous plans of the setting on waste half-sheets of paper. At noon he was telephoning at Tom regarding the question of whether there ought to be one desk or two on the stage.

He skipped the evening meal at Mrs. Arty's, dining with literary pensiveness at the Armenian, for he had subtle problems to meditate. He bought a dollar fountain-pen, which had large gold-like bands and a rather scratchy pen-point, and a box of fairly large sheets of paper. Pressing his literary impedimenta tenderly under his arm, he attended four moving-picture and vaudeville theaters. By eleven he had seen three more one-act plays and a dramatic playlet.

He slipped by the parlor door at Mrs. Arty's.

His room was quiet. The lamplight on the delicately green walls was like that of a regular author's den, he was quite sure. He happily tested the fountain-pen by writing the names Nelly and William Wrenn on a bit of wrapping-paper (which he guiltily burned in an ash-tray); washed his face with water which he let run for a minute to cool; sat down before his table with a grunt of content; went back and washed his hands; fiercely threw off the bourgeois encumbrances of coat and collar; sat down again; got up to straighten a picture; picked up his pen; laid it down, and glowed as he thought of Nelly, slumbering there, near at hand, her exquisite cheek nestling silkenly against her arm, perhaps, and her white dreams—

Suddenly he roared at himself, "Get on the job there, will yuh?" He picked up the pen and wrote:

THE MILLIONAIRE'S DAUGHTER

A ONE ACT DRAMATIC PLAYLET

by

WILLIAM WRENN

CHARACTERS

John Warrington, a railway president; quite rich.
Nelty Warrington, Mr. Warrington's daughter.
Reginald Thorne, his secretary.

He was jubilant. His pen whined at top speed, scattering a shower of tiny drops of ink.

Stage Scene: An office. Very expensive. Mr. Warrington and Mr. Thorne are sitting there. Miss Warrington comes in. She says:

He stopped. He thought. He held his head. He went over to the stationary bowl and soaked his hair with water. He lay on the bed and kicked his heels, slowly and gravely smoothing his mustache. Fifty minutes later he gave a portentous groan and went to bed.

He hadn't been able to think of what Miss Warrington says beyond "I have come to tell you that I am married, papa," and that didn't sound just right; not for a first line it didn't, anyway.

At dinner next night—Saturday—Tom was rather inclined to make references to "our author," and to remark: "Well, I know where somebody was last night, but of course I won't tell. Say, them authors are a wild lot."

Mr. Wrenn, who had permitted the teasing of even Tim, the hatter, "wasn't going to stand for no kidding from nobody—not when Nelly was there," and he called for a glass of water with the air of a Harvard assistant professor forced to eat in a lunch-wagon and slapped on the back by the cook.

Nelly soothed him. "The play *is* going well, *isn't* it?"

When he had, with a detached grandeur of which he was immediately ashamed, vouchsafed that he was already "getting right down to brass tacks on it," that he had already investigated four more plays and begun the actual writing, every one looked awed and asked him assorted questions.

At nine-thirty that evening he combed and tightly brushed his hair, which he had been pawing angrily for an hour and a half, went down the hall to Nelly's hall bedroom, and knocked with: "It's Mr. Wrenn. May I ask you something about the play?"

"Just a moment," he heard her say.

He waited, panting softly, his lips apart. This was to be the first time he had ever seen Nelly's room. She opened the door part way, smiling shyly, timidly, holding her pale-blue dressing-gown close. The pale blueness was a modestly brilliant spot against the whiteness of the room—white bureau, hung with dance programs and a yellow Upton's Grove High School banner, white tiny rocker, pale-yellow matting, white-and-silver wall-paper, and a glimpse of a white soft bed.

He was dizzy with the exaltation of that purity, but he got himself to say:

"I'm kind of stuck on the first part of the play, Miss Nelly. Please tell me how you think the heroine would speak to her dad. Would she call him 'papa' or 'sir,' do you think?"

"Why—let me see—"

"They're such awful high society—"

"Yes, that's so. Why, I should think she'd say 'sir.' Maybe oh, what was it I heard in a play at the Academy of Music? 'Father, I have come back to you!'"

"Sa-a-ay, that's a fine line! That'll get the crowd going right from the first.... I *told* you you'd help me a lot."

"I'm awfully glad if I *have* helped you," she said, earnestly. Good night—and good, "awfully glad, but luck with the play. Good night."

"Good night. Thank you a lot, Miss Nelly. Church in the morning, remember! Good night."

"Good night."

As it is well known that all playwrights labor with toy theaters before them for working models, Mr. Wrenn ran to earth a fine unbroken pasteboard box in which a ninety-eight-cent alarm-clock had recently arrived. He went out for some glue and three small corks. Setting up his box stage, he glued a pill-box and a match-box on the floor—the side of the box it had always been till now—and there he had the mahogany desks. He thrust three matches into the corks, and behold three graceful actors—graceful for corks, at least. There was fascination in having them enter, through holes punched in the back of the box, frisk up to their desks and deliver magic emotional speeches that would cause any audience to weep; speeches regarding which he knew everything but the words; a detail of which he was still quite ignorant after half an hour of playing with his marionettes.

Before he went despairingly to bed that Saturday night he had added to his manuscript:

> *Mr. Thorne* says: Here are the papers, sir. As a great railway pres-
> ident you should—

The rest of that was to be filled in later. How the dickens could he let the public know how truly great his president was?

> *(Daughter, Miss Nelly, comes in.)*
>
> *Miss Nelly:* Father, I have come back to you, sir.
>
> *Mr. Warrington:* My Daughter!
>
> *Nelly:* Father, I have something to tell you; something—

Breakfast at Mrs. Arty's was always an inspiration. In contrast to the lonely dingy meal at the Hustler Dairy Lunch of his Zapp days, he sat next to a trimly shirtwaisted Nelly, fresh and enthusiastic after nine hours' sleep. So much for ordinary days. But Sunday morning—that was paradise! The oil-stove glowed and purred like a large tin pussy cat; it toasted their legs into dreamy comfort, while they methodically stuffed themselves with toast and waffles and coffee. Nelly and he always felt gently superior to Tom Poppins, who would be a-sleeping late, as they talked of the joy of not having to go to the office, of approaching Christmas, and of the superiority of Upton's Grove and Parthenon.

This morning was to be Mr. Wrenn's first attendance at church with Nelly. The previous time they had planned to go, Mr. Wrenn had spent Sunday morning in unreligious fervor at the Chelsea Dental Parlors with a young man in a white jacket instead of at church with Nelly.

This was also the first time that he had attended a church service in nine years, except for mass at St. Patrick's, which he regarded not as church, but as beauty. He felt tremendously reformed, set upon new paths of virtue and achievement. He thought slightingly of those lonely bachelors, Morton and Mittyford, Ph. D. They just didn't know what it meant to a fellow to be going to church with a girl like Miss Nelly, he reflected, as he re brushed his hair after breakfast.

He walked proudly beside her, and made much of the gentility of entering the church, as one of the well-to-do and intensely bathed congregation. He even bowed to an almost painfully washed and brushed young usher with gold-rimmed eye-glasses. He thought scornfully of his salad days, when he had bowed to the Brass-button Man at the Nickelorion.

The church interior was as comfortable as Sunday-morning toast and marmalade—half a block of red carpet in the aisles; shiny solid-oak pews, gorgeous stained-glass windows, and a general polite creaking of ladies' best stays and gentlemen's stiff shirt-bosoms, and an odor of the best cologne and moth-balls.

It lacked but six days till Christmas. Mr. Wrenn's heart was a little garden, and his eyes were moist, and he peeped tenderly at Nelly as he saw the holly and ivy and the frosted Christmas mottoes, "Peace on Earth, Good Will to Men," and the rest, that brightened the spaces between windows.

Christmas—happy homes—laughter…. Since, as a boy, he had attended the Christmas festivities of the Old Church Sunday-school at Parthenon, and got highly colored candy in a net bag, his holidays had been celebrated by buying himself plum pudding at lonely Christmas dinners at large cheap restaurants, where there was no one to wish him "Merry Christmas" except his waiter, whom he would quite probably never see again, nor ever wish to see.

But this Christmas—he surprised himself and Nelly suddenly by hotly thrusting out his hand and touching her sleeve with the searching finger-tips of a child comforted from night fears.

During the sermon he had an idea. What was it Nelly had told him about "Peter Pan"? Oh yes; somebody in it had said "Do you believe in fairies?" *Say,* why wouldn't it be great to have the millionaire's daughter say to her father, "Do you believe in love?"

"Gee, *I* believe in love!" he yearned to himself, as he felt Nelly's arm unconsciously touch his.

Tom Poppins had Horatio Hood Teddem in that afternoon for a hot toddy.

Horatio looked very boyish, very confiding, and borrowed five dollars from Mr. Wrenn almost painlessly, so absorbed was Mr. Wrenn in learning from Horatio how to sell a play. To know the address of the firm of Wendelbaum & Schirtz, play-brokers, located in a Broadway theater building, seemed next door to knowing a Broadway manager.

When Horatio had gone Tom presented an idea which he had ponderously conceived during his Sunday noon-hour at the cigar-store.

"Why not have three of us—say me and you and Mrs. Arty—talk the play, just like we was acting it?"

He enthusiastically forced the plan on Mr. Wrenn. He pounded down-stairs and brought up Mrs. Arty. He dashed about the room, shouting directions. He dragged out his bureau for the railroad-president's desk, and a table for the secretary, and, after some consideration and much rubbing of his chin, with two slams and a bang he converted his hard green Morris-chair into an office safe.

The play was on. Mr. T. Poppins, in the role of the president, entered, with a stern high expression on his face, threw a "Good morning, Thorne," at Wrenn, his secretary, and peeled off his gloves. (Mr. Wrenn noted the gloves; they were a Touch.)

Mr. Wrenn approached diffidently, his face expressionless, lest Mrs. Arty laugh at him. "Here—

"Say, what do you think would be a good way for the secretary to tell the crowd that the other guy is the president? Say, how about this: `The vice-president of the railway would like to have you sign these, sir, as president'?"

"That's fine!" exclaimed Mrs. Arty, whose satin dress was carefully spread over her swelling knees, as she sat in the oak rocker, like a cheerful bronze monument to Sunday propriety. "But don't you think he'd say, `when it's convenient to you, sir'?"

"Gee, that's dandy!"

The play was on.

It ended at seven. Mr. Wrenn took but fifteen minutes for Sunday supper, and wrote till one of the morning, finishing the first draft of his manuscript.

Revision was delightful, for it demanded many conferences with Nelly, sitting at the parlor table, with shoulders confidentially touching. They were the more intimate because Tom had invited Mr. Wrenn, Nelly, and Mrs. Arty to the Grand Christmas Eve Ball of the Cigar-Makers' Union at Melpomene Hall. Nelly asked of Mr. Wrenn, almost as urgently as of Mrs. Arty, whether she should wear her new white mull or her older rose-colored China silk.

Two days before Christmas he timidly turned over the play for typing to a haughty public stenographer who looked like Lee Theresa Zapp. She yawned at him when he begged her to be careful of the manuscript. The gloriously pink-bound and red-underlined typed manuscript of the play was mailed to Messrs. Wendelbaum & Schirtz, play-brokers, at 6.15 P.M., Christmas Eve.

The four walked down Sixth Avenue to the Cigar-Makers' Ball. They made an Indian file through the Christmas shopping crowds, and stopped frequently and noisily before the street-booths' glamour of tinsel and teddy-bears. They shrieked all with one rotund mad laughter as Tom Poppins capered over and bought for seven cents a pink bisque doll, which he pinned to the lapel of his plaid overcoat. They drank hot chocolate at the Olympic Confectionery Store, pretending to each other that they were shivering with cold.

It was here that Nelly reached up and patted Mr. Wrenn's pale-blue tie into better lines. In her hair was the scent which he had come to identify as hers. Her white furs brushed against his overcoat.

The cigar-makers, with seven of them in full evening-dress and two in dinner-coats, were already dancing on the waxy floor of Melpomene Hall when they arrived. A full orchestra was pounding and scraping itself into an hysteria of merriment on the platform under the red stucco-fronted balcony, and at the bar behind the balcony there was a spirit of beer and revelry by night.

Mr. Wrenn embarrassedly passed large groups of pretty girls. He felt very light and insecure in his new gun-metal-finish pumps now that he had taken off his rubbers and essayed the slippery floor. He tried desperately not to use his handkerchief too conspicuously, though he had a cold.

It was not till the choosing of partners for the next dance, when Tom Poppins stood up beside Nelly, their arms swaying a little, their feet tapping, that Mr. Wrenn quite got the fact that he could not dance.

He had casually said to the others, a week before, that he knew only the square dances which, as a boy, he had learned at parties at Parthenon. But they had reassured him: "Oh, come on—we'll teach you how to dance at the ball—it won't be formal. Besides, we'll give you some lessons before we go." Playwriting and playing Five Hundred had prevented their giving him the lessons. So he now sat terrified as a two-step began and he saw what seemed to be thousands of glittering youths and maidens whirling deftly in a most involved course, getting themselves past each other in a way which he was sure he could never imitate. The orchestra yearned over music as rich and smooth as milk chocolate, which made him intensely lonely for Nelly, though she was only across the room from him.

Tom Poppins immediately introduced Nelly to a facetious cigar salesman, who introduced her to three of the beaux in evening clothes, while Tom led out Mrs. Arty. Mr. Wrenn, sitting in a row of persons who were not at all interested in his sorrows, glowered out across the hall, and wished, oh! so bitterly, to flee home. Nelly came up, glowing, laughing, with black-mustached and pearl-waistcoated men, and introduced him to them, but he glanced at them disapprovingly; and always she was carried off to dance again.

She found and hopefully introduced to Mr. Wrenn a wallflower who came from Yonkers and had never heard of Tom Poppins or aeroplanes or Oxford or any other topic upon which Mr. Wrenn uneasily tried to discourse as he watched Nelly waltz and smile up at her partners. Presently the two sat silent. The wallflower excused herself and went back to her mama from Yonkers.

Mr. Wrenn sat sulking, hating his friends for having brought him, hating the sweetness of Nelly Croubel, and saying to himself, "Oh—*sure*—she dances with all those other men—me, I'm only the poor fool that talks to her when she's tired and tries to cheer her up."

He did not answer when Tom came and told him a new story he had just heard in the barroom.

Once Nelly landed beside him and bubblingly insisted on his coming out and trying to learn to dance. He brightened, but shyly remarked, "Oh no, I don't think I'd better." Just then the blackest-mustached and pearl-waistcoatedest of all the cigar salesmen came begging for a dance, and she was gone, with only: "Now get up your courage. I'm going to *make* you dance."

At the intermission he watched her cross the floor with the hateful cigar salesman, slender in her tight crisp new white mull, flourishing her fan and talking with happy rapidity. She sat down beside him. He said nothing; he still stared out across the glassy floor. She peeped at him curiously several times, and made a low tapping with her fan on the side of her chair.

She sighed a little. Cautiously, but very casually, she said, "Aren't you going to take me out for some refreshments, Mr. Wrenn?"

"Oh sure—I'm good enough to buy refreshments for her!" he said to himself.

Poor Mr. Wrenn; he had not gone to enough parties in Parthenon, and he hadn't gone to any in New York. At nearly forty he was just learning the drab sulkiness and churlishness and black jealousy of the lover.... To her: "Why didn't you go out with that guy with the black mustache?" He still stared straight ahead.

She was big-eyed, a tear showing. "Why, Billy—" was all she answered.

He clenched his hands to keep from bursting out with all the pitiful tears which were surging in his eyes. But he said nothing.

"Billy, what—"

He turned shyly around to her; his hand touched hers softly.

"Oh, I'm a beast," he said, rapidly, low, his undertone trembling to her ears through the laughter of a group next to them. "I didn't mean that, but I was—I felt like such a mutt—not being able to dance. Oh, Nelly, I'm awfully sorry. You know I didn't mean—*Come on!* Let's go get something to eat!"

As they consumed ice-cream, fudge, doughnuts, and chicken sandwiches at the refreshment counter they were very intimate, resenting the presence of others. Tom and Mrs. Arty joined them. Tom made Nelly light her first cigarette. Mr. Wrenn admired the shy way in which, taking the tiniest of puffs, she kept drawing out her cigarette with little pouts and nose wriggles and pretended sneezes, but he felt a lofty gladness when she threw it away after a minute, declaring that she'd never smoke again, and that she was going to make all three of her companions stop smoking, "now that she knew how horrid and sneezy it was, so there!"

With what he intended to be deep subtlety Mr. Wrenn drew her away to the barroom, and these two children, over two glasses of ginger-ale, looked their innocent and rustic love so plainly that Mrs. Arty and Tom sneaked away. Nelly cut out a dance, which she had promised to a cigar-maker, and started homeward with Mr. Wrenn.

"Let's not take a car—I want some fresh air after that smoky place," she said. "But it *was* grand…. Let's walk up Fifth Avenue."

"Fine…. Tired, Nelly?"

"A little."

He thought her voice somewhat chilly.

"Nelly—I'm so sorry—I didn't really have the chance to tell you in there how sorry I was for the way I spoke to you. Gee! it was fierce of me—but I felt—I couldn't dance, and—oh—"

No answer.

"And you did mind it, didn't you?"

"Why, I didn't think you were so very nice about it—when I'd tried so hard to have you have a good time—"

"Oh, Nelly, I'm so sorry—"

There was tragedy in his voice. His shoulders, which he always tried to keep as straight as though they were in a vise when he walked with her, were drooping.

She touched his glove. "Oh don't, Billy; it's all right now. I understand. Let's forget—"

"Oh, you're too good to me!"

Silence.

As they crossed Twenty-third on Fifth Avenue she took his arm. He squeezed her hand. Suddenly the world was all young and beautiful and wonderful. It was the first time in his life that he had ever walked thus, with the arm of a girl for whom he cared cuddled in his. He glanced down at her cheap white furs. Snowflakes, tremulous on the fur, were turned into diamond dust in the light from a street-lamp which showed as well a tiny place where her collar had been torn and mended ever so carefully. Then, in a millionth of a second, he who had been a wanderer in the lonely gray regions of a detached man's heart knew the pity of love, all its emotion, and the infinite care for the beloved that makes a man of a rusty sales-clerk. He lifted a face of adoration to the misty wonder of the bare trees, whose tracery of twigs filled Madison Square; to the Metropolitan Tower, with its vast upward stretch toward the ruddy sky of the city's winter night. All these mysteries he knew and sang. What he *said* was:

"Gee, those trees look like a reg'lar picture!… The Tower just kind of fades away. Don't it?"

"Yes, it is pretty," she said, doubtfully, but with a pressure of his arm.

Then they talked like a summer-time brook, planning that he was to buy a Christmas bough of evergreen, which she would smuggle to breakfast in the morning. Through their chatter persisted the new intimacy which had been born in the pain of their misunderstanding.

On January 10th the manuscript of "The Millionaire's Daughter" was returned by play-brokers Wendelbaum & Schirtz with this letter:

DEAR SIR,—We regret to say that we do not find play available. We inclose our reader's report on the same. Also inclose bill for ten dollars for reading-fee, which kindly remit at early convenience.

He stood in the hall at Mrs. Arty's just before dinner. He reread the letter and slowly opened the reader's report, which announced:

"Millionaire's Daughter." One-act vlle. Utterly impos. Amateurish to the limit. Dialogue sounds like burlesque of Laura Jean Libbey. Can it.

Nelly was coming down-stairs. He handed her the letter and report, then tried to stick out his jaw. She read them. Her hand slipped into his. He went quickly toward the basement and made himself read the letter—though not the report—to the tableful. He burned the manuscript of his play before going to bed. The next morning he waded into The Job as he never had before. He was gloomily certain that he would never get away from The Job. But he thought of Nelly a hundred times a day and hoped that sometime, some spring night of a burning moon, he might dare the great adventure and kiss her. Istra— Theoretically, he remembered her as a great experience. But what nebulous bodies these theories are!

That slow but absolutely accurate Five-Hundred player, Mr. William Wrenn, known as Billy, glanced triumphantly at Miss Proudfoot, who was his partner against Mrs. Arty and James T. Duncan, the traveling-man, on that night of late February. His was the last bid in the crucial hand of the rubber game. The others waited respectfully. Confidently, he bid "Nine on no trump."

"Good Lord, Billl" exclaimed James T. Duncan.

"I'll make it."

And he did. He arose a victor. There was no uneasiness, but rather all the social polish of Mrs. Arty's at its best, in his manner, as he crossed to Mrs. Ebbitt's chair and asked: "How is Mr. Ebbitt to-night? Pretty rheumatic?" Miss Proudfoot offered him a lime tablet, and he accepted it judicially. "I believe these tablets are just about as good as Park & Tilford's," he said, cocking his head. "Say, Dunk, I'll match you to see who rushes a growler of beer. Tom'll be here pretty soon—store ought to be closed by now. We'll have some ready for him."

"Right, Bill," agreed James T. Duncan.

Mr. Wrenn lost. He departed, after secretively obtaining not one, but two pitchers, in one of which he got a "pint of dark" and in the other a surprise. He bawled upstairs to Nelly, "Come on down, Nelly, can't you? Got a growler of ice-cream soda for the ladies!"

It is true that when Tom arrived and fell to conversational blows with James T. Duncan over the merits of a Tom Collins Mr. Wrenn was not brilliant, for the reason that he took Tom Collins to be a man instead of the drink he really is.

Yet, as they went up-stairs Miss Proudfoot said to Nelly: "Mr. Wrenn is quiet, but I do think in some ways he's one of the nicest men I've seen in the house for years. And he is so earnest. And I think he'll make a good pinochle player, besides Five Hundred."

"Yes," said Nelly.

"I think he was a little shy at first…. *I* was always shy…. But he likes us, and I like folks that like folks."

"*Yes!*" said Nelly.

CHAPTER XVII

HE IS BLOWN BY THE WHIRLWIND

"He was blown by the whirlwind and followed a wandering flame through perilous seas to a happy shore." — *Quoth Francois.*

On an April Monday evening, when a small moon passed shyly over the city and the streets were filled with the sound of hurdy-gurdies and the spring cries of dancing children, Mr. Wrenn pranced down to the basement dining-room early, for Nelly Croubel would be down there talking to Mrs. Arty, and he gaily wanted to make plans for a picnic to occur the coming Sunday. He had a shy unacknowledged hope that he might kiss Nelly after such a picnic; he even had the notion that he might some day—well, other fellows had been married; why not?

Miss Mary Proudfoot was mending a rent in the current table-cloth with delicate swift motions of her silvery-skinned hands. She informed him: "Mr. Duncan will be back from his Southern trip in five days. We'll have to have a grand closing progressive Five Hundred tournament." Mr. Wrenn was too much absorbed in wondering whether Miss Proudfoot would make some of her celebrated—and justly celebrated—minced-ham sandwiches for the picnic to be much interested. He was not much more interested when she said, "Mrs. Ferrard's got a letter or something for you."

Then, as dinner began, Mrs. Ferrard rushed in dramatically and said, "There's a telegram for you, Mr. Wrenn!"

Was it death? Whose death? The table panted, Mr. Wrenn with them…. That's what a telegram meant to them.

Their eyes were like a circle of charging bayonets as he opened and read the message—a ship's wireless.

Meet me *Hesperida.* —ISTRA.

"It's just—a—a business message," he managed to say, and splashed his soup. This was not the place to take the feelings out of his thumping heart and examine them.

Dinner was begun. Picnics were conversationally considered in all their more important phases—historical, dietetical, and social. Mr. Wrenn talked much and a little wildly. After dinner he galloped out to buy a paper. The S.S. *Hesperiida* was due at ten next morning.

It was an evening of frightened confusion. He tottered along Lexington Avenue on a furtive walk. He knew only that he was very fond of Nelly, yet pantingly eager to see Istra. He damned himself—"damned" is literal—every other minute for a cad, a double-faced traitor, and all the other horrifying things a man is likely to declare himself to be for making the discovery that two women may be different and yet equally likable. And every other minute he reveled in an adventurous gladness that he was going to see Istra—actually, incredibly going to see her, just the next day! He returned to find Nelly sitting on the steps of Mrs. Arty's.

"Hello."

"Hello."

Both good sound observations, and all they could say for a time, while Mr. Wrenn examined the under side of the iron steps rail minutely.

"Billy—was it something serious, the telegram?"

"No, it was—Miss Nash, the artist I told you about, asked me to meet her at the boat. I suppose she wants me to help her with her baggage and the customs and all them things. She's just coming from Paris."

"Oh yes, I see."

So lacking in jealousy was Nelly that Mr. Wrenn was disappointed, though he didn't know why. It always hurts to have one's thunderous tragedies turn out realistic dialogues.

"I wonder if you would like to meet her. She's awful well educated, but I dunno—maybe she'd strike you as kind of snobbish. But she dresses I don't think I ever seen anybody so elegant. In dressing, I mean. Course"—hastily—"she's got money, and so she can afford to. But she's—oh, awful nice, some ways. I hope you like—I hope she won't—"

"Oh, I sha'n't mind if she's a snob. Of course a lady gets used to that, working in a department store," she said, chillily; then repented swiftly and begged: "Oh, I *didn't* mean to be snippy, Billy. Forgive me! I'm sure Miss Nash will be real nice. Does she live here in New York?"

"No—in California.... I don't know how long she's going to stay here."

"Well—well—hum-m-m. I'm getting *so* sleepy. I guess I'd better go up to bed. Good night."

Uneasy because he was away from the office, displeased because he had to leave his beloved letters to the Southern trade, angry because he had had difficulty in getting a pass to the wharf, and furious, finally, because he hadn't slept, Mr. Wrenn nursed all these cumulative emotions attentively and waited for the coming of the *Hesperida*. He was wondering if he'd want to see Istra at all. He couldn't remember just how she looked. Would he like her?

The great steamer swung side-to and was coaxed alongside the wharf. Peering out between rows of crowding shoulders, Mr. Wrenn coldly inspected the passengers lining the decks. Istra was not in sight. Then he knew that he was wildly agitated about her. Suppose something had happened to her!

The smallish man who had been edging into the crowd so politely suddenly dashed to the group forming at the gang-plank and pushed his way rudely into the front rank. His elbow dug into the proper waistcoat of a proper plump old gentleman, but he didn't know it. He stood grasping the rope rail of the plank, gazing goggle-eyed while the plank was lifted to the steamer's deck and the long line of smiling and waving passengers disembarked. Then he saw her—tall, graceful, nonchalant, uninterested, in a smart check suit with a lively hat of black straw, carrying a new Gladstone bag.

He stared at her. "Gee!" he gasped. "I'm crazy about her. I am, all right."

She saw him, and their smiles of welcome made them one. She came from the plank and hastily kissed him.

"Really here!" she laughed.

"Well, well, well, well! I'm so glad to see you!"

"Glad to see you, Mouse dear."

"Have good tr—"

"Don't ask me about it! There was a married man *sans* wife who persecuted me all the way over. I'm glad *you* aren't going to fall in love with me."

"Why—uh—"

"Let's hustle over and get through the customs as soon as we can. Where's N? Oh, how clever of it, it's right by M. There's one of my trunks already. How are you, Mouse dear?"

But she didn't seem really to care so very much, and the old bewilderment she always caused was over him.

"It is good to get back after all, and—Mouse dear, I know you won't mind finding me a place to live the next few days, will you?" She quite took it for granted. "We'll find a place this morning, *n'est-ce pas?* Not too expensive. I've got just about enough to get back to California."

Man fashion, he saw with acute clearness the pile of work on his desk, and, man fashion, responded, "No; be glad tuh."

"How about the place where you're living? You spoke about its being so clean and all."

The thought of Nelly and Istra together frightened him.

"Why, I don't know as you'd like it so very much."

"Oh, it'll be all right for a few days, anyway. Is there a room vacant."

He was sulky about it. He saw much trouble ahead.

"Why, yes, I suppose there is."

"Mouse dear!" Istra plumped down on a trunk in the confused billows of incoming baggage, customs officials, and indignant passengers that surged about them on the rough floor of the vast dock-house. She stared up at him with real sorrow in her fine eyes.

"Why, Mouse! I thought you'd be glad to see me. I've never rowed with you, have I? I've tried not to be temperamental with you. That's why I wired you, when there are others I've known for years."

"Oh, I didn't mean to seem grouchy; I didn't! I just wondered if you'd like the house."

He could have knelt in repentance before his goddess, what time she was but a lonely girl in the clatter of New York. He went on:

"And we've got kind of separated, and I didn't know — But I guess I'll always — oh — kind of worship you."

"It's all right, Mouse. It's — Here's the customs men."

Now Istra Nash knew perfectly that the customs persons were not ready to examine her baggage as yet. But the discussion was ended, and they seemed to understand each other.

"Gee, there's a lot of rich Jew ladies coming back this time!" said he.

"Yes. They had diamonds three times a day," she assented.

"Gee, this is a big place!"

"Yes." So did they testify to fixity of friendship till they reached the house and Istra was welcomed to "that Teddem's" room as a new guest.

Dinner began with the ceremony due Mrs. Arty. There was no lack of the sacred old jokes. Tom Poppins did not fail to bellow "Bring on the dish-water," nor Miss Mary Proudfoot to cheep demurely "Don't y' knaow" in a tone which would have been recognized as fascinatingly English anywhere on the American stage. Then the talk stopped dead as Istra Nash stood agaze in the doorway—pale and intolerant, her red hair twisted high on her head, tall and slim and uncorseted in a gray tight-fitting gown. Every head turned as on a pivot, first to Istra, then to Mr. Wrenn. He blushed and bowed as if he had been called on for a speech, stumblingly arose, and said: "Uh—uh—uh—you met Mrs. Ferrard, didn't you, Istra? She'll introduce you to the rest."

He sat down, wondering why the deuce he'd stood up, and unhappily realized that Nelly was examining Istra and himself with cool hostility. In a flurry he glowered at Istra as she nonchalantly sat down opposite him, beside Mrs. Arty, and incuriously unfolded her napkin. He thought that in her cheerful face there was an expression of devilish amusement.

He blushed. He furiously buttered his bread as Mrs. Arty remarked to the assemblage:

"Ladies and gentlemen, I want you all to meet Miss Istra Nash. Miss Nash— you've met Mr. Wrenn; Miss Nelly Croubel, our baby; Tom Poppins, the great Five-Hundred player; Mrs. Ebbitt, Mr. Ebbitt, Miss Proudfoot."

Istra Nash lifted her bowed eyes with what seemed shyness, hesitated, said "Thank you" in a clear voice with a precise pronunciation, and returned to her soup, as though her pleasant communion with it had been unpleasantly interrupted.

The others began talking and eating very fast and rather noisily. Miss Mary Proudfoot's thin voice pierced the clamor:

"I hear you have just come to New York, Miss Nash."

"Yes."

"Is this your first visit to—"

"No."

Miss Proudfoot rancorously took a long drink of water.

Nelly attempted, bravely:

"Do you like New York, Miss Nash?"

"Yes."

Nelly and Miss Proudfoot and Tom Poppins began discussing shoe-stores, all at once and very rapidly, while hot and uncomfortable Mr. Wrenn tried to think of something to say…. Good Lord, suppose Istra "queered" him at Mrs. Arty's!… Then he was angry at himself and all of them for not appreciating her. How exquisite she looked, with her tired white face!

As the soup-plates were being removed by Annie, the maid, with an elaborate confusion and a general passing of plates down the line, Istra Nash peered at the maid petulantly. Mrs. Arty frowned, then grew artificially pleasant and said:

"Miss Nash has just come back from Paris. She's a regular European traveler, just like Mr. Wrenn."

Mrs. Samuel Ebbitt piped: "Mr. Ebbitt was to Europe. In 1882."

"No 'twa'n't, Fannie; 'twas in 1881," complained Mr. Ebbitt.

Miss Nash waited for the end of this interruption as though it were a noise which merely had to be endured, like the Elevated.

Twice she drew in her breath to speak, and the whole table laid its collective knife and fork down to listen. All she said was:

"Oh, will you pardon me if I speak of it now, Mrs. Ferrard, but would you mind letting me have my breakfast in my room to-morrow? About nine? Just something simple—a canteloupe and some shirred eggs and chocolate?"

"Oh no; why, yes, certainly, "mumbled Mrs. Arty, while the table held its breaths and underneath them gasped:

"Chocolate!"

"A canteloupe!"

"Shirred eggs!"

"*In her room—at nine!*"

All this was very terrible to Mr. Wrenn. He found himself in the position of a man scheduled to address the Brewers' Association and the W. C. T. U. at the same hour. Valiantly he attempted:

"Miss Nash oughta be a good person for our picnics. She's a regular shark for outdoor tramping."

"Oh yes, Mr. Wrenn and I tramped most all night in England one time," said Istra, innocently.

The eyes of the table asked Mr. Wrenn what he meant by it. He tried to look at Nelly, but something hurt inside him.

"Yes," he mumbled. "Quite a long walk."

Miss Mary Proudfoot tried again:

"is it pleasant to study in Paris? Mrs. Arty said you were an artist."

"No."

Then they were all silent, and the rest of the dinner Mr. Wrenn alternately discussed Olympia Johns with Istra and picnics with Nelly. There was an undertone of pleading in his voice which made Nelly glance at him and even become kind. With quiet insistence she dragged Istra into a discussion of rue de la Paix fashions which nearly united the shattered table and won Mr. Wrenn's palpitating thankfulness.

After dessert Istra slowly drew a plain gold cigarette-case from a brocade bag of silvery gray. She took out a match and a thin Russian cigarette, which she carefully lighted. She sat smoking in one of her best attitudes, pointed elbows on the table, coolly contemplating a huge picture called "Hunting the Stag" on the wall behind Mr. Wrenn.

Mrs. Arty snapped to the servant, "Annie, bring me *my* cigarettes." But Mrs. Arty always was penitent when she had been nasty, and—though Istra did not at once seem to know that the landlady *had* been nasty—Mrs. Arty invited her up to the parlor for after-dinner so cordially that Istra could but grant "Perhaps I will," and she even went so far as to say, "I think you're all to be envied, having such a happy family."

"Yes, that's so," reflected Mrs. Arty.

"Yes," added Mr. Wrenn.

And Nelly: "That's so."

The whole table nodded gravely, "Yes, that's so."

"I'm sure"—Istra smiled at Mrs. Arty—"that it's because a woman is running things. Now think what cat-and-dog lives you'd lead if Mr. Wrenn or Mr.—Popple, was it?—were ruling."

They applauded. They felt that she had been humorous. She was again and publicly invited up to the parlor, and she came, though she said, rather shortly, that she didn't play Five Hundred, but only bumblepuppy bridge, a variety of whist which Mr. Wrenn instantly resolved to learn. She reclined ("reclined" is perfectly accurate) on the red-leather couch, among the pillows, and smoked two cigarettes, relapsing into "No?"'s for conversation.

Mr. Wrenn said to himself, almost spitefully, as she snubbed Nelly, "Too good for us, is she?" But he couldn't keep away from her. The realization that Istra was in the room made him forget most of his melds at pinochle; and when Miss Proudfoot inquired his opinion as to whether the coming picnic should be held on Staten island or the Palisades he said, vaguely, "Yes, I guess that would be better."

For he was wanting to sit down beside Istra Nash, just be near her; he *had* to be! So he ventured over and was instantly regarding all the rest as outsiders whom his wise comrade and himself were studying.

"Tell me, Mouse dear, why do you like the people here? The peepul, I mean. They don't seem so very remarkable. Enlighten poor Istra."

"Well, they're awful kind. I've always lived in a house where the folks didn't hardly know each other at all, except Mrs. Zapp—she was the landlady—and I didn't like her very much. But here Tom Poppins and Mrs. Arty and—the rest— they really like folks, and they make it just like a home…. Miss Croubel is a very nice girl. She works for Wanamacy's—she has quite a big job there. She is assistant buyer in the—"

He stopped in horror. He had nearly said "in the lingery department." He changed it to "in the clothing department," and went on, doubtfully: "Mr. Duncan is a traveling-man. He's away on a trip."

"Which one do you play with? So Nelly likes to—well, make b'lieve—'magine?"

"How did you—"

"Oh, I watched her looking at you. I think she's a terribly nice pink-face. And just now you're comparing her and me."

"Gee!" he said.

She was immensely pleased with herself. "Tell me, what do these people think about; at least, what do you talk about?"

"*Say!*"

"'S-s-s-h! Not so loud, my dear."

"Say, I know how you mean. You feel something like what I did in England. You can't get next to what the folks are thinking, and it makes you sort of lonely."

"Well, I—"

Just then Tom Poppins rolled jovially up to the couch. He had carried his many and perspiring pounds over to Third Avenue because Miss Proudfoot reflected, "I've got a regular sweet tooth to-night." He stood before Istra and Mr. Wrenn theatrically holding out a bag of chocolate drops in one hand and peanut brittle in the other; and grandiloquently:

"Which shall it be, your Highness? Nobody loves a fat man, so he has to buy candy so's they'll let him stick around. Le's see; you take chocolates, Bill. Name your drink, Miss Nash." She looked up at him, gravely and politely—too gravely and politely. She didn't seem to consider him a nice person.

"Neither, thank you," sharply, as he still stood there. He moved away, hurt, bewildered.

Istra was going on, "I haven't been here long enough to be lonely yet, but in any case—" when Mr. Wrenn interrupted:

"You've hurt Tom's feelings by not taking any candy; and, gee, he's awful kind!"

"Have I?" mockingly.

"Yes, you *have*. And there ain't any too many kind people in this world."

"Oh yes, of course you' re right. I *am* sorry, really I am."

She dived after Tom's retreat and cheerfully addressed him:

"Oh, I do want some of those chocolates. Will you let me change my mind? Please do."

"Yes *ma'am*, you sure can!" said broad Tom, all one pleased chuckle, poking out the two bags.

Istra stopped beside the Five-Hundred table to smile in a lordly way down at Mrs. Arty and say, quite humanly:

"I'm so sorry I can't play a decent game of cards. I'm afraid I'm too stupid to learn. You are very lucky, I think."

Mr. Wrenn on the couch was horribly agitated…. Wasn't Istra coming back?

She was. She detached herself from the hubbub of invitations to learn to play Five Hundred and wandered back to the couch, murmuring: "Was bad Istra good? Am I forgiven? Mouse dear, I didn't mean to be rude to your friends."

As the bubbles rise through water in a cooking-pot, as the surface writhes, and then, after the long wait, suddenly the water is aboil, so was the emotion of Mr. Wrenn now that Istra, the lordly, had actually done something he suggested.

"Istra—" That was all he could say, but from his eyes had gone all reserve.

Her glance back was as frank as his—only it had more of the mother in it; it was like a kindly pat on the head; and she was the mother as she mused:

"So you *have* missed me, then?"

"Missed you—"

"Did you think of me after you came here? Oh, I know—I was forgotten; poor Istra abdicates to the pretty pink-face."

"Oh, Istra, *don't*. I—can't we just go out for a little walk so—so we can talk?"

"Why, we can talk here."

"Oh, gee!—there's so many people around…. Golly! when I came back to

America—gee!—I couldn't hardly sleep nights—"

From across the room came the boisterous, somewhat coarse-timbred voice of Tom, speaking to Nelly:

"Oh yes, of course you think you're the only girl that ever seen a vodville show. *We* ain't never seen a vodville show. Oh no!"

Nelly and Miss Proudfoot dissolved in giggles at the wit.

Mr. Wrenn gazed at them, detached; these were not his people, and with startled pride he glanced at Istra's face, delicately carven by thought, as he stumbled hotly on.

"—just couldn't sleep nights at all…. Then I got on the job…."

"Let's see, you're still with that same company?"

"Yes. Souvenir and Art Novelty Company. And I got awfully on the job there, and so I managed to forget for a little while and—"

"So you really do like me even after I was so beastly to you in England."

"Oh, that wasn't nothing…. But I was always thinking of you, even when I was on the job—"

"It's gratifying to have some one continue taking me seriously…. Really, dear, I do appreciate it. But you mustn't—you mustn't—"

"Oh, gee! I just can't get over it—you here by me—ain't it curious!… "Then he persisted with the tale of his longing, which she had so carefully interrupted: "The people here are *awful* kind and good, and you can bank on 'em. But—oh—"

From across the room, Tom's pretended jeers, lighted up with Miss Proudfoot's giggles, as paper lanterns illumine Coney Island. From Tom:

"Yes, you're a hot dancer, all right. I suppose you can do the Boston and all them swell dances. Wah-h-h-h-h!"

"—but Istra, oh, gee! you're like poetry—like all them things a feller can't get but he tries to when he reads Shakespeare and all those poets."

"Oh, dear boy, you mustn't! We will be good friends. I do appreciate having some one care whether I'm alive or not. But I thought it was all understood that we weren't to take playing together seriously; that it was to be merely playing—nothing more."

"But, anyway, you will let me play with you here in New York as much as I can? Oh, come on, *let's* go for a walk—let's—let's go to a show."

"I'm awf'ly sorry, but I promised—a man's going to call for me, and we're going to a stupid studio party on Bryant Park. Bore, isn't it, the day of landing? And poor Istra dreadfully landsick."

"Oh, then," hopefully, "don't go. Let's—"

"I'm sorry, Mouse dear, but I'm afraid I can't break the date…. Fact, I must go up and primp now—"

"Don't you care a bit?" he said, sulkily.

"Why, yes, of course. But you wouldn't have Istra disappoint a nice Johnny after he's bought him a cunnin' new weskit, would you?... Good night, dear." She smiled—the mother smile—and was gone with a lively good night to the room in general.

Nelly went up to bed early. She was tired, she said. He had no chance for a word with her. He sat on the steps outside alone a long time. Sometimes he yearned for a sight of Istra's ivory face. Sometimes, with a fierce compassion that longed to take the burden from her, he pictured Nelly working all day in the rushing department store on which the fetid city summer would soon descend.

They did have their walk the next night, Istra and Mr. Wrenn, but Istra kept the talk to laughing burlesques of their tramp in England. Somehow—he couldn't tell exactly why—he couldn't seem to get in all the remarks he had inside him about how much he had missed her.

Wednesday—Thursday—Friday; he saw her only at one dinner, or on the stairs, departing volubly with clever-looking men in evening clothes to taxis waiting before the house.

Nelly was very pleasant; just that—pleasant. She pleasantly sat as his partner at Five Hundred, and pleasantly declined to go to the moving pictures with him. She was getting more and more tired, staying till seven at the store, preparing what she called "special stunts" for the summer white sale. Friday evening he saw her soft fresh lips drooping sadly as she toiled up the front steps before dinner. She went to bed at eight, at which time Istra was going out to dinner with a thin, hatchet-faced sarcastic-looking man in a Norfolk jacket and a fluffy black tie. Mr. Wrenn resented the Norfolk jacket. Of course, the kingly men in evening dress would be expected to take Istra away from him, but a Norfolk jacket—He did not call it that. Though he had worn one in the fair village of Aengusmere, it was still to him a "coat with a belt."

He thought of Nelly all evening. He heard her—there on the same floor with him—talking to Miss Proudfoot, who stood at Nelly's door, three hours after she was supposed to be asleep.

"No," Nelly was saying with evidently fictitious cheerfulness, "no, it was just a little headache.... It's much better. I think I can sleep now. Thank you very much for coming."

Nelly hadn't told Mr. Wrenn that she had a severe headache—she who had once, a few weeks before, run to him with a cut in her soft small finger, demanding that he bind it up.... He went slowly to bed.

He had lain awake half an hour before his agony so overpowered him that he flung out of bed. He crouched low by the bed, like a child, his legs curled under him, the wooden sideboard pressing into his chest in one long line of hot pain, while he prayed:

"O God, O God, forgive me, forgive me, oh, forgive me! Here I been forgetting Nelly (and I *love* her) and comparing her with Istra and not appreciating her, and

Nelly always so sweet to me and trusting me so—O God, keep me away from wickedness!"

He huddled there many minutes, praying, the scorching pressure of the bed-side growing more painful. All the while the camp-fire he had shared with Istra was burning within his closed eyes, and Istra was visibly lording it in a London flat filled with clever people, and he was passionately aware that the line of her slim breast was like the lip of a shell; the line of her pallid cheek, defined by her flame-colored hair, something utterly fine, something he could not express.

"Oh," he groaned, "she is like that poetry stuff in Shakespeare that's so hard to get…. I'll be extra nice to Nelly at the picnic Sunday…. Her trusting me so, and then me—O God, keep me away from wickedness!"

As he was going out Saturday morning he found a note from Istra waiting in the hall on the hat-rack:

> Do you want to play with poor Istra tomorrow Sat. afternoon and perhaps evening, Mouse? You have Saturday afternoon off, don't you? Leave me a note if you can call for me at 1.30.
>
> I. N.

He didn't have Saturday afternoon off, but he said he did in his note, and at one-thirty he appeared at her door in a new spring suit (purchased on Tuesday), a new spring hat, very fuzzy and gay (purchased Saturday noon), and the walk-ing-stick he had bought on Tottenham Court Road, but decently concealed from the boarding-house.

Istra took him to what she called a "futurist play." She explained it all to him several times, and she stood him tea and muffins, and recalled Mrs. Cattermole's establishment with full attention to Mrs. Cattermole's bulbous but earnest nose. They dined at the Brevoort, and were back at nine-thirty; for, said Istra, she was "just a bit tired, Mouse."

They stood at the door of Istra's room. Istra said, "You may come in—just for a minute."

It was the first time he had even peeped into her room in New York. The old shyness was on him, and he glanced back.

Nelly was just coming up-stairs, staring at him where he stood inside the door, her lips apart with amazement.

Ladies distinctly did not entertain in their rooms at Mrs. Arty's.

He wanted to rush out, to explain, to invite her in, to—to— He stuttered in his thought, and by now Nelly had hastened past, her face turned from them.

Uneasily he tilted on the front of a cane-seated rocking-chair, glaring at a pile of books before one of Istra's trunks. Istra sat on the bedside nursing her knee. She burst out:

"O Mouse dear, I'm so bored by everybody—every sort of everybody…. Of course I don't mean you; you're a good pal…. Oh—Paris is *too* complex—especially when you can't quite get the nasal vowels—and New York is too youthful and earnest; and Dos Puentes, California, will be plain hell.... And all my little parties—I start out on them happily, always, as naive as a kiddy going to a birthday party, and then I get there and find I can't even dance square dances, as the kiddy does, and go home—Oh damn it, damn it, damn it! Am I shocking you? Well, what do I care if I shock everybody!"

Her slim pliant length was flung out along the bed, and she was crying. Her beautiful hands clutched the corners of a pillow bitterly.

He crept over to the bed, patting her shoulder, slowly and regularly, too frightened of her mood even to want to kiss her.

She looked up, laughing tearfully. "Please say, `There, there, there; don't cry.' It always goes with pats for weepy girls, you know…. O Mouse, you will be good to some woman some day."

Her long strong arms reached up and drew him down. It was his head that rested on her shoulder. It seemed to both of them that it was he who was to be petted, not she. He pressed his cheek against the comforting hollow of her curving shoulder and rested there, abandoned to a forlorn and growing happiness, the happiness of getting so far outside of his tight world of Wrennishness that he could give comfort and take comfort with no prim worried thoughts of Wrenn.

Istra murmured: "Perhaps that's what I need—some one to need me. Only—" She stroked his hair. "Now you must go, dear."

"You—It's better now? I'm afraid I ain't helped you much. It's kinda t' other way round."

"Oh yes, indeed, it's all right now! Just nerves. Nothing more. Now, good night."

"Please, won't you come to the picnic to-morrow? It's—"

"No. Sorry, but can't possibly."

"Please think it over."

"No, no, no, no, dear! You go and forget me and enjoy yourself and be good to your pink-face—Nelly, isn't it? She seems to be terribly nice, and I know you two will have a good party. You must forget me. I'm just a teacher of playing games who hasn't been successful at any game whatever. Not that it matters. I don't care. I don't, really. Now, good night."

CHAPTER XVIII

AND FOLLOWS A WANDERING FLAME THROUGH PERILOUS SEAS

They had picnic dinner early up there on the Palisades:

Nelly and Mr. Wrenn, Mrs. Arty and Tom, Miss Proudfoot and Mrs. Samuel Ebbitt, the last of whom kept ejaculating: "Well! I ain't run off like this in ten years!" They squatted about a red-cotton table-cloth spread on a rock, broadly discussing the sandwiches and cold chicken and lemonade and stuffed olives, and laughing almost to a point of distress over Tom's accusation that Miss Proudfoot had secreted about her person a bottle of rye whisky.

Nelly was very pleasant to Mr. Wrenn, but she called him neither Billy nor anything else, and mostly she talked to Miss Proudfoot, smiling at him, but saying nothing when he managed to get out a jest about Mrs. Arty's chewing-gum. When he moved to her side with a wooden plate of cream-cheese sandwiches (which Tom humorously termed "cold-cream wafers") Mr. Wrenn started to explain how he had come to enter Istra's room.

"Why shouldn't you?" Nelly asked, curtly, and turned to Miss Proudfoot.

"She doesn't seem to care much," he reflected, relieved and stabbed in his humble vanity and reattracted to Nelly, all at once. He was anxious about her opinion of Istra and her opinion of himself, and slightly defiant, as she continued to regard him as a respectable person whose name she couldn't exactly remember.

Hadn't he the right to love Istra if he wanted to? he desired to know of himself. Besides, what had he *done?* Just gone out walking with his English hotel acquaintance Istra! He hadn't been in her room but just a few minutes. Fine reason that was for Nelly to act like a blooming iceberg! Besides, it wasn't as if he were engaged to Nelly, or anything like that. Besides, of course Istra would never care for him. There were several other besideses with which he harrowed himself while trying to appear picnically agreeable. He was getting very much confused, and was slightly abrupt as he said to Nelly, "Let's walk over to that high rock on the edge."

A dusky afterglow filled the sky before them as they silently trudged to the rock and from the top of the sheer cliff contemplated the smooth and steely-gray Hudson below. Nelly squeaked her fear at the drop and clutched his arm, but suddenly let go and drew back without his aid.

He groaned within, "I haven't the right to help her." He took her arm as she hesitatingly climbed from the rock down to the ground.

She jerked it free, curtly saying, "No, thank you."

She was repentant in a moment, and, cheerfully:

"Miss Nash took me in her room yesterday and showed me her things. My, she's got such be-*yoo*-ti-ful jewels! La V'lieres and pearls and a swell amethyst brooch. My! She told me all about how the girls used to study in Paris, and how sorry she would be to go back to California and keep house."

"Keep house?"

Nelly let him suffer for a moment before she relieved him with, "For her father."

"Oh…. Did she say she was going back to California soon?"

"Not till the end of the summer, maybe."

"Oh…. Oh, Nelly—"

For the first time that day he was perfectly sincere. He was trying to confide in her. But the shame of having emotions was on him. He got no farther.

To his amazement, Nelly mused, "She is very nice."

He tried hard to be gallant. "Yes, she is interesting, but of course she ain't anywheres near as nice as you are, Nelly, be—"

"Oh, don't, Billy!"

The quick agony in her voice almost set them both weeping. The shared sorrow of separation drew them together for a moment. Then she started off, with short swift steps, and he tagged after. He found little to say. He tried to comment on the river. He remarked that the apartment-houses across in New York were bright in the sunset; that, in fact, the upper windows looked "like there was a fire in there." Her sole comment was "Yes."

When they rejoined the crowd he was surprised to hear her talking volubly to Miss Proudfoot. He rejoiced that she was "game," but he did not rejoice long. For a frightened feeling that he had to hurry home and see Istra at once was turning him weak and cold. He didn't want to see her; she was intruding; but he had to go—go at once; and the agony held him all the way home, while he was mechanically playing the part of stern reformer and agreeing with Tom Poppins that the horrors of the recent Triangle shirt-waist-factory fire showed that "something oughta be done—something sure oughta be."

He trembled on the ferry till Nelly, with a burst of motherly tenderness in her young voice, suddenly asked: "Why, you're shivering dreadfully! Did you get a chill?"

Naturally, he wanted the credit of being known as an invalid, and pitied and nursed, but he reluctantly smiled and said, "Oh no, it ain't anything at all."

Then Istra called him again, and he fumed over the slowness of their landing.

And, at home, Istra was out.

He went resolutely down and found Nelly alone, sitting on a round pale-yellow straw mat on the steps.

He sat by her. He was very quiet; not at all the jovial young man of the picnic properly following the boarding-house-district rule that males should be jocular and show their appreciation of the ladies by "kidding them." And he spoke with a quiet graciousness that was almost courtly, with a note of weariness and spiritual experience such as seldom comes into the boarding-houses, to slay joy and bring wisdom and give words shyness.

He had, as he sat down, intended to ask her to go with him to a moving-picture show. But inspiration was on him. He merely sat and talked.

When Mr. Wrenn returned from the office, two evenings later, he found this note awaiting him:

> DEAR MOUSE,—Friend has asked me to join her in studio & have beat it. Sorry not see you & say good-by. Come see me sometime—phone before and see if I'm in—Spring xxx—address xx South Washington Sq. In haste,
>
> ISTRA.

He spent the evening in not going to the studio. Several times he broke away from a pinochle game to rush upstairs and see if the note was as chilly as he remembered. It always was.

Then for a week he awaited a more definite invitation from her, which did not come. He was uneasily polite to Nelly these days, and tremulously appreciative of her gentleness. He wanted to brood, but he did not take to his old habit of long solitary walks. Every afternoon he planned one for the evening; every evening found that he "wanted to be around with folks."

He had a sort of youthful defiant despair, so he jested much at the card-table, by way of practising his new game of keeping people from knowing what he was thinking. He took sophisticated pleasure in noting that Mrs. Arty no longer condescended to him. He managed to imitate Tom's writing on a card which he left with a bunch of jonquils in Nelly's room, and nearly persuaded even Tom himself that Tom was the donor. Probably because he didn't much care what happened he was able to force Mr. Mortimer R. Guilfogle to raise his salary to twenty-three dollars a week. Mr. Guilfogle went out of his way to admit that the letters to the Southern trade had been "a first-rate stunt, son."

John Henson, the head of the Souvenir Company's manufacturing department, invited Mr. Wrenn home to dinner, and the account of the cattle-boat was much admired by Mrs. Henson and the three young Hensons.

A few days later, in mid-June, there was an unusually cheerful dinner at the boarding-house. Nelly turned to Mr. Wrenn—yes, he was quite sure about it; she was speaking exclusively to him, with a lengthy and most merry account of the manner in which the floor superintendent had "called down" the unkindest of the aislesmen.

He longed to give his whole self in his answer, to be in the absolute community of thought that lovers know. But the image of Istra was behind his chair. Istra — he had to see her — now, this evening. He rushed out to the corner drug-store and reached her by telephone.

Yes-s, admitted Istra, a little grudgingly, she was going to be at the studio that evening, though she — well, there was going to be a little party — some friends — but — yes, she'd be glad to have him come.

Grimly, Mr. Wrenn set out for Washington Square.

Since this scientific treatise has so exhaustively examined Mr. Wrenn's reactions toward the esthetic, one need give but three of his impressions of the studio and people he found on Washington Square — namely:

(a) That the big room was bare, ill kept, and not comparable to the red-plush splendor of Mrs. Arty's, for all its pretension to superiority. Why, a lot of the pictures weren't framed! And you should have seen the giltness and fruit-borderness of the frames at Mrs. Arty's!

(b) That the people were brothers-in-talk to the inmates of the flat on Great James Street, London, only far less, and friendly.

(c) That Mr. Wrenn was now a man of friends, and if the "blooming Bohemians," as he called them, didn't like him they were permitted to go to the dickens.

Istra was always across the room from him somehow. He found himself glad. It made their parting definite.

He was going back to his own people, he was deciding.

As he rose with elaborate boarding-house apologies to the room at large for going, and a cheerful but not intimate "Good night" to Istra, she followed him to the door and into the dark long hallway without.

"Good night, Mouse dear. I'm glad you got a chance to talk to the Silver Girl. But was Mr. Hargis rude to you? I heard him talking Single Tax — or was it Matisse? — and he's usually rude when he talks about them."

"No. He was all right."

"Then what *is* worrying you?"

"Oh — nothing. Good ni —"

"You *are* going off angry. *Aren't* you?"

"No, but — oh, there ain't any use of our — of me being — *Is* there?"

"N-no —"

"Matisse — the guy you just spoke about — and these artists here tonight in bobtail dress-suits — I wouldn't know when to wear one of them things, and when a swallow-tail — if I had one, even — or when a Prince Albert or —"

"Oh, not a Prince Albert, Mouse dear. Say, a frock-coat."

"Sure. That's what I mean. It's like that Matisse guy. I don't know about none of the things you're interested in. While you've been away from Mrs. Arty's—Lord, I've missed you so! But when I try to train with your bunch, or when you spring Matisse" (he seemed peculiarly to resent the unfortunate French artist) "on me I sort of get onto myself—and now it ain't like it was in England; I've got a bunch of my own I can chase around with. Anyway, I got onto myself tonight. I s'pose it's partly because I been thinking you didn't care much for *my* friends."

"But, Mouse dear, all this isn't news to me. Surely you, who've gipsied with me, aren't going to be so obvious, so banal, as to blame *me* because you've cared for me, are you, child?"

"Oh no, no, no! I didn't mean to do that. I just wanted—oh, gee! I dunno—well, I wanted to have things between us definite."

"I do understand. You're quite right. And now we're just friends, aren't we?"

"Yes."

"Then good-by. And sometime when I'm back in New York—I'm going to California in a few days—I think I'll be able to get back here—I certainly hope so—though of course I'll have to keep house for friend father for a while, and maybe I'll marry myself with a local magnate in desperation—but, as I was saying, dear, when I get back here we'll have a good dinner, *nicht wahr?*"

"Yes, and—good-by."

She stood at the top of the stairs looking down. He slowly clumped down the wooden treads, boiling with the amazing discoveries that he had said good-by to Istra, that he was not sorry, and that now he could offer to Nelly Croubel everything.

Istra suddenly called, "O Mouse, wait just a moment."

She darted like a swallow. She threw her arm about his shoulder and kissed his cheek. Instantly she was running up-stairs again, and had disappeared into the studio.

Mr. William Wrenn was walking rapidly up Riverside Drive, thinking about his letters to the Southern merchants.

While he was leaving the studio building he had perfectly seen himself as one who was about to go through a tumultuous agony, after which he would be free of all the desire for Istra and ready to serve Nelly sincerely and humbly.

But he found that the agony was all over. Even to save his dignity as one who was being dramatic, he couldn't keep his thoughts on Istra.

Every time he thought of Nelly his heart was warm and he chuckled softly. Several times out of nothing came pictures of the supercilious persons whom he had heard solving the problems of the world at the studio on Washington Square, and he muttered: "Oh, hope they choke. Istra's all right, though; she learnt me an awful lot. But—gee! I'm glad she ain't in the same house; I suppose I'd ag'nize round if she was."

Suddenly, at no particular street corner on Riverside Drive, just *a* street, he fled over to Broadway and the Subway. He had to be under the same roof with Nelly. If it were only possible to see her that night! But it was midnight. However, he formulated a plan. The next morning he would leave the office, find her at her department store, and make her go out to Manhattan Beach with him for dinner that night.

He was home. He went happily up the stairs. He would dream of Nelly, and—

Nelly's door opened, and she peered out, drawing her *peignoir* about her.

"Oh," she said, softly, "is it you?"

"Yes. My, you're up late."

"Do you—Are you all right?"

He dashed down the hall and stood shyly scratching at the straw of his newest hat.

"Why yes, Nelly, course. Poor—Oh, don't tell me you have a headache again?"

"No—I was awful foolish, of course, but I saw you when you went out this evening, and you looked so savage, and you didn't look very well."

"But now it's all right."

"Then good night."

"Oh no—listen—please do! I went over to the place Miss Nash is living at, because I was pretty sure that I ain't hipped on her—sort of hypnotized by her—any more. And I found I ain't! *I ain't!* I don't know what to say, I want to—I want you to know that from going to try and see if I can't get you to care for me." He was dreadfully earnest, and rather quiet, with the dignity of the man who has found himself. "I'm scared," he went on, "about saying this, because maybe you'll think I've got an idea I'm kind of a little tin god, and all I've got to do is to say which girl I'll want and she'll come a-running, but it isn't that; *it isn't.* It's just that I want you to know I'm going to give *all* of me to you now if I can get you to want me. And I *am* glad I knew Istra—she learnt me a lot about books and all, so I have more to me, or maybe will have, for you. It's —Nelly—promise you'll be—my friend— promise—If you knew how I rushed back here tonight to see you!"

"Billy—"

She held out her hand, and he grasped it as though it were the sacred symbol of his dreams.

"To-morrow," she smiled, with a hint of tears, "I'll be a reg'lar lady, I guess, and make you explain and explain like everything, but now I'm just glad. Yes," defiantly, "I *will* admit it if I want to! I *am* glad!"

Her door closed.

CHAPTER XIX

TO A HAPPY SHORE

Upon an evening of November, 1911, it chanced that of Mrs. Arty's flock only Nelly and Mr. Wrenn were at home. They had finished two hot games of pinochle, and sat with their feet on a small amiable oil-stove. Mr. Wrenn laid her hand against his cheek with infinite content. He was outlining the situation at the office.

The business had so increased that Mr. Mortimer R. Guilfogle, the manager, had told Rabin, the head traveling-salesman, that he was going to appoint an assistant manager. Should he, Mr. Wrenn queried, try to get the position? The other candidates, Rabin and Henson and Glover, were all good friends of his, and, furthermore, could he "run a bunch of guys if he was over them?"

"Why, of course you can, Billy. I remember when you came here you were sort of shy. But now you're 'most the star boarder! And won't those others be trying to get the job away from you? Of course!"

"Yes, that's so."

"Why, Billy, some day you might be manager!"

"Say, that would be great, wouldn't it! But hones', Nell, do you think I might have a chance to land the assistant's job?"

"I certainly do."

"Oh, Nelly—gee! you make me—oh, learn to bank on myself—"

He kissed her for the second time in his life.

"Mr. Guilfogle," stated Mr. Wrenn, next day, "I want to talk to you about that assistant managership."

The manager, in his new office and his new flowered waistcoat, had acted interested when Our steady and reliable Mr. Wrenn came in. But now he tried to appear dignified and impatient.

"That—" he began.

"I've been here longer than any of the other men, and I know every line of the business now, even the manufacturing. You remember I held down Henson's job when his wife was sick."

"Yes, but—"

"And I guess Jake thinks I can boss all right, and Miss Leavenbetz, too."

"Now will you kindly 'low *me* to talk a little, Wrenn? I know a *little* something about how things go in the office myself! I don't deny you're a good man. Maybe some day you may get to be assistant manager. But I'm going to give the first try at it to Glover. He's had so much more experience with meeting people directly—personally. But you're a good man—"

"Yes, I've heard that before, but I'll be gol-darned if I'll stick at one desk all my life just because I save you all the trouble in that department, Guilfogle, and now—"

"Now, now, now, now! Calm down; hold your horses, my boy. This ain't a melodrama, you know."

"Yes, I know; I didn't mean to get sore, but you know—"

"Well, now I'll tell you what I'm going to do. I'm going to make you head of the manufacturing department instead of getting in a new man, and shift Henson to purchasing. I'll put Jake on your old job, and expect you to give him a lift when he needs it. And you'd better keep up the most important of the jollying-letters, I guess."

"Well, I like that all right. I appreciate it. But of course I expect more pay—two men's work—"

"Let's see; what you getting now?"

"Twenty-three."

"Well, that's a good deal, you know. The overhead expenses have been increasing a lot faster than our profits, and we've—"

"Huh!"

"—got to see where new business is coming in to justify the liberal way we've treated you men before we can afford to do much salary-raising—though we're just as glad to do it as you men to get it; but—"

"Huh!"

"—if we go to getting extravagant we'll go bankrupt, and then we won't any of us have jobs…. Still, I *am* willing to raise you to twenty-five, though—"

"Thirty-five!"

Mr. Wrenn stood straight. The manager tried to stare him down. Panic was attacking Mr. Wrenn, and he had to think of Nelly to keep up his defiance. At last Mr. Guilfogle glared, then roared: "Well, confound it, Wrenn, I'll give you twenty-nine-fifty, and not a cent more for at least a year. That's final. *Understand?*"

"All right," chirped Mr. Wrenn.

"Gee!" he was exulting to himself, "never thought I'd get anything like that. Twenty-nine-fifty! More 'n enough to marry on now! I'm going to get *twenty-nine-fifty!*"

"Married five months ago to-night, honey," said Mr. Wrenn to Nelly, his wife, in their Bronx flat, and thus set down October 17, 1913, as a great date in history.

"Oh, I *know* it, Billy. I wondered if you'd remember. You just ought to see the dessert I'm making—but that's a s'prise."

"Remember! Should say I did! See what I've got for somebody!"

He opened a parcel and displayed a pair of red-worsted bed-slippers, a creation of one of the greatest red-worsted artists in the whole land. Yes, and he could afford them, too. Was he not making thirty-two dollars a week—he who had been poor! And his chances for the assistant managership "looked good."

"Oh, they'll be so comfy when it gets cold. You're a dear! Oh, Billy, the janitress says the Jewish lady across the court in number seventy is so lazy she wears her corsets to bed!"

"Did the janitress get the coal put in, Nell?"

"Yes, but her husband is laid off again. I was talking to her quite a while this afternoon.... Oh, dear, I do get so lonely for you, sweetheart, with nothing to do. But I did read some *Kim* this afternoon. I liked it."

"That's fine!"

"But it's kind of hard. Maybe I'll—Oh, I don't know. I guess I'll have to read a lot."

He patted her back softly, and hoped: "Maybe some day we can get a little house out of town, and then you can garden.... Sorry old Siddons is laid off again.... Is the gas-stove working all right now?"

"Um-huh, honey. I fixed it."

"Say, let me make the coffee, Nell. You'll have enough to do with setting the table and watching the sausages."

"All rightee, hun. But, oh, Billy, I'm so, shamed. I was going to get some potato salad, and I've just remembered I forgot." She hung her head, with a fingertip to her pretty lips, and pretended to look dreadfully ashamed. "Would you mind so ver-ee much skipping down to Bachmeyer's for some? Ah-h, is it just fearful neglected when it comes home all tired out?"

"No, indeedy. But you got to kiss me first, else I won't go at all."

Nelly turned to him and, as he held her, her head bent far back. She lay tremblingly inert against his arms, staring up at him, panting. With her head on his shoulder—a soft burden of love that his shoulder rejoiced to bear—they stood gazing out of the narrow kitchen window of their sixth-story flat and noticed for the hundredth time that the trees in a vacant lot across were quite as red and yellow as the millionaire trees in Central Park along Fifth Avenue.

"Sometime," mused Mr. Wrenn, "we'll live in Jersey, where there's trees and trees and trees—and maybe there'll be kiddies to play under them, and then you won't be lonely, honey; they'll keep you some busy!"

"You skip along now, and don't be talking nonsense, or I'll not give you one single wee bit of dinner!" Then she blushed adorably, with infinite hope.

He hastened out of the kitchen, with the happy glance he never failed to give the living-room—its red-papered walls with shiny imitation-oak woodwork; the rows of steins on the plate-rack; the imitation-oak dining-table, with a vase of newly dusted paper roses; the Morris chair, with Nelly's sewing on a tiny wicker table beside it; the large gilt-framed oleograph of "Pike's Peak by Moonlight."

He clattered down the slate treads of the stairs. He fairly vaulted out of doors. He stopped, startled.

Across the ragged vacant lots to the west a vast sunset processional marched down the sky. It had not been visible from their flat, which looked across East River to the tame grassy shore of a real-estate boomer's suburb. "Gee!" he mourned, "it's the first time I've noticed a sunset for a month! I used to see knights' flags and Mandalay and all sorts of stuff in sunsets!"

Wistfully the exile gazed at his lost kingdom, till the October chill aroused him.

But he learned a new way to cook eggs from the proprietor of the delicatessen store; and his plans for spending the evening playing pinochle with Nelly, and reading the evening paper aloud, set him chuckling softly to himself as he hurried home through the brisk autumn breeze with seven cents' worth of potato salad.

THE END.

Lector House believes that a society develops through a two-fold approach of continuous learning and adaptation, which is derived from the study of classic literary works spread across the historic timeline of literature records. Therefore, we aim at reviving, repairing and redeveloping all those inaccessible or damaged but historically as well as culturally important literature across subjects so that the future generations may have an opportunity to study and learn from past works to embark upon a journey of creating a better future.

This book is a result of an effort made by Lector House towards making a contribution to the preservation and repair of original ancient works which might hold historical significance to the approach of continuous learning across subjects.

HAPPY READING & LEARNING!

LECTOR HOUSE LLP
E-MAIL: lectorpublishing@gmail.com

9 789390 058761